Cracking the
ASVAB

The Princeton Review

Cracking the ASVAB

NICOLE MOSS, ANDY KIEHL, AND DAVID WINN

FIRST EDITION

RANDOM HOUSE, INC.
NEW YORK

www.PrincetonReview.com

The Independent Education Consultants Association recognizes The Princeton Review as a valuable resource for high school and college students applying to college and graduate school.

Princeton Review Publishing, L.L.C.
2315 Broadway
New York, NY 10024
E-mail: booksupport@review.com

ISBN 0-375-76243-4

Editor: Jeff Soloway
Production Editor: Maria Dente
Production Coordinator: Jennifer Arias

Manufactured in the United States of America.

10 9 8 7 6 5 4 3 2

First Edition

ACKNOWLEDGMENTS

The authors would like to thank Dan Chudnof, Udo Fissenewert, Jim Lupton, Jeff Rubenstein, Jeff Soloway, Maria Dente, Stephen White, Anthony Moore, David Anderson and Jennifer Arias for their invaluable help in the production of this book. Their guidance, advice, and wisdom were greatly appreciated.

CONTENTS

PART I

Orientation

1

INTRODUCTION

WHAT IS THE ASVAB?

The ASVAB, which stands for Armed Services Vocational Aptitude Battery, is used by the armed services to assess the abilities of recruits and help place them in jobs that they're most suitable for. The test is administered on paper or computer, depending on the site where you take it. It generally lasts about three hours. The ASVAB includes 10 subtests given in the order presented below.

1

General Science
11 Minutes
25 Questions
Measures knowledge of general science, including biological, physical, astronomical, and earth science.

2

Arithemetic Reasoning
36 Minutes
30 Questions
Measures ability to solve arithmetic word problems.

3

Word Knowledge
11 Minutes
35 Questions
Measures vocabulary

4

Paragraph Comprehension
13 Minutes
15 Questions
Measures ability to obtain information from written passages.

5

Numerical Operations
3 Minutes
50 Questions
Measures ability to solve simple arithmetic operations quickly and accurately.

6

Coding Speed
7 Minutes
84 Questions
Measures ability to quickly and accurately find the correct code from a key.

7

Auto and Shop Information
11 Minutes
25 Questions
Measures knowledge of automobiles, shop practices, and tools.

8

Mathematics Knowledge
24 Minutes
25 Questions
Measures ability to solve general mathematical problems. More emphasis on algebra and geometry.

9

Mechanical Comprehension
19 Minutes
25 Questions
Measures knowledge of mechanical principles.

10

Electronics Information
9 Minutes
20 Questions
Measures knowlege of electrical, radio, and electronics information.

THE SUBTESTS

Each of the 10 subtests is designed to assess different skills. Some of the subtests are very straightforward and simply assess your knowledge level in a particular area. Others are designed to measure how well you perform under time constraints. Let's look at each subtest now.

GENERAL SCIENCE

The General Science test is designed to assess your knowledge of basic high school science. It contains questions covering biology, earth science, chemistry, physics, and astronomy. If you've studied all of these in school you should do well. If you're not familiar with these subjects, be sure to read our review chapter carefully, and spend extra time on those areas that seem the most foreign. For this section, you're given 11 minutes to answer 25 questions.

ARITHMETIC REASONING

This test is designed to assess your ability to solve word problems. The math covered in this test is mostly arithmetic—nothing too complex. The topics often include percents, decimals, proportions, and averages. Of course, to do well you'll need a strong background in the basics: addition, subtraction, multiplication, and division. If you're weak in any of these areas, you better practice, since every question on this test requires at least one of these skills, and usually more. For this section, you're given 36 minutes to answer 30 questions.

WORD KNOWLEDGE

The Word Knowledge test is designed to assess your vocabulary. Luckily, you've probably seen and used most of the words on the test. The vocabulary here is not as tough as that of the SAT, for example. There shouldn't be too many surprises. But since you're only given 11 minutes to answer 35 questions, the hard part of this test is getting through it all. We'll talk about how to deal with the time pressure later on.

PARAGRAPH COMPREHENSION

This test assesses your ability to comprehend written text. You're given several reading passages and then asked questions about them. For the most part, the passages are pretty straightforward and easy to understand. The challenge here, like in the Word Knowledge test, lies in the time limit. You're given only 13 minutes to answer 15 questions, and that includes time for reading the passages. Later on, we'll discuss techniques that will save you time and improve your accuracy on this section.

NUMERICAL OPERATIONS

This test is all about speed. You're given only 3 minutes to solve 50 simple mathematical computations. You probably won't be able to answer every question here, so just do as many as you can. The questions are all simple addition, subtraction, multiplication, or division problems. Once again, a strong background in these areas will really help you on this test.

CODING SPEED

This is another test that's all about speed. It's also one of the strangest tests on the ASVAB. In this test you are given a "key." The key is a list of ten words with a unique numerical code assigned to each. Following each key are twelve "questions" that simply give you one of the words from the key. Your task is to choose the correct numerical code for that word. There are 84 questions and you have only 7 minutes. Again, you probably won't be able to finish the entire section—very few people can. The important thing is to correctly answer as many as possible.

AUTO AND SHOP INFORMATION

This test assesses your knowledge of auto mechanics and common shop practices. Some of the topics covered include the major systems in an automobile engine, common hand tools, fastening devices, and rivets. If you've taken a course in auto mechanics or shop or even if you've just worked on cars a lot, you should do pretty well on this test. If you haven't, most of the questions will look pretty unfamiliar. For this section, you're given 11 minutes to answer 25 questions.

MATHEMATICS KNOWLEDGE

This test is more difficult than the Arithmetic Reasoning test. The concepts covered on this test come primarily from algebra and geometry. You will see questions asking you to solve for x, factor, and find the area of geometric figures. Luckily, there is no trigonometry or calculus on this test. You are given 24 minutes to solve 25 problems, which is difficult for many test takers. Don't worry though, we will talk about time-saving techniques later.

MECHANICAL COMPREHENSION

The Mechanical Comprehension test assesses your knowledge of basic mechanical principles. Topics could include levers, block-and-tackles, wheels, axles, inclined planes, wedges, gears, force, friction, power, and work. If you're familiar with these subjects, the test shouldn't be too difficult for you. If you're not, you may have a hard time with it. For this section, you're given 19 minutes to answer 25 questions.

ELECTRICAL INFORMATION

This test measures your knowledge of basic electrical principles, including currents, flow, resistance, circuits, and Ohm's law. If you're familiar with these subjects the questions shouldn't be too challenging. For this question, you're given 9 minutes to answer 20 questions.

PERCEPTUAL ABILITIES*

Some recent versions of the ASVAB have included an eleventh test that assesses your ability to visualize three-dimensional figures and piece them together when they're taken apart. Since this subtest is so new, we don't know much about it. What we do know, however, is that your score on this test does not affect your chances of being accepted to the armed services. What it is used for is unclear. One theory is that it is used to help identify people who may be successful at certain, specific jobs within the military. We will not be discussing this subtest in the book, but wanted to make you aware of its existence in case you see it.

   *Note: some recent versions include this test.

YOUR SCORE

The ASVAB is used as a qualification test for the armed services. It is designed to measure general abilities in various subjects. You'll receive a separate score for each subtest, as well as three academic composite scores. The three composite scores measure your academic achievement and assess your ability to learn more through further training. These three scores are generated as follows:

> The Verbal Ability Composite is generated by adding the scores from the Word Knowledge and Paragraph Comprehension tests. It is intended to measure the student's capacity for verbal activities.

> The Math Ability Composite is generated by adding the scores from the Arithmetic Reasoning and Mathematics Knowledge tests. It is intended to measure the student's capacity for mathematical activities.

> The Academic Ability Composite is generated by adding the scores from the Verbal Ability Composite and Math Ability Composite. It is intended to indicate the student's potential for further education.

Recruiters use these composites to help identify areas the recruit may be successful in.

To enlist in the armed services, you must receive a minimum score on the ASVAB. That score is different for each branch of the army. To find out what you need to enlist in the service of your choice, contact your local recruiter. While the minimum score may be different, how the scores are generated is the same for all branches. The scores from the Arithmetic Reasoning, Word Knowledge, Paragraph Comprehension, and Mathematics Knowledge tests are used to generate a raw score. The formula for this is:

(score from the Word Knowledge test × 2) + (score from the Paragraph Comprehension test × 2) + (score from the Arithmetic Reasoning test) + (score from the Mathematics Knowledge test) = Your Raw Score

That raw score is then converted into a percentile score. Your percentile score tells you how well you did on the ASVAB compared to other people. For example, if you score in the 50th percentile, that means you scored higher than 49 percent of the people who took the test. Each branch of the military has a minimum percentile score they require of new recruits.

You also receive a Military Careers Score when you take the ASVAB. This score is used to help recruits determine their chances of qualifying for various occupations within the military. It is a combination of the scores from the Academic Ability composite and the Mechanical Comprehension and Electronics Information tests. The score range is 140 to 240, with an average of 200. When receiving their test results, recruits receive a copy of the book *Military Careers*. *Military Careers* describes most of the positions available in the armed services, along with the requirements for the job, the training provided, civilian counterparts, and a graph showing chances of acceptance based on the Military Careers Score. For example, a recruit with a Military Careers Score of 215 stands a 90 percent chance of qualifying for a job as a Diver, whereas someone with a 175 has less than a 10 percent chance of qualifying.

The test scores from the General Science, Auto and Shop Information, Numerical Operations, and Coding Speed subtests are not used to derive the percentile score or the Military Careers Score. Rather, they are used by recruiters to help identify other areas in which the recruit may be successful. It's important to note that the recruiter only looks at these scores if the recruit has scored above the minimum percentile score required by that branch. If you don't achieve a high enough score on the Arithmetic Reasoning, Word Knowledge, Paragraph Comprehension, and Mathematics Knowledge subtests, you won't be able to enlist.

TAKING CONTROL OF THE ASVAB

In buying this book, you've taken an important first step towards doing well on the ASVAB. Here's how to get the most out of your purchase:

HOW TO USE THIS BOOK

- **Subject Review Chapters**: We've reviewed the most important concepts that you may see on the ASVAB. As you read through the chapters, take notes of the main points. Many people find that they remember things better if they write them down. You may also find it helpful to underline or highlight important concepts in the book.

- **Quick Quizzes**: To reinforce the important concepts, we've included "Quick Quizzes" in the review chapters. These quizzes follow each of the major sections in the chapters and review what has just been covered. Use them to test your understanding of the material you just studied. If you miss several questions, you know you will need to spend a little more time studying before you move on.

- **Practice ASVAB tests**: At the back of the book you'll find three full-length practice ASVABs. We made these tests as similar to real ASVABs as possible. We suggest you use one test as an assessment of your strengths and weaknesses *before* you begin to study. This will give you an idea of what you really need to focus on during your preparation. We also recommend that you use the second test for timed drills just after you finish reviewing the ASVAB material, and the third as a full-timed practice tests to get an idea of the what taking the real test will be like. We'll give more details on how to use these tests later.

- **Answer Explanations**: We have provided an explanation for every question in the practice tests. Use these to review questions you answered incorrectly and for tips on how to get them right the next time.

- **The Hit Parade**: Chapter 4 contains the Hit Parade, a list of words that every ASVAB-taker should know. While we can't guarantee that you will see these words on the test, we wouldn't be surprised if at least a few of them popped up. In addition, they serve as a good assessment of your vocabulary. If you know most of the words on the Hit Parade, you're probably in pretty good shape. If a lot of them look unfamiliar to you, you better start studying!

DEVELOPING YOUR STUDY STRATEGY

The first thing you should do to start preparing for the ASVAB is to develop a strategy. Set up a realistic schedule for studying and stick to it. But before you decide how to allocate your time, take a full-length practice test. This will help you identify what you need to focus on. If you're interested in a particular job opportunity, ask your recruiter which tests are important for that job. You may be able to ignore complete sections of the test if they're not needed for what you want to do.

Once you know what you need to study, you can dive into the review chapters. Plan on spending a few hours at a time studying. Trying to do too much in one sitting is exhausting and usually futile. As you work through the chapters, use the Quick Quizzes to test your comprehension of the material. If you miss any of the questions, make sure to go back and review the section covering that material before you move on. After you finish each review chapter, use the corresponding section from the second practice test as a timed drill. For example, when you finish reviewing the science section, use the General Science subtest from the second practice test as a timed drill. When you have reviewed everything you need to, use the third practice test to simulate the real ASVAB.

When taking the practice tests, make sure you're in a quiet area where you won't be disturbed. If you're taking a full-timed test or a timed drill, make sure to use a clock, watch, or timer. Try to take the first and third practice tests all in one sitting—just as if you were taking the real thing. You won't be given any breaks between the sections, so try not to take any on the practice tests either. In other words, make them as much like the real ASVAB as possible.

HOW TO CRACK THE ASVAB

In addition to providing a thorough review of the material on the ASVAB, we've developed some test-taking techniques that will help you boost your score and make the test easier. Some techniques work great for the entire test, while others work just for a particular section or type of question. Below are some techniques that will help throughout the entire test. Techniques specific to a particular section or question type will be covered in the appropriate review chapter.

LETTER OF THE DAY

There is no guessing penalty on the ASVAB. That means if you answer a question wrong, it won't hurt you (it just won't help you). That's why it's always in your best interest to answer every question. That doesn't mean you need to understand or even read every question. It just means that you want to put down an answer for every question on the test. That's where your letter of the day comes in.

Every question on the ASVAB is accompanied by four answer choices: A, B, C, and D. When we say that you should choose a "letter of the day," we simply mean that you should choose one of those four letters to fill in questions that you can't answer. For example, if you are running out of time on the Word Knowledge test (which a lot of people do, by the way), you should just fill in B (or whatever letter you chose) on all the remaining questions. You won't get every one right, but you'll probably pick up a few extra points. Leaving questions blank will get you absolutely nothing.

Use your letter of the day whenever you are about to run out of time on a section. If you know that you won't be able to finish a section, save a little time at the end, perhaps the last minute or the last 30 seconds, to fill in your letter for the remaining questions.

PROCESS OF ELIMINATION

The ASVAB is a multiple-choice test. That means you get to see the correct answer for every question on the test—it's one of the four choices you're given. You also get to see three incorrect answers. Your job is to pick out the correct answer from among the incorrect answers. If you don't know the answer right away, your best option is to use a technique called Process of Elimination (POE for short). Process of Elimination is the single most important tool you can use on any standardized test.

POE is useful for those questions where you don't quite know the answer. It helps you get rid of the answers that you know are wrong, thereby increasing your chances of finding the right answer. Every time you can eliminate an answer choice, your chances of choosing the correct answer increase.

Try the following question:

1. What is the capital of Malawi?

If you happen to be from Malawi, this question will be easy for you. If not, then probably all you can do is guess, but you might be able to improve your chances of guessing correctly by using POE. Let's look at the answer choices:

    A. Wasington, D.C.
    B. Paris
    C. London
    D. Lilongwe

You may not know the answer, but three of the choices are obviously wrong. This leaves you with only one answer left, the correct one!

Even when POE doesn't get rid of all of the wrong answers, it can still help you. Let's look at another example:

2. What is the capital of Qator?

    A. Paris
    B. Dukham
    C. Tokyo
    D. Doha

This time you can probably eliminate only two choices. That leaves you with two to choose from. But that's still much better than where you started from—you're much more likely to choose the correct answer when you have only two choices, instead of four.

As you work through this book, keep some scrap paper handy. When you answer a question, write A, B, C, and D on the paper. As you work through the answer choices, use your pencil to cross off answers that you can eliminate. The paper test doesn't allow you to write in the test booklet, and obviously you can't write on the computer test either, so it's a good idea to get used to using scrap paper. If you practice this now, it will be second nature when you take the real thing!

TWO-PASS SYSTEM

Every question on the ASVAB, no matter how hard or how easy, is worth one point. That's why it makes no sense to spend four minutes working on a hard problem when you can answer two easier questions in the same amount of time. Using the Two-Pass system allows you to skip the hard, time-consuming questions, and go right to the easy, quick questions, thereby scoring the most points in the shortest amount of time. Here's how the system works:

Work through the section in two passes. The first time you go through it, do all the questions that seem easy to you—the ones where you know the answer right away—and skip the harder ones. This ensures that you pick up all of the easy points in the test. When you've reached the end of the section, stop and go back to the beginning. In the second pass, answer the questions you skipped before. If you come across a really hard question that you don't know how to answer, or that will take a long time, use POE to eliminate what you can and guess. Don't spend too much time on any one question.

This technique works only on the paper ASVAB. Unfortunately, if you take the ASVAB on computer, you will have to answer the questions in the order you seem them—you can't skip questions on the computer test. In addition, the two-pass technique is only necessary on certain tests. It shouldn't be used on the Numerical Operations, or Coding Speed tests. These tests have questions that are almost universally equivalent in level of difficulty, making the Two-Pass System unnecessary.

Your Scrap Paper

You are given scrap paper to do your work on. Use it! It is much easier to work out problems on paper than in your head. Using scrap paper also helps you avoid careless mistakes. This is particularly important on the Arithmetic Reasoning and Mathematics Knowledge tests. Many of the questions in these two tests require several steps to solve. Trying to solve them in your head will only lead to mistakes and slow you down. In addition, you can use your scrap paper to help you with POE, like we discussed earlier.

In Conclusion

As we stated earlier, these techniques will work well for most of the test. As you work through the book, however, pay attention to other techniques as we discuss them. There are some great tricks that will help you with particular questions. Some of the hardest questions on the test become much easier once you know how to handle them.

PART II

How to Crack
the ASVAB

2

GENERAL SCIENCE

INTRODUCTION TO THE GENERAL SCIENCE TEST

The ASVAB General Science Test covers basic concepts taught in most high school science courses. It's a broad survey of important topics from the life sciences, physical sciences, and earth sciences. More specifically, the following areas are covered:

- Life Sciences: biology, ecology, human anatomy, nutrition, botany, and zoology

- Physical Sciences: chemistry, units of measurement, and physics

- Earth Sciences: geology, astronomy, meteorology, and oceanography

While the test covers a broad range of topics, it's only 25 questions long. Most of those questions will focus on the life and physical sciences, with just a few about the earth sciences. The questions tend to be short and relatively straightforward. Here's an example:

1. Which organelle is considered the "control center" of the cell?

   A. ribosome
   B. cytoplasm
   C. lysosome
   D. nucleus

   You'll have only 11 minutes to answer all 25 questions, so you'll need to move quickly. That's why it's important that you feel comfortable with the concepts being tested. Since science is such a broad field, it's impossible for us to review everything here. Don't worry, though—we'll cover all the important concepts and terms you need to know!

Study Tips for the General Science Section

- Don't try to learn everything in one or two "cram" sessions. Plan ahead and study a little bit at a time.

- Make flashcards to help you remember key concepts and definitions.

- Have friends or family members quiz you on the topics after you have studied them.

- Pay close attention to topics you didn't cover in school. You may need to study those a little more.

- Use the quiz at the end of each section to make sure you didn't miss anything important.

- Review any topics that you missed in the quizzes.

THE LIFE SCIENCES

The life sciences include biology, ecology, human anatomy, nutrition, botany, and zoology. That's a lot of information to know, but the ASVAB only tests certain concepts from each field of study. We will review all of the most important concepts. Pay close attention to the words in bold, because you'll need to know what they mean. After the review, we'll test your knowledge with a quiz. So let's get started…

BIOLOGY

CLASSIFICATION OF LIVING THINGS

Since the beginning of human civilization, scientists have worked to understand how living organisms are related to each other. To do this, they need a system of classification that assigns plants and animals to groups based on shared traits. Species are first classified into large groups that have fewer traits in common and then smaller groups with more traits in common.

Those groups are:

Kingdom, Phylum, Class, Order, Family, Genus, and Species.

To help remember the order of classification, use the following mnemonic:

King	(Kingdom)
Philip	(Phylum)
Came	(Class)
Over	(Order)
From	(Family)
Germany	(Genus)
Soaked	(Species)

Here's how the classification system works:

- Each kingdom is made up of many phyla.

- Each phylum (the plural is "phyla") is made up of many classes.

- Each class is made up of many orders.

- Each order is made up of many families.

- Each family is made up of many genuses.

- Each genus is made up of many species.

The 5 Kingdoms	Characteristics	Examples
1. Monera Prokaryotes	single-celled; microscopic	Bacteria
2. Protista Eukaryotes	mainly unicellular or colonial	Protozoa
3. Fungi	plantlike, but cannot carry on photosynthesis	Mushrooms
4. Plantae Multicellular	carry out photosynthesis	Trees
5. Animalia Multicellular	possess complex organ systems	Humans

Humans belong to the Animalia Kingdom. Therefore, it's important that you know the characteristics of the phyla in the Animalia Kingdom.

CLASSIFICATION OF ANIMALS

Phylum	Characteristics	Examples	
1. Porifera	Two layers of cells with pores	Sponge	
2. Coelenterata	Two layers of cells; hollow digestive cavity with tentacles	Hydra, jellyfish	
3. Platyhelminthes (Flatworms)	Three layers of cells; flat; bilateral symmetry	Tapeworm, planaria, fluke	
4. Nematoda (Roundworms)	Digestive system with a mouth and anus; round	Hookworm	
5. Rotifera	Digestive system	Rotifer	
6. Annelida (Segmented worms)	Long, segmented body; digestive system; closed circulatory system	Earthworm	
7. Mollusca	Soft bodies; hard shell	Clam, snail	
8. Arthropoda	Segmented body; jointed legs; exoskeleton		
Class Crustacea	Gills for breathing; jointed legs	Crab, lobster	
Insecta	Three body parts; one pair of antennae; six legs; tracheal breathing system	Bee, grasshopper	
Arachnida	Two body parts; eight legs	Spider	
Chilopoda	One pair of legs per segment	Centipede	
Diplopoda	Two pairs of legs per segment	Millipede	
9. Echinodermata (Spiny-skinned)	Spiny exoskeleton; complete digestive system	Starfish, sea urchin, sea cucumber	

THE HUMAN BODY

The human body is made up of several complex systems that work together to obtain and distribute nutrients throughout the body, remove wastes, adapt to the environment, and reproduce. We will review each system separately.

The Musculoskeletal System

The musculoskeletal system is responsible for holding the body together. Without a skeleton, humans would be just a pile of skin and organs. Humans wear their skeletons on the inside, which is called an **endoskeleton**. Organisms who wear their skeleton on the outside, such as insects, have **exoskeletons**. Both endoskeletons and exoskeletons provide support and protection for the organism.

The human skeleton is made up of **cartilage** and **bone**. Cartilage is found at the end of all bones, at the joints, in the nose, and in the ear. It is more flexible than bone and is used as a buffer between bones and as a support in the ear and nose. Bones provide the primary support for the body. They also protect the organs, produce blood cells, and store minerals, such as calcium.

Muscles work with the skeleton to support, protect, and move the body. There are three types of muscle in the body: **cardiac**, **skeletal**, and **smooth**. Cardiac muscles are found in the heart. Their movements are what you feel when you say your heart is pounding. Skeletal muscles are attached to the skeleton and move your body around. They are responsible for all voluntary movements you make. Smooth muscles are found in the stomach, intestines, and bladder. They are involuntary, meaning that you have no control over their movements.

The Digestive System

The digestive system is responsible for breaking down the food you eat into molecules that the body can absorb. It consists of the mouth, esophagus, small intestine, large intestine, rectum, and anus.

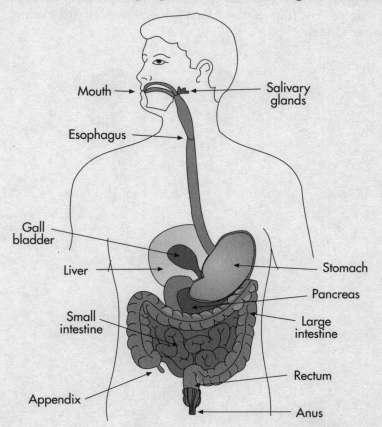

Mouth: Food enters the mouth, and the tongue and teeth begin the process of breaking food down by chewing.

Esophagus: The chewed food moves from the mouth into the esophagus. Contractions push the food through the esophagus and into the stomach.

Stomach: The food is mixed with gastric acids and **pepsin**, which break the food down further.

Small Intestine: The food moves from the stomach to the small intestine. The small intestine is very long, about 23 feet long on average. The food is broken down completely by enzymes produced in the walls of the small intestine and the pancreas. Bile, which is produced by the liver, breaks down fats. The broken-down food is absorbed into the bloodstream from the small intestine and carried throughout the body.

Large Intestine: The remaining matter moves into the large intestine where water and minerals are absorbed into the body.

Rectum: The solid waste matter is stored here.

Anus: Solid waste matter is periodically released through the anus. Liquid waste (urine) is sent to the bladder and released through the urethra.

The Excretory System

The organ that regulates excretion is the **kidney**. The kidneys are made up of millions of tiny structures called **nephrons**. The function of the nephrons is to filter the blood. The fluid filtered out of the blood is called filtrate. The filtrate travels through the nephron to the ureter and then into the bladder, where it is stored. The filtrate, now called urine, remains in the bladder until it is excreted out of the body through the **urethra**.

The Respiratory System

You need oxygen to survive. The job of the respiratory system is to collect air from the environment, filter out oxygen from the air, and deliver the oxygen to the circulatory system.

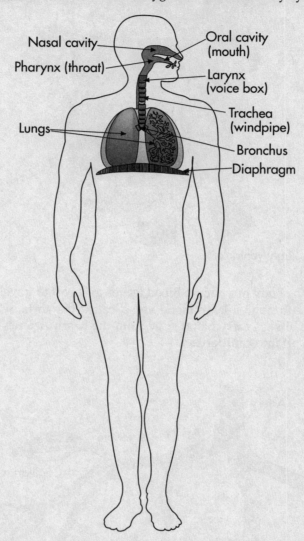

Air enters the body through the mouth or nose and passes through the **pharynx** and **larynx**. It then enters the **trachea**, which is covered by the **epiglottis**. The epiglottis prevents food from going down the wrong pipe. The trachea branches into the **left and right bronchi**. These two tubes break down into smaller tubes called **bronchioles**. Each bronchiole ends in a small sac called an **alveolus**. In the alveolus, the oxygen crosses from the lungs into the blood stream.

The Circulatory System

The purpose of the **circulatory system** is to transport nutrients and oxygen throughout the body and to get rid of wastes. The main organ in the circulatory system is the **heart**. The heart pumps blood through the body. It is divided into four chambers, two on the left and two on the right. Once in the blood stream, the circulatory system moves the oxygen throughout the body. The circulatory system also brings carbon dioxide back to the alveolus so the respiratory system can get rid of it when you exhale.

Left atrium

Right atrium

Left ventricle

Right ventricle

Blood flows through the body in a circuit. Blood leaves the heart to travel through the body from the left ventricle. It flows through a large blood vessel called the **aorta**, which then branches into smaller **arteries**. Arteries always carry blood *away* from the heart. Arteries branch off into smaller **arterioles**, which branch off into **capillaries**.

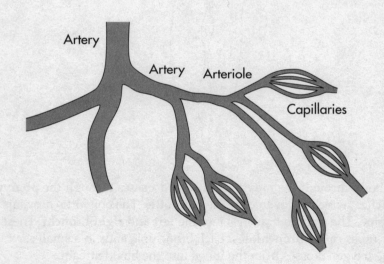

Artery

Artery   Arteriole

Capillaries

You have thousands of capillaries in your body. Capillaries exchange oxygen, nutrients, and wastes with the tissues of your body.

Once the blood has been through the tissues and returned to the capillaries it has very little oxygen left. It moves from the capillaries to vessels called **venules**. The venules meet up with larger vessels called **veins**. The veins carry the blood *into* the heart through the right atrium and then the right ventricle. The blood is sent from the right ventricle directly to the lungs for more oxygen. Once the blood has become **oxygenated** it moves back into the heart through the left atrium. From the left atrium it is sent into the left ventricle, which is where we started. To review, here is the path the blood takes through the body:

Left Ventricle → Artery → Arterioles → Capillaries → Tissue → Capillaries → Venules → Veins → Right Atrium → Right Ventricle → Lungs → Left Atrium → Left Ventricle

Blood consists of two things:

- **Plasma** (the liquid part of blood)
- **Cells** (the stuff suspended in the liquid)

As we've already discussed, blood carries oxygen, nutrients, and wastes throughout the body. It also carries three types of cells: red blood cells (also called erythrocytes), white blood cells (called leukocytes), and platelets.

- **Red blood cells:** The oxygen-carrying cells of the blood.
- **White blood cells:** The cells that fight infections by destroying foreign organisms.
- **Platelets:** Cell fragments that are involved in blood clotting.

All blood cells are made in the bone marrow, which is located in the center of the bones.

Blood comes in four different types: A, B, AB, and O. Type O is the **universal donor**, which means that it can be given to anyone in a blood transfusion. Type AB is the **universal recipient**, which means that it won't react negatively to any type of new blood that is introduced to it during a blood transfusion. In other words, a person with type AB blood can receive any kind of blood.

The Lymphatic System

The lymphatic system is a network of vessels that follow the routes of blood vessels. The job of the lymphatic system is to collect and return fluids to the blood and to fight infection, using **lymphocytes**.

Lymph nodes are bulges found along the path of a lymph vessel. Lymph nodes contain lots of lymphocytes. Since lymphocytes are important in fighting infection, the lymph nodes often swell up when you are sick.

The Nervous System

The nervous system consists of the brain, spinal cord, and billions of nerve cells called **neurons**. The nervous system serves two primary purposes: to control the functions of the body and to receive stimuli from the environment.

There are two parts to the nervous system, the **central nervous system** and the **peripheral nervous system**. The central nervous system includes the neurons in the brain and the spinal cord. The peripheral nervous system is made up of all other neurons, including neurons in the skin, organs, and blood vessels. It can broken down further into the **somatic nervous system** and the **autonomic nervous system**. The somatic nervous system controls voluntary actions, such as waving your hand or dancing. The autonomic nervous system controls involuntary actions, such as your heartbeat and your digestive system. The autonomic nervous system can be broken down into the **sympathetic** and **parasympathetic** nervous systems. Both of these systems are responsible for preparing the body to defend itself, also known as the "fight or flight" response. The sympathetic nervous system raises your heart and respiration rates, causes your blood vessels to constrict, increases glucose levels, and produces "goosebumps" when you feel threatened. The job of the parasympathetic nervous system is to return the body to normal when the danger is over. To remember the divisions of the nervous system, take a look at the following flow chart:

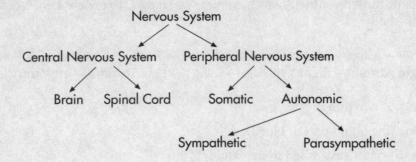

The **brain** is made up of the cerebrum, cerebellum, hypothalamus, and medulla.

Divisions Within the Brain	
Parts of the Brain	**Function**
Cerebrum	Controls all voluntary activities; receives and interprets sensory information
Cerebellum	Coordinates muscle activity
Hypothalamus	Regulates homeostasis and secretes hormones
Medulla	Controls involuntary actions such as breathing and swallowing

The brain is called the "control center" of the body, because information from every part of the body and the surrounding environment is sent to the brain for processing. The brain responds to this information by sending out messages through neurons.

Neurons are specialized cells found in the nervous system. Their job is to send impulses between body parts. Here is what a typical neuron looks like:

Neuron

A neuron consists of a **cell body**, **dendrites**, **nucleus**, and **axon**. The cell body contains the nucleus and other objects. The nucleus is the "brain" of the neuron. The dendrites receive impulses and transmit them through the cell body and axon. If the impulse is strong enough, the axon will send it on to the next neuron, which will pick it up via its dendrites and start the process over again.

The Endocrine System

We've seen how the nervous system controls body functions. It works very quickly and its results last only a short time. The **endocrine system** also works to control the body but works slower and the results last longer. It works through the release of **hormones**. Hormones are chemical messengers that are made by endocrine glands and secreted into the blood stream. Once in the blood stream, they go everywhere in the body, but only affect organs that have receptors for that particular hormone. These organs are called target organs. Here is a summary of the hormones and their effects on the body:

Organ	Hormone(s)	Effect
Anterior Pituitary	FSH	Stimulates activity in ovaries and testes
	LH	Stimulates activity in ovary (release of ovum) and production of testosterone
	ACTH	Stimulates the adrenal cortex
	TSH	Stimulates thyroid gland
	Growth Hormone	Stimulates bone and muscle growth
	Prolactin	Causes milk secretion
Posterior Pituitary	Oxytocin	Causes uterus to contract
	Vasopressin	Causes kidney to reabsorb water
Thyroid	Thyroid Hormone	Regulates metabolic rate
	Calcitonin	Lowers blood calcium levels
Parathyroid	Parathyroid Hormone	Increases blood calcium concentration
Adrenal Cortex	Aldosterone	Increases Na^+ and H_2O reabsorption in kidney
Adrenal Medulla	Epinephrine Norepinephrine	Increases blood glucose level and heart rate
Pancreas	Insulin	Decreases blood sugar concentration
	Glucagon	Increases blood sugar concentration
Ovaries	Estrogen	Promotes female secondary sex characteristics
	Progesterone	Thickens endometrial lining
Testes	Testosterone	Promotes male secondary sex characteristics

While both the nervous system and endocrine system work to control the body, there are important differences between the two that you should know:

- The nervous system sends impulses using neurons, whereas the endocrine system secretes hormones.

- Nerve impulses act quickly and control short-lived events such as muscle contractions, whereas hormones are slower acting but can last much longer—for example, the testosterone produced during puberty is a hormone.

The Reproductive System

Reproduction involves two sets of organs, the male reproductive organs and the female reproductive organs. During reproduction, the male spermatozoon fuse with the female ovum, creating a **zygote**. The zygote eventually develops into a fetus.

The **male reproductive system** produces **sperm** in the testes in small tubes called the **seminiferous tubules**. These tiny tubules merge to form a large duct called the **vas deferens**. The vas deferens connects with the urethra, which then carries the sperm out of the body. The sperm is carried out in a fluid called semen. Semen is secreted by several glands and provides nutrients for the sperm.

The main organs involved in the **female reproductive system** are the **ovaries** and the **uterus**. The ovaries store the ova and release one ovum every menstrual cycle. The ovum travels through the fallopian tube to the uterus. If the ovum is fertilized by a sperm, the fertilized ovum implants itself in the lining of the uterus, and pregnancy follows. If the ovum is not fertilized, the lining of the uterus breaks down and is eventually passed out of the body through the vagina in a process called **menstruation,** and then a new cycle begins.

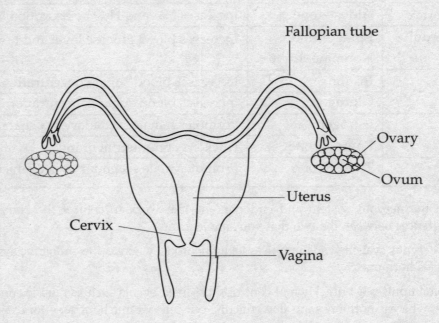

NUTRITION

A healthy diet requires protein, carbohydrates, fat, fiber, minerals, and vitamins. Protein, carbohydrates, and fat are necessary for your body to produce energy. Fiber, vitamins, and minerals are necessary for your body to function properly.

Protein: Protein is necessary for the body's growth and repair. It can be found in meat, fish, eggs, cheese, peas, legumes, and grains.

Carbohydrates: There are two types of carbohydrates—sugars and starches. These are the main energy sources necessary for the body's metabolism. Starches are found in bread, cereal, and pasta. Sugars come from fruit, cane sugar, and beets.

Fats: Fats also provide energy for metabolism. There are three types of fats: saturated, monosaturated, and polyunsaturated. Saturated fats tend to increase the levels of bad cholesterol in the blood, while monosaturated and polysaturated fats tend to decrease levels of bad cholesterol. Fat can be found in meat, dairy products, fish, and oil.

Fiber: Fiber passes through the body unchanged but is necessary for a healthy diet. It provides bulk, which allows the large intestine to carry away waste matter.

Minerals: Small amounts of minerals are needed for a balanced diet. Most people get enough. Some necessary minerals are iron, zinc, calcium, magnesium, and sodium chloride (salt).

Vitamins: Vitamins help regulate the metabolism. Below is a table of vitamins necessary for good health.

Vitamin	Sources	Result of Deficiency
A	Eggs, fruit, butter, liver, vegetables	Night blindness, skin infections loss of appetite, diarrhea
B_1	Wheat germ, bran, grains, poultry, eggs, pasta, beans	Loss of appetite, Beriberi
B_2	Liver, dairy, whole grains, green vegetables	Weakness, skin infections
B_{12}	Meat, dairy, eggs, fish	Anemia
C	Citrus fruit, tomatoes, vegetables, strawberries	Scurvy
D	Milk, eggs, dairy, fish	Rickets
E	Vegetable oils, nuts, meat cereals, egg yolk	Anemia
K	Green vegetables, egg yolk, cheese, pork, liver	Excessive bleeding

THE CELL

Every living organism—plants, animals, and others—is made up of cells. The smallest organisms, like bacteria, are called **unicellular**, because they are made up of only one cell. Larger organisms, like humans, are made up of billions of cells and are called **multicellular**. Inside of all cells are small structures called **organelles**. There are several different organelles, each with their own distinct functions. Here is what a typical cell looks like:

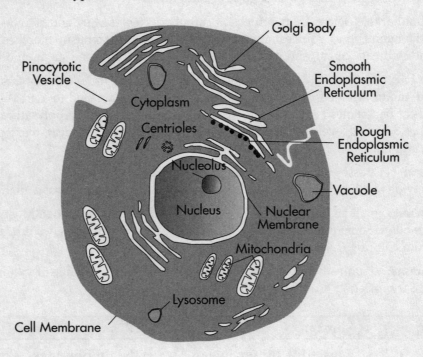

Organelle	Function
Cell membrane	Outer membrane of the cell. Controls what enters and leaves the cell.
Centrioles	Form spindle fibers during cellular division.
Golgi Body	Sorts and packages proteins.
Lysosomes	Digest old organelles and foreign substances.
Mitochondria	Produces energy for the cell.
Nucleolus	Part of the nucleus. Makes ribosomes.
Nucleus	Control center of the cell. Contains the chromosomes.
Ribosomes	Site of the protein synthesis.
Rough endoplasmic reticulum(ER)	Makes proteins to be exported out of cell.
Smooth endoplasmic reticulum	Makes lipids and detoxifies enzymes.
Vacuole	Stores wastes and other materials.

The cells of plants and animals are similar, with just a few differences. Those differences are the following:

- Both plant and animal cells have a cell membrane that surrounds the cell. Plant cells, however, also have a rigid, protective outer covering, called the **cell wall**, which surrounds the cell membrane.

- Plant cells possess **chloroplasts,** while animal cells do not. Chloroplasts are involved in photosynthesis (the process through which plants make their own food).

- The vacuoles in a plant cell are much larger and tend to crowd the other organelles.

A Quick Word about Chromosomes

Chromosomes are located in the nucleus of cells. They contain **DNA**—the hereditary blueprint of the cell. DNA determines the genetic makeup of organisms. It tells the cell how to function, when to reproduce, and when to die. Things like eye color, hair color, height, weight, and even some diseases are controlled by DNA. That's why people who are related look alike—they share similar DNA! Every human cell, except for the sex cells, has 46 chromosomes. A human cell with 46 chromosomes is **diploid**. That means it has two sets of 23 chromosomes each. Sex cells, which have only 23 chromosomes, are called **haploid**. We will talk more about this later. For now all you need to remember is that most human cells have 46 chromosomes.

THE CELL CYCLE

Thousands of cells are dying in your body right now. Cells have only a limited life span and die when that life span is over. But don't worry—your body is making new cells as quickly as the old ones die out. In fact, your skin cells die off so fast that you have an entirely new skin every few weeks. The body produces all these new cells through a process called **cell division**.

Cell division, also called **mitosis**, is a process that allows our body to replace the aging cells with fresh new ones. There are two periods in a cell's life span: interphase and mitosis.

Interphase

Interphase is the time period after the cell's birth, and before it undergoes mitosis, when it copies itself. During interphase the cell is carrying out it's normal functions. Before interphase ends the cell makes a copy of all its chromosomes. The duplicated chromosome is connected to the original chromosome by the centromere. Each individual chromosome is called a **chromatid**.

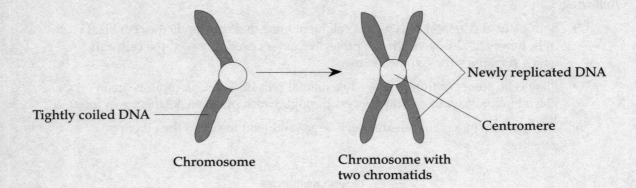

Tightly coiled DNA

Chromosome

Newly replicated DNA

Centromere

Chromosome with
two chromatids

When interphase is over, all 46 of the original chromosomes have duplicated. The cell now has 46 chromosomes with 2 chromatids each. The cell is now ready for mitosis.

Mitosis

Mitosis is the process a cell goes through when it divides. There are four stages to mitosis, with the end result being a new cell.

> **Stage 1: Prophase.** During prophase the nuclear membrane begins to break up. The chromosomes thicken and form coils. The centrioles move away from each other and form a system of microtubules called **spindle fibers**. The spindle fibers attach to the chromosomes and help them move around.

Nuclear
envelope pieces

Centrioles

Condensed
chromosome

Mitotic
spindle

Note: In the drawing above, only 4 chromosomes are shown. This is only to keep the drawing simple. Remember, in a real cell there are 46 chromosomes, all doing exactly the same thing.

> **Stage 2: Metaphase.** Now that the spindle fibers are attached to the chromosomes, they help them line up in the middle of the cell. The area of the cell is called the **metaphase plate**.

metaphase plate

Stage 3: Anaphase. During this stage, the spindle fibers pull the chromatids apart. The separated chromatids are pulled to opposite poles.

Stage 4: Telophase. The last stage is telophase. During this stage, a nuclear membrane forms around each set of chromosomes. Then the cytoplasm splits in a process called **cytokinesis**. The cell membrane forms around each new cell and two daughter cells are formed, each with 46 chromosomes.

Once the daughter cells are formed they enter interphase and the whole process starts up again. Here is a mnemonic device you can use to help you remember all that:

I've Probably Mixed All This Up!

I've	Interphase	I is for Interlude
Probably	Prophase	P is for Prepare
Mixed	Metaphase	M is for Meet
All	Anaphase	A is for Apart
This	Telophase	T is for Tear
Up!	Up	Up to the top and start over again

Meiosis

Recall from our discussion of chromosomes that sex cells are **haploid**, which means they contain only 23 chromosomes. This is because the sex cells, the sperm and ova, combine during fertilization to create a new cell, called a zygote. If they both had 46 chromosomes, then the new zygote would have 92 chromosomes, twice the number it should have. Therefore, sex cells are made differently from all other cells. The process by which sex cells are made is called **meiosis**. Meiosis occurs only in sex organs called gonads. In males, the sex organs are the **testes**; in females they're the **ovaries**.

Meiosis, unlike mitosis, takes place in two rounds of cell division, called meosis 1 and meiosis 2. Before meiosis starts, a diploid cell (a cell with 46 chromosomes) undergoes interphase. Just like in mitosis, the chromosomes replicate into 46 paired sets. Once this has occurred, the cell is ready to undergo meiosis 1.

> **Meiosis 1:** is made up of four stages that should sound familiar: prophase 1, metaphase 1, anaphase 1, and telophase 1.
>
> **Prophase1:** During prophase 1, the nuclear membrane disappears and the centrioles move to opposite poles of the nucleus, just like in mitosis.

Unlike in mitosis, however, the chromosomes do not split up. Instead, they undergo **synapsis**. Synapsis occurs when two sets of chromosomes combine, forming a tetrad. The tetrad consists of four chromatids. Once synapsis has occurred, the four chromatids exchange segments in a process called **crossing over**.

In the picture above, the gray chromosome is swapping segments with the black chromosome. When crossing over is complete, each chromosome will consist of one gray segment and one black segment.

Metaphase 1: The tetrads line up at the metaphase plate just like in mitosis. The only difference is that the chromosomes are lined up in pairs (tetrads) during meosis. Recall that during mitosis, the chromosomes are lined up individually.

Anaphase 1: The tetrads separate and move to opposite poles. Compare this to mitosis, where the chromatids separated.

Telophase 1: The nuclear membrane forms around each set of chromosomes. The cells undergo cytokinesis and two daughter cells are the result. Notice that the cells are still diploid.

Earlier in our discussion we said that sex cells are haploid. At this point we have two diploid daughter cells. That means that meiosis isn't finished yet. We still need to go through the second stage of meiosis.

Meiosis 2 is almost identical to mitosis. The only difference is that at the beginning of mitosis there are two sets of chromosomes in the nucleus. In meosis 2, there is only one set. The cell undergoes all of the stages of mitosis: prophase, metaphase, anaphase, and telophase. Since the cell starts with 46 chromosomes and divides in half during meiosis 2, the resulting cells are haploid (23 chromosomes).

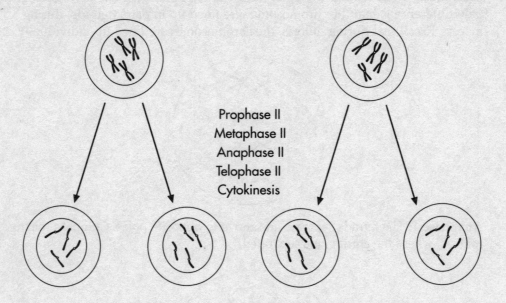

Prophase II
Metaphase II
Anaphase II
Telophase II
Cytokinesis

The resulting haploid cells are used during reproduction. The chromosomes in the cells determine the offspring's genetic makeup. In the next section, we will discuss how those chromosomes combine to create unique individuals with their own genetic characteristics.

GENETICS

Genetics is the study of heredity. Heredity is the process by which traits are passed from parents to children. Let's start by covering some basic definitions:

A **trait**, or characteristic, is produced through heredity by **genes**.

Genes, which are located in the chromosomes of cells, tell the cells how to behave. Genes consist of a pair of hereditary factors called **alleles**. Each organism carries two alleles for a trait.

An allele can be **dominant** or **recessive**. If an individual has two identical alleles for a trait—either two dominant alleles or two recessive alleles—then the individual is **homozygous**. If an individual has two different alleles for a trait, then he or she is **heterozygous**.

We indicate dominant alleles by using uppercase letters such as *B*. When denoting recessive alleles use lowercase letters such as *b*.

If an organism has one dominant allele, it will exhibit the trait of that allele, even if the other allele in the pair is recessive. For example, an organism with a *Bb* pair will express the dominant trait linked to the **B**. If an organism has only recessive alleles (*bb*), it will express the recessive trait.

When discussing the physical characteristics of a person we refer to his or her **phenotype**. When discussing genetic makeup, we are talking about **genotype**.

One way the ASVAB may test you about genetics is by asking you to predict phenotypes and genotypes. This might sound difficult but it's actually quite simple if you use Punnett squares.

A Punnett square is just a four-chambered box like the one on the following page.

On the sides of the Punnett square you list the genotypes of the two parents. Then you fill in the box according to what you wrote on the outside. This gives you the probability of each phenotype in the offspring. Let's look at an example using eye color.

Suppose the allele for blue eyes is recessive and the allele for brown eyes is dominant. We would express this using B for the dominant allele brown, and b for the recessive allele blue. Now let's assume we have two parents with the following genotypes:

Parent A   Parent B
   bb   Bb

We would fill in the Punnett square using this information.

By looking at the genotypes of the parents, we can see that Parent A is homozygous for the blue phenotype bb and Parent B is heterozygous for the brown phenotype Bb. Now let's look at the offspring.

Two of the offspring have the heterozygous genotype Bb, which means they have brown eyes, and the other two have the homozygous genotype bb, which means they have blue eyes. This means that 50 percent of the offspring will have the brown phenotype and 50 percent will have the blue phenotype.

Let's try one more problem. Suppose that a plant produces flowers that are either white or pink. White is the dominant trait and pink is recessive. Let's look at a cross between two plants with these genotypes:

Parent A   Parent B
   Ww   Ww

Here is what the Punnett square looks like:

Both parents have the genotype Ww, which means that both parents have white flowers, because W denotes the dominant gene. However, both parents also carry the recessive gene for pink flowers, w. The parents in this example are both heterozygous. Now let's discuss the offspring.

Our four results in the Punnett square are WW, Ww, Ww, and ww. What do each of these mean?

- WW means the plant is homozygous for the white trait and has a white phenotype.
- Ww means the plant is heterozygous for the white trait and has a white phenotype.
- ww means the plant is homozygous for the pink trait and has a pink phenotype.

Therefore, 75 percent of the plants will have the white phenotype, and 25 percent will have the pink phenotype.

Sex Determination

The sex of offspring is determined by genes located in the sex chromosomes. Females carry the homozygous genotype XX, and males the heterozygous genotype XY. As you will recall, conception occurs when a sperm fertilizes an egg. At this time, each parent contributes one sex chromosome to the offspring. The mother always contributes an X chromosome. The sperm that fertilizes the egg determines the sex of the offspring. If the sperm carries another X chromosome, the offspring will be female (XX). If it contributes a Y chromosome, the offspring will be male (XY).

PLANTS

So far, most of our review has focused on animals, humans in particular. You may see some questions, however, asking you about plants.

Plants, like humans, are multicellular. As we mentioned above, plant cells differ from animal cells in that they possess a cell wall. The purpose of the cell wall is to provide support for the plant and to help prevent it from drying out. Another difference that we mentioned before is that plant cells possess **chloroplasts**. Chloroplasts are essential for photosynthesis.

Photosynthesis

As you have probably noticed, plants do not need to search for food—they don't hunt, cook, or grocery shop. But like all living things, they do need nutrients to survive. What makes plants special is that they produce their own food. The process by which plants make food is called **photosynthesis**.

Photosynthesis is a process by which plants turn energy from the sun into chemical energy. The chemical reaction for photosynthesis is:

$$\text{sunlight}$$
$$6CO_2 + 12H_2O \quad \rightarrow \quad C_6H_{12}O_6 + 6O_2 + 6H_2O$$

The plant uses carbon dioxide (CO_2), water (H_2O), and sunlight to make the simple sugars that the plant uses for energy ($C_6H_{12}O_6$), in addition to byproducts of oxygen and water. Photosynthesis occurs in the chloroplasts of the plant.

Classification of Plants

Just as we classified the animal kingdom earlier, we can also classify the plant kingdom.

As you can see from the flow chart, all plants fall into one of two categories: bryophytes and tracheophytes. Bryophytes are more primitive plants, lacking true stems and leaves. Some bryophytes you may be familiar with are mosses and liverworts. Tracheophytes are what you probably think of when you think of plants. They have stems, leaves, and roots. All trees, flowers, shrubs, and ferns are tracheophytes.

FUNGI

Fungi are often mistaken for plants, but are a separate kingdom completely. They are multicellular like plants, but differ in that they do not carry on photosynthesis. They live on decomposing matter. Some common fungi are mushrooms, yeasts, and molds.

ECOLOGY

Ecology is the study of the interactions between living things and their environments. Just as biologists classify living organisms, ecologists have a system of classification.

Biosphere:	This is the area of the earth where all living things exist. It is made up of the soil, water, and air. It can be divided up into regions called biomes.
Biome:	A large region of the earth. Biomes are areas that are grouped together because of similar climate, vegetation, and animal life.
Ecosystem:	The interaction of living and nonliving things.
Community:	The area in which a group of populations live.
Population:	A group of individuals that belong to the same species.

THE BIOME

The biosphere is divided into several large regions called biomes. You may need to know the various biomes and the plant and animal life they contain for the ASVAB.

Biome 1: The Tundra. Tundra climates are found in the northern parts of Alaska, Europe, and Asia. The soil in a tundra is permanently frozen, so it is difficult for plants to grow roots. Therefore, very few trees can be found in the tundra. Common vegetation includes short shrubs, grasses, and mosses. There aren't many animals living in this rugged environment, but reindeer, caribou, wolves, and bears manage to survive here, as well as several types of insects.

Biome 2: The Taiga. Taiga is found a little south of the tundra (note that neither the taiga nor the tundra are found in the southern hemisphere). It's known as coniferous forest, because it contains many conifers (evergreen trees). Taigas have long, severe winters. Animals that can be found here include bears, wolves, elk, beavers, deer, squirrels, rabbits, and moose.

Biome 3: The Deciduous Forests. Deciduous forests are found south of the taiga. The climate here has distinct hot and cold seasons and a lot of rain. A wide variety of plants and animals can be found in these forests. Trees here, unlike coniferous trees, lose their leaves in the winter and regrow them in the spring. Some animals you might find include deer, beavers, raccoons, squirrels, foxes, bears, and rabbits.

Biome 4: The Grasslands (Savanna). Characterized by grasses and a few trees, grasslands can be found in the American Midwest, Africa, Eurasia, and South America. Summers here are hot, winters cold, and rainfall is unpredictable. Animals found in the grasslands include antelope, kangaroo, zebra, giraffe, elephants, ferrets, snakes, and lizards.

Biome 5: Tropical Rain Forests. Tropical rain forests are characterized by the heaviest rainfall anywhere on earth and the largest variety of plants and animals. They are found in South America, Africa, and Southeast Asia. The trees here tend to grow very tall, forming a canopy of leaves that prevents sunlight from reaching the ground. Animals found here include monkeys, birds, lizards, snakes, tapirs, and insects.

Biome 6: The Desert. Deserts are the driest places on earth. People often associate heat with deserts, but deserts can be hot or cold. Plant and animal life is scarce and must be adapted to the arid environment. Plants consist primarily of cactuses. Animals include jackrabbits, owls, snakes, lizards, kangaroo, and small rodents.

THE COMMUNITY

All biomes can be divided into ecosystems, which are further divided into communities. A community is made up of living things that interact with each other. All members of a community fall into one of three roles: producers, consumers, or decomposers.

Producers, also known as autotrophs, make their own food. They don't have to rely upon other species for survival. Plants, which make their own food through photosynthesis, are producers.

Consumers, also know as heterotrophs, can't produce their own food. They are forced to get it from outside sources. Primary consumers are organisms that feed on producers directly. Cows are primary consumers, since they only eat plants (they are called herbivores). Above primary consumers on the food chain are secondary consumers. They eat other primary consumers, usually animals (so they are called carnivores). Some examples are lions, wolves, and sharks. Tertiary consumers eat producers, primary consumers, and secondary consumers. Organisms that eat both plants and animals are called omnivores. Humans are an example of omnivores.

Decomposers are organisms that break down organic matter into simple products. Examples are fungi and bacteria. Eventually everything in the food chain will succumb to decomposers.

As you can see, decomposers have been left off the diagram. They are usually not considered a part of the food chain. Just remember that they decompose all living matter.

QUICK QUIZ 1

Well that's it, everything you need to know about the life sciences. Test your knowledge with the quiz below. You can check your answers at the end of the chapter. If you miss any questions, be sure to go back and review. Good luck!

1. Match the organelle on the left with its function/description on the right.

    _____ Cell membrane   A. control center of the cell, contains DNA

    _____ Centrioles   B. synthesizes proteins to be exported out of the cell

    _____ Golgi apparatus   C. site of protein synthesis

    _____ Lysosomes   D. site of cellular respiration and energy production

    _____ Rough ER   E. makes lipids and detoxifies enzymes

    _____ Ribosomes   F. stores waste and other substances

    _____ Nucleolus   G. sorts and packages membrane and secreted proteins

    _____ Vacuole   H. related to the formation of spindle during mitosis

    _____ Smooth ER   I. site of ribosome synthesis in the nucleus

    _____ Mitochondria   J. barrier that controls what enters and leaves the cell

    _____ Nucleus   K. digest foreign substances and worn organelles

2. Put the following in order from largest to smallest:

Family   Class   Phylum   Order   Kingdom   Species   Genus

K _____

P _____

C _____

O _____

P _____

G _____

S _____

3. The process by which a plant produces its own food is called _____.

4. The soil here is permanently frozen. Deep root growth is difficult, so there are very few trees. Animals such as reindeer, wolves, bears, and caribou are found here. Which biome is being described?

A.   desert

B.   grasslands

C.   taiga

D.   tundra

5. Earlobes can be attached or unattached. Attached earlobes are the dominant trait.

Parent A   Parent B
   Aa   Aa

Fill in the Punnett Square below:

A   a

A | AA | Aa

a | aA | aa

The probability that the parents produce offspring with attached earlobes is _____ percent.

The probability that the parents produce offspring with unattached earlobes is _____ percent.

6. Match the description on the right with the stage of mitosis on the left.

    _____ Interphase   A. nuclear membrane forms, cytokinesis occurs

    _____ Prophase   B. chromatids split and chromosomes move to opposite poles

    _____ Metaphase   C. chromosomes replicate

    _____ Anaphase   D. chromosomes line up

    _____ Telophase   E. nuclear membrane breaks up, spindles form, centrioles move to opposite poles

7. Fill in the blanks.

The nervous system can be divided into two parts: _____ and _____. The brain and the spinal cord are parts of the _____. The peripheral nervous system can be divided into the _____ and _____. The _____ controls voluntary actions. The _____ controls involuntary actions. The autonomic system can be divided into the _____ and _____.

8. Which organism in the food chain is a primary consumer?

    A. birds

    B. insects

    C. plants

    D. snakes

    E. mice

9. Match the description/deficiency to the vitamin.

    _____ Vitamin A   A. a lack of this may cause sterility

    _____ Vitamin B_1 B. a lack of this may cause rickets

    _____ Vitamin B_2 C. a lack of this may cause night blindness

    _____ Vitamin B_{12} D. a lack of this may cause weakness or skin infections

    _____ Vitamin C   E. a lack of this may cause appetite loss or Beriberi

    _____ Vitamin D   F. a lack of this may cause anemia

    _____ Vitamin E   G. a lack of this may cause excessive bleeding

    _____ Vitamin K   H. a lack of this may cause scurvy

10. True or False: Type O blood is the universal recipient. __false__

                                        universal donor

11. Which of the following is a bryophyte?

    A. fern

    B. oak tree

    C. moss

    D. mushroom

    E. rose

12. Which of the following are functions of the kidney?

      I. filtration of blood to remove wastes

     II. blood pressure regulation

    III. pH regulation

    A.   I only
    B.   I and II only
    C.   I and III only
    D.   II and III only
    E.   I, II, and III

13. All of the following are true about the endocrine system EXCEPT

    A.   it relies on chemical messengers that travel through the bloodstream
    B.   it is a control system that has extremely rapid effects on the body
    C.   the hormones affect only certain "target" organs
    D.   it is involved in maintaining body homeostasis
    E.   its organs secrete hormones directly into the bloodstream, rather than through ducts

14. Plants that have true roots, stems, and leaves are classified as _____.

15. Which of the following groups have the most in common with one another?

    A.   members of the same kingdom
    B.   members of the same genus
    C.   members of the same phylum
    D.   members of the same class
    E.   members of the same family

16. An organism that feeds at several trophic levels is

    A.   a carnivore
    B.   an omnivore
    C.   a primary consumer
    D.   a herbivore
    E.   a primary producer

17. Which of the following animals would you be most likely to find in a grassland biome?

    A.   caribou
    B.   beaver
    C.   bear
    D.   zebra
    E.   lizard

18. The _____ is a large duct that conducts sperm from the testes to the urethra.

19. The three types of muscle are:

   1)_____skeletay_____
   2)_____smooth_____
   3)_____cardiac_____

20. A cell that has just completed meiosis 1

   A. has 23 chromosomes
   B. has 46 chromosomes
   C. is diploid
   D. Both A and C
   E. Both B and C

21. Food moves through the digestive system in which order?

   A. mouth, esophagus, stomach, small intestine, large intestine, rectum, anus
   B. mouth, stomach, esophagus, large intestine, small intestine, rectum, anus
   C. mouth, stomach, small intestine, large intestine, esophagus, rectum, anus
   D. mouth, esophagus, small intestine, stomach, large intestine, rectum, anus
   E. mouth, esophagus, stomach, large intestine, small intestine, rectum, anus

22. Circle the appropriate word to complete the sentence.

   Ova travel from the [ovaries/uterus] through the [cervix/fallopian tubes] to the [ovaries/uterus].

23. Two parents are homozygous for the dominant trait X. Their child's genotype will be:

   A. Xx
   B. XX
   C. XY
   D. Xx or XY
   E. not enough information to determine

24. The area of the lungs where oxygen and carbon dioxide are exchanged is called

   A. bronchioles
   B. trachea
   C. alveolus
   D. capillary
   E. epiglottis

EARTH SCIENCE AND ASTRONOMY

Earth science is the study of the earth and the universe around it. It encompasses geology, oceanography, meteorology, and astronomy. A few questions on the ASVAB will test your knowledge of earth science. Let's start by looking back in time...

GEOLOGY

Geology is the study of the origin, history, and structure of the earth. Geologists look inside the earth for clues about what it was like thousands and even millions of years ago. The surface of the earth is always changing, due to erosion, volcanic eruptions, earthquakes, and the weather. These changes are recorded in the earth's layers, and geologists have created a geologic time scale to track them.

Geologic Time Periods

There are four geologic time periods, also called **eras**.

- **Precambrian Era:** This era began at the formation of the earth, approximately 4.6 billion years ago, and ended about 570 million years ago. It is by far the longest era. There are very few fossils from this time period. Those found tend to be bacteria and algae, but a few fossils of primitive sponges, worms, and corals from the end of the era have also been found.

- **Paleozoic Era:** The next era, the Paleozoic, lasted about 325 million years. A wide variety of fossils of plants and animals have been found from this era.

- **Mesozoic Era:** This era started about 245 million years ago and ended about 65 million years ago. Fossils from this time period show a variety of lizards, turtles, snakes, and dinosaurs. Towards the end of this era, the mass extinction of numerous species occurred, including all dinosaurs.

- **Cenozoic Era:** This era started 65 million years ago and continues today. During this period, a wide range of mammals have flourished, including humans.

Layers of the Earth

The earth is made up of three major layers. The outermost layer, the crust, makes up only about 1 percent of the earth's total mass. Directly below that is the mantle. The mantle is a thick layer of rock that makes up about two-thirds of the earth's mass. The center of the earth is the core. The core has a dense liquid outer layer and a solid inner layer of iron. It makes up almost one-third of the earth's mass.

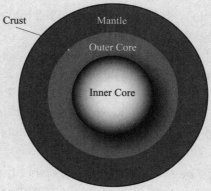

Types of Rocks

There are three major types of rocks.

- **Igneous Rock:** rocks formed when magma, which is called lava when it reaches the earth's surface, cools.

- **Sedimentary Rock:** small pieces of rock, minerals, and organic matter that are put under immense pressure and cemented together.

- **Metamorphic Rock:** existing rock that is changed by certain forces and processes, such as extreme heat, pressure, and chemical reactions.

Rocks gradually change on the earth's surface through weathering. Weathering that occurs as a result of temperature changes, ice, plants, water, wind, and other physical causes is called **mechanical weathering**. Weathering that is the result of chemical reactions that alter the internal structure of the rock is called chemical weathering. A common type of chemical weathering is oxidation. Oxidation occurs when metallic elements in the rock combine with oxygen. The reddish tint of soil in the southern United States is due to oxidation.

Weathered rocks are sometimes moved by a process called erosion. Water, gravity, glaciers, and wind all cause rocks to erode.

Plate Tectonics and Earthquakes

The crust of the earth is actually made up of two layers, one on top of the other. The top layer of the crust is made up of approximately 30 separate pieces called plates. These plates float on the bottom layer of the crust much like a boat floats in water. Since the top layer is floating, it tends to drift slowly. The continents and oceans tend to move as the crust drifts—but the movement is so slow that's it's only noticeable after millions of years.

The area where one plate ends and another plate begins is called a **fault line.** When two or more fault lines move against each other, the ground vibrates and an earthquake results. The reason there are so many earthquakes along the west coast of the United States is because a long fault line runs up the coast. When an earthquake occurs, scientists use the Richter scale to measure its magnitude. This scale uses a 1 to 10 system, with 1 being for the smallest earthquake and 10 for the largest earthquake.

OCEANOGRAPHY

Oceanography is the study of the earth's oceans. Since nearly three-fourths of the earth's surface is covered by oceans, studying them can be a big job. Oceanographers study waves, tides, currents, plants, and marine animals.

Marine Biomes

Recall from our discussion of ecology that the earth is divided into biomes. The ocean is also divided into biomes. There are three that you need to know.

- **Biome 1: The Intertidal Zone.** This is where the land and water meet. This zone alternates between total submersion in water and dryness as the tides rise and fall. Organisms found here include crabs, mussels, clams, snails, starfish, and sponges.

- **Biome 2: The Neritic Zone.** This zone starts where the intertidal zone ends and extends to the edge of the continental shelf. Organisms found here include starfish, sea urchins, seaweed, and many species of fish.

- **Biome 3: The Oceanic Zone.** This zone includes all of the open ocean. Due to the depth of the water there is very little vegetation, as the seawater filters out all light before it can reach the ocean floor. Organisms living here tend to be very large and carnivorous. This includes marine mammals such as dolphins and whales, sharks, large squids, and sea turtles.

Two other zones to remember are the photopic and the aphotic. The **photopic zone** begins at the water's surface and extends down as far as light will penetrate. The **aphotic zone** is the area that no light reaches.

Marine Biomes

METEOROLOGY

Meteorology is the study of the earth's atmosphere, including the atmospheric conditions that cause weather.

Layers of the Atmosphere

The atmosphere is divided into four large layers that lie on top of each other, extending out from the surface of the earth.

- **The Troposphere:** The layer closest to the earth is the troposphere. Depending on the latitude and the season, the troposphere can range from 6 km thick to 17 km thick. The majority of the water vapor and carbon dioxide in the atmosphere is found here. As you travel away from the earth's surface, the temperature of the air drops, until you reach the upper boundary of the troposphere. This area is called the tropopause. An interesting fact about the tropopause is that the temperature remains almost constant here.

- **The Stratosphere:** The stratosphere starts at the tropopause and extends about 50 km above the earth. This layer is home to the ozone layer. The temperature as you enter the stratosphere is about –60°C. As you approach the upper boundary of the stratosphere, called the stratopause, the temperature begins to rise, as a result of direct solar energy.

- **The Mesosphere:** This layer starts above the stratosphere and extends about 80 km above the earth. Here, the temperature begins to drop again as you move further away from the earth. This is the coldest layer of the atmosphere—temperatures can drop as low as –90°C. As you approach the upper boundary of the mesosphere, the mesopause, the temperature stabilizes.

- **The Thermosphere:** In this layer, the highest in the atmosphere, the temperature rises the farther from the earth that you get, as nitrogen and oxygen atoms absorb more solar energy from the sun. Temperatures as high as 2,000°C have been recorded here. The thermosphere is divided into two regions, the ionosphere and the exosphere. The lower region, the ionosphere, starts about 80 km above the earth and continues to about 550 km. The exosphere is almost a complete vacuum—it contains almost no matter. It extends for thousands of kilometers above the earth.

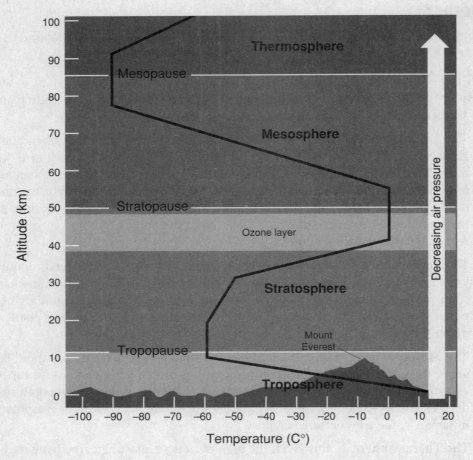

Humidity

Humidity is the measure of the water vapor in the air. As water evaporates into the air, humidity rises. The amount of water vapor the air can hold increases as the temperature rises and decreases as the temperature drops. When the air holds the maximum amount of water vapor that it can, it is saturated.

Fronts

You've probably heard meteorologists talking about warm fronts and cold fronts on your local news. A front is just a boundary between two unlike air masses. When a warm air mass overtakes colder air, you have a warm front. When a cold air mass overtakes warmer air, you have a cold front. Sometimes two air masses meet and neither is displaced. This is called a stationary front. When cold air overtakes warm air very quickly, it sometimes pushes the warm air up high into the atmosphere. This is called an occluded front.

ASTRONOMY

Astronomy is the study of the universe beyond the earth. Astronomers study the moon, planets, solar system, galaxy, and everything farther away. It is one of the oldest branches of science, dating back to ancient times. In fact, some scientists theorize that the pyramids in Egypt were actually used for astronomical purposes.

For the purposes of the ASVAB, you only need to know about a few astronomical objects. All of them are in our part of the universe, the solar system.

THE SOLAR SYSTEM

The solar system is where we live. It is made up of the sun and the objects revolving around it, including the earth. For a long time, scientists believed that the earth was the center of the solar system. Nicolaus Copernicus, a Polish astronomer, was the first to introduce the idea of a heliocentric, or sun-centered, model of the solar system. It has now been proven that our solar system is indeed heliocentric. Our solar system looks like this:

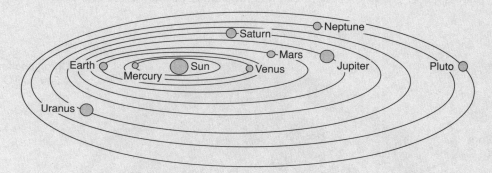

Terrestrial Planets

The four planets closest to the sun—Mercury, Venus, Earth, and Mars—are called the terrestrial planets, or inner planets. They consist mainly of rock with metal cores. They do not have rings, but some, such as the earth, have moons.

Outer Planets

The five planets farthest from the sun—Jupiter, Saturn, Uranus, Neptune, and Pluto—are called the outer planets. The first four are also called the Jovian planets because their structure is similar to that of Jupiter. The Jovian planets are the largest in the solar system. They all have numerous moons, ranging from 8 to approximately 20. They also all have rings. The last of the outer planets, Pluto, is the smallest planet in the solar system. It has a moon almost half its size. Some scientists speculate that Pluto was once one of Neptune's moons and that a large object passing by pulled it out of Neptune's orbit.

Asteroids, Comets, and Meteoroids

The solar system also contains millions of smaller objects. Asteroids are large pieces of rock that orbit the sun, just as the planets do. Most asteroids are located between Mars and Jupiter in an area that is called the asteroid belt. Comets are made up of rock, dust, methane, and ice. Like asteroids, they also orbit the sun. Meteoroids are small pieces of rock and metal. Sometimes meteoroids enter the earth's atmosphere. When that happens, they are called meteors. Usually the meteor will burn up when passing through the atmosphere. However, on rare occasions they hit the earth and are then called meteorites.

The Earth's Orbit

At this very moment the earth is traveling around the sun at an average speed of about 106,000 km per hour. It takes the earth about 365 days (one year) to make one trip—or revolution—around the earth. As the earth revolves around the sun it is also spinning on its axis. This spinning is called rotation. It takes the earth 24 hours (one day) to make one complete rotation.

Structure of the Sun

The sun is made up of two main regions.

- **The Core:** The core, the center of the sun, is extremely hot, about 15,000,000 degrees Celsius. At that temperature the only matter that can exist is gas. Because of this intense heat, nuclear reactions are constantly occurring in the core.

- **The Inner Zones:** The area surrounding the core is called the radiative zone. In this zone, the energy from the core is turned into radiation. Beyond the radiative zone is the convective zone. This zone carries the radiation to the surface of the sun, the photosphere. The photosphere extends thousands of kilometers into space.

Chromosphere
4,000° C TO 50,000° C

Core
15,000,000° C

Photosphere
6,000° C

Radioactive zone
2,500,000° C

Connective zone
1,000,000° C

Eclipses

Eclipses occur when a planet or moon passes through the shadow of another. There are two types of eclipses: solar and lunar.

- **Solar Eclipse:** A solar eclipse occurs when the moon moves between the sun and the earth. The moon blocks the light of the sun, casting a shadow over a certain part of the earth. During a total eclipse, all of the sun's light is blocked. During a partial eclipse, only part of the sun is being blocked.

- **Lunar Eclipse:** A lunar eclipse occurs when the earth moves between the sun and the moon. When this happens, the earth blocks the sunlight, casting a shadow over the moon. A total eclipse occurs when the earth's shadow obscures all of the moon, and a partial eclipse occurs when the earth's shadow obscures only a part of the moon.

Solar Eclipse

Sun

Total Solar Eclipse

Earth

Partial Solar Eclipse

Lunar Eclipse

Sun

Earth

Earth's Shadow

Moon

QUICK QUIZ 2

That concludes our review of the Earth Sciences and Astronomy. The following quiz will test you on what we just covered. You can check your answers at the end of the chapter. If you miss any questions, be sure to go back and review.

1. Match the type of rock on the left to the description on the right.

    _____ Igneous   A. small pieces of rock, minerals, and organic matter that have been compressed and cemented together

    _____ Sedimentary   B. starts as magma and then cools and hardens

    _____ Metamorphic   C. changes from one type of rock into another due to extreme heat, pressure, or chemical processes

2. Name the front.

    A. A cold air mass overcomes a warm air mass. _____

    B. Cold and warm air masses meet but neither is displaced. _____

    C. A cold air mass rushes in and pushes up a warm air mass. _____

3. Put the geologic periods in the correct order:

    A. Cenozoic, Mesozoic, Paleozoic, Precambrian

    B. Precambrian, Paleozoic, Mesozoic, Cenozoic

    C. Paleozoic, Mesozoic, Precambrian, Cenozoic

    D. Precambrian, Cenozoic, Mesozoic, Paleozoic

4. Which marine biome fits this description?

    It extends to the continental shelf. Organisms found here include starfish, crustaceans, seaweed, and many species of fish.

    A. Intertidal Zone

    B. Neritic Zone

    C. Oceanic Zone

5. Put the layers in the correct order:

    A. Thermosphere, Stratosphere, Mesosphere, Troposphere

    B. Troposphere, Mesosphere, Stratosphere, Thermosphere

    C. Mesosphere, Stratosphere, Thermosphere, Troposphere

    D. Troposphere, Stratosphere, Mesosphere, Thermosphere

6. It takes the earth _____ to revolve around the sun. It takes the earth _____ to rotate once.

7. The weathering of rocks occurs as a result of:

   I. wind
   II. water
   III. ice
   IV. plants and animals

   A.   I and II
   B.   I, II, and III
   C.   II and III
   D.   I, II, III, and IV

8. A _____ occurs when the earth moves between the sun and the moon, casting a shadow over the moon. A _____ occurs when the moon moves between the sun and the earth, casting a shadow over the earth.

9. True or False. A meteoroid is a large rock that orbits the sun, usually somewhere between the planets Mars and Jupiter. _____.

10. Fill in the diagram below with the layers of the earth.

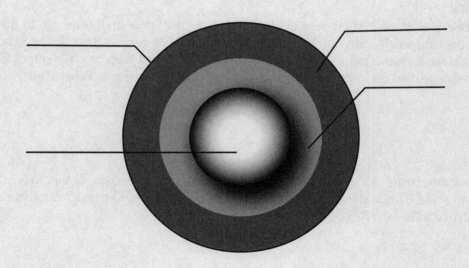

PHYSICAL SCIENCE

MEASUREMENT

The **metric system** is used around the world to measure length, mass, volume, and temperature. It is a decimal system based on multiples and fractions of ten.

Length

The standard unit of measurement is the meter. A meter is bit more than 3 feet long. A meter can be broken into smaller units, called **centimeters**. Centimeters are divided into **millimeters**. To measure long distances, **kilometers** are used. A kilometer is 1000 meters.

> 1 meter (m) = 100 centimeters (cm) = 1000 millimeters (mm)
> 1000 meters = 1 kilometer (km)

Mass

Grams (g), **kilograms** (kg), and **milligrams** (mg) are used to measure mass. A kilogram is about 2.2 pounds.

> 1 kg = 1000 g = 1,000,000 mg

Volume

Volume is the amount of space an object occupies. You can obtain the volume of an object by multiplying its length × its width × its height. In the metric system, volumes are measure in **milliliters** (ml), **cubic centimeters** (cm3), or **liters** (L).

> $1cm^3$ = 1 ml
> 1 liter (L) = 1,000 milliliters (ml)

Temperature

Temperature can be measured on the **Celsius** (C) scale or the **Fahrenheit** (F) scale. In the U.S., we usually use the Fahrenheit scale. On this scale, water freezes at 32 degrees F (or "F°") and boils at 212 degrees F. On the Celsius scale, water freezes at 0 degrees C and boils at 100 degrees C. Use the equations below to convert from Fahrenheit to Celsius, or from Celsius to Fahrenheit.

$$F° = \frac{9}{5}C° + 32$$

$$C° = \frac{5}{9}(F° - 32)$$

Another temperature scale, one that's commonly used by scientists, is the **Kelvin** scale, or absolute zero scale. This scale starts at absolute zero (-273 degrees Celsius). Water freezes at 273 degrees Kelvin and boils at 373 degrees Kelvin.

STATES OF MATTER

As a substance gives off or absorbs heat, two things can happen: Its temperature can change, or it can change states. All matter can exist in three states: solid, liquid, or gas. Water, for example, is a solid (ice) until it reaches 32 degrees Fahrenheit or 0 degrees Celsius, at which point it becomes a liquid. When it reaches 212 degrees Fahrenheit or 100 degrees Celsius it changes to a gas (water vapor, or steam). All types of matter can change properties, but they do so at different temperatures.

The Phase Change Diagram

PHYSICS

IMPORTANT FORMULAS

Memorize these important terms and formulas; you may need them on the test.

- **Momentum:** The tendency for an object to continue moving in the same direction. Momentum = mass × speed.

- **Power:** The rate at which work is done. Power is measured in watts. Work is energy expended, measured in joules (J).
  Power = work ÷ time.

- **Speed (or Velocity):** The distance traveled by an object over a certain amount of time. Speed = distance ÷ time.

FORMS OF ENERGY

Energy can be defined as the capacity to do work. It can never be created or destroyed; it only changes forms. There are many forms of energy, including chemical, light, heat, electrical, nuclear, sound, and mechanical. Energy can be either potential or kinetic. Potential energy is the energy stored in an object as a result of its position, shape, or state. Kinetic energy is the energy that a moving object has.

WAVES

Sound and light energy travel in waves. Sound waves are produced when an object vibrates, disturbing the medium surrounding it. If the vibrations are in a certain range, they will be detected by the human ear. Sometimes the frequency of the sound waves that humans detect are not the same frequency as what the source is emitting. This is called the Doppler effect. The Doppler effect occurs when the source of the sound waves, the detector of the sound waves, or both, are moving. For example, if you are sitting in your car waiting for a train to pass, the sound of the train changes as it moves closer to you and then past you. The sound waves being emitted from the train are not changing, just your position in relation to the train, and therefore the sound waves that your ear perceives are different.

Light waves are subject to the Doppler effect. For example, when you look up at the night sky, what you see is light coming from the stars and planets. That light can be measured in wavelengths. If you measure the wavelengths on the star or planet and compare them to a measurement taken on the earth, you would see that they are different. This difference occurs because the stars, planets, and the earth are in constant motion.

ELECTROMAGNETIC SPECTRUM

The light that you see only makes up a small part of the electromagnetic spectrum. This spectrum is comprised of radiowaves, microwaves, infrared, visible light, ultraviolet, x-rays, and gamma rays. Visible light waves are in the middle of the spectrum. Different frequencies of light waves are perceived as different colors. Red, for example, has the lowest frequency, and violet the highest. When light waves enter your eye, they strike rods and cones in the back of your eyeball. The rods and cones send neural impulses to the brain. The brain determines what color you're seeing based on the frequency of the wavelengths that entered your eye. When you look at a red apple, the light waves that are entering your eye are in the range on the electromagnetic spectrum for red light. This is because the apple is absorbing all of the waves except for the red light waves. Those are being reflected by the apple. A green object, like a leaf, is absorbing all light except for green light waves.

Electromagnetic Spectrum

frequency (Hz)

Wavelength (m)

10^{22}	10^{-14}
10^{21}	10^{-13}
10^{20}	10^{-12}
10^{19}	10^{-11}
10^{18}	10^{-10}
10^{17}	10^{-9}
10^{16}	10^{-8}
10^{15}	10^{-7}
10^{14}	10^{-6}
10^{13}	10^{-5}
10^{12}	10^{-4}
10^{11}	10^{-3}
10^{10}	10^{-2}
10^{9}	10^{-1}
10^{8}	1
10^{7}	10^{1}
10^{6}	10^{2}
10^{5}	10^{3}

γ-rays

X-rays

Ultraviolet

Visible light

Infrared

Microwaves

Radiowaves

Violet: $3.90 - 4.55 \times 10^{-7}$m
Blue: $4.55 - 4.92 \times 10^{-7}$m
Green: $4.92 - 5.77 \times 10^{-7}$m
Yellow: $5.77 - 5.97 \times 10^{-7}$m
Orange: $5.97 - 6.22 \times 10^{-7}$m
Red: $6.22 - 7.70 \times 10^{-7}$m

REFRACTION

Refraction is the bending of light. For example, when sunlight enters a prism, the light refracts, or bends, and all of its different frequencies separate, creating a rainbow. White light (like sunlight) is a combination of all of the colors in the visible spectrum.

CONVEX AND CONCAVE

A mirror or lens can either be concave or convex. A concave lens is caved in and a convex lens is curved out.

HEAT

Heat energy is transferred by conduction, convection, or radiation. **Conduction** occurs when heat is transferred from a source with a high temperature to something with a lower temperature. For example, when you cook on a stove you're transferring heat from the stove to the food. **Convection** occurs when a gas or liquid changes density due to higher heat. For example, a hot air balloon rises in the air because of convection. The air inside the balloon is heated up, causing it to rise and taking the balloon with it. **Radiation** occurs when electromagnetic waves transmit heat. For example, the sun heats up a sidewalk because the sun is sending out electromagnetic waves, which are absorbed by the cement.

MAGNETISM

Have you ever heard the saying "opposites attract"? Well, in the case of magnets, it's true. Magnets have a north pole and a south pole. The north poles of two magnets will repel each other, and the south poles of two magnets will repel each other. But, if you bring the north pole of one magnet close to the south pole of another magnet, they will attract each other.

CHEMISTRY

Let's start with some basic terms you should know:

- **Element:** An element is a substance that can't be broken down any further by a chemical reaction. Some examples of elements are hydrogen, carbon, and oxygen. All of the elements are listed in the **Periodic Table**.

- **Atom:** An atom is the smallest component of an element that still retains the properties of that element. Atoms are often known as the building blocks of matter. Atoms are made up of protons, neutrons, and electrons.

- **Proton:** Protons are found in an atom's nucleus. A proton has a positive electric charge.

- **Neutron:** Neutrons are also found in an atom's nucleus. A neutron does not have a charge. It is neutral.

- **Electron:** Electrons are found outside of the nucleus. They have a negative charge.

Periodic Table of the Elements

1 **H** 1.0																	2 **He** 4.0
3 **Li** 6.9	4 **Be** 9.0											5 **B** 10.8	6 **C** 12.0	7 **N** 14.0	8 **O** 16.0	9 **F** 19.0	10 **Ne** 20.2
11 **Na** 23.0	12 **Mg** 24.3											13 **Al** 27.0	14 **Si** 28.1	15 **P** 31.0	16 **S** 32.1	17 **Cl** 35.5	18 **Ar** 39.9
19 **K** 39.1	20 **Ca** 40.1	21 **Sc** 45.0	22 **Ti** 47.9	23 **V** 50.9	24 **Cr** 52.0	25 **Mn** 54.9	26 **Fe** 55.8	27 **Co** 58.9	28 **Ni** 58.7	29 **Cu** 63.5	30 **Zn** 65.4	31 **Ga** 69.7	32 **Ge** 72.6	33 **As** 74.9	34 **Se** 79.0	35 **Br** 79.9	36 **Kr** 83.8
37 **Rb** 85.5	38 **Sr** 87.6	39 **Y** 88.9	40 **Zr** 91.2	41 **Nb** 92.9	42 **Mo** 95.9	43 **Tc** (98)	44 **Ru** 101.1	45 **Rh** 102.9	46 **Pd** 106.4	47 **Ag** 107.9	48 **Cd** 112.4	49 **In** 114.8	50 **Sn** 118.7	51 **Sb** 121.8	52 **Te** 127.6	53 **I** 126.9	54 **Xe** 131.3
55 **Cs** 132.9	56 **Ba** 137.3	57 **La*** 138.9	72 **Hf** 178.5	73 **Ta** 180.9	74 **W** 183.9	75 **Re** 186.2	76 **Os** 190.2	77 **Ir** 192.2	78 **Pt** 195.1	79 **Au** 197.0	80 **Hg** 200.6	81 **Tl** 204.4	82 **Pb** 207.2	83 **Bi** 209.0	84 **Po** (209)	85 **At** (210)	86 **Rn** (222)
87 **Fr** (223)	88 **Ra** 226.0	89 **Ac**† 227.0	104 **Unq** (261)	105 **Unp** (262)	106 **Unh** (263)	107 **Uns** (262)	108 **Uno** (265)	109 **Une** (267)									

58 **Ce** 140.1	59 **Pr** 140.9	60 **Nd** 144.2	61 **Pm** (145)	62 **Sm** 150.4	63 **Eu** 152.0	64 **Gd** 157.3	65 **Tb** 158.9	66 **Dy** 162.5	67 **Ho** 164.9	68 **Er** 167.3	69 **Tm** 168.9	70 **Yb** 173.0	71 **Lu** 175.0
90 **Th** 232.0	91 **Pa** (231)	92 **U** 238.0	93 **Np** (237)	94 **Pu** (244)	95 **Am** (243)	96 **Cm** (247)	97 **Bk** (247)	98 **Cf** (251)	99 **Es** (252)	100 **Fm** (257)	101 **Md** (258)	102 **No** (259)	103 **Lr** (260)

As you can see from the periodic table, every element has a number above it. That number is called the atomic number. The atomic number tells you how many protons are in the nucleus of one atom of that element. The number of protons in the nucleus determines which element the atom is. For example, the element hydrogen has an atomic number of 1. That means it has 1 proton in its nucleus.

Oxygen has 8 protons in its nucleus. Its atomic number is 8. The atomic number for potassium (K) is 19. It has 19 protons.

IONS

When an atom has the same number of protons and electrons, it is neutral. Sometimes, however, an atom loses or gains an electron. When this happens the number of protons and electrons is not equal, and the atom is no longer neutral. If it gains a neutron the atom is negatively charged, and if it loses one it is positively charged. When an atom isn't electrically neutral anymore it is called an ion.

MASS NUMBER

Atoms have two things in their nuclei: protons and neutrons. Each proton and neutron has a mass that is approximately equal to 1 atomic mass unit (amu). Electrons have practically no mass, so an atom's mass is determined by the number of protons and neutrons it has. For example, if a carbon atom has 6 protons and 6 neutrons, its mass is 12.

ISOTOPES

In the carbon example above, the number of protons and the number of neutrons were equal. But that isn't always the case. Atoms can have an unequal number of protons and neutrons. When two atoms of the same element have different numbers of neutrons in their nuclei, they are called isotopes. For example, a carbon atom with 8 neutrons and a carbon atom with 6 neutrons are isotopes.

MOLECULES

As we know, an atom is the smallest possible part of an element. Atoms often have strong attraction to each other, however, and can attach to each other. When different atoms bind together they are called molecules. The chemical formula for water, H_2O, indicates that one molecule of water is made up of 2 hydrogen atoms and 1 oxygen atom. The smallest unit of water is one molecule.

COMPOUNDS AND MIXTURES

A substance made up of two or more elements is called a compound. Water (H_2O) is a compound of hydrogen (H) and oxygen (O). A mixture is made up of different elements that are not chemically bonded to each other. For example, granite is made up of three different types of matter: quartz, mica, and feldspar. If you look at granite, you can see the separate layers of matter. The three layers are not chemically bonded to each other.

ACIDS, BASES, AND pH

Acids are substances that release hydrogen ions when added to water. Some common acids are vinegar and lemon juice. They taste sour. Bases are substances that take up hydrogen ions. Some common bases are soap and ammonia. They feel slippery and taste bitter. The concentration of hydrogen ions in a substance is measured on the pH scale. The pH scale ranges from 0 to 14. A pH of 7 means that the substance is neutral. Acids have a pH of less than 7. The lower the number, the stronger the acid is. Bases have a pH greater than 7. The higher the number, the stronger the base.

SOLUTIONS, SOLVENTS, AND CONCENTRATIONS

Solutions are mixtures of solutes and solvents. **Solutes** are substances that dissolve into something. **Solvents** are the mediums that the solutes are dissolved into. For example, saltwater is a solution made up of salt (the solute) and water (the solvent). The amount of solute in a solvent is called the **concentration**. The concentration would tell us how salty the water was. The higher the concentration, the saltier the water.

METALS

Metals are elements that share certain characteristics. Metals tend to be shiny, malleable (capable of being shaped, perhaps by hammering or by pressure), and good conductors of heat and electricity. The most important thing to remember about metals, though, is that they tend to give up electrons when they bond. Approximately 75 percent of the elements are metals. Nonmetals tend to share or gain electrons when they bond. Some common metals are copper, gold, silver, and iron.

CHEMICAL REACTIONS

A chemical reaction is a process that changes one or more substances into different substances. There are two types of chemical reactions that you should be familiar with:

- **Combination/synthesis reactions:** When two different substances combine to form a new substance.

- **Decomposition reactions:** When one substance breaks down into two or more separate substances.

QUICK QUIZ 3

That's everything you need to know about physics and chemistry. Think you got it all? Take this little quiz to find out. You can check your answers at the end of the chapter. As always, if you get any question wrong, go back and review the topic. Good luck!

1. Energy that is stored in an object as a result of its position, shape, or state is called _____ energy. Energy that a moving object has is called _____ energy.

2. True or False. Warming up your hands in front of a fire is an example of convection. _____.

3. An atom is made up of: _____, _____, and _____.

4. Match the definition to the word on the left.

   _____ Isotope   A. found in the nucleus, positively charged

   _____ Molecule   B. the smallest unit of a particular element

   _____ Ion   C. found in the nucleus, not charged

   _____ Atom   D. found outside the nucleus, negatively charged

   _____ Proton   E. two atoms of the same element with unequal neutrons

   _____ Neutron   F. an atom with a charge, either positive or negative

   _____ Electron   G. the smallest unit of a chemical

5. Fill in the blanks.

   1 meter = _____centimeters = _____millimeters

   1 kilometers = _____meters

   1 kilogram = _____grams

   1 liter = _____milliliters

6. When water reaches 212 degrees Fahrenheit it

   I.   freezes
   II. boils
   III. has a temperature equivalent to 100 degrees Celsius
   IV. has a temperature equivalent to 273 degrees Kelvin

   A. II only
   B. II and III only
   C. II, III, and IV only
   D. I, III, and IV only

7. The atomic number for the element sodium (Na) is 11. Based on this we know that sodium always:

   I.   has 11 neutrons
   II. has 11 protons
   III. has 11 electrons

   A. I only
   B. II only
   C. III only
   D. I, II, and III

8. Circle the correct word.

   A substance with a pH of 9 is [an acid/a base/neutral]. A substance with a pH of 7 is [an acid/a base/neutral]. A substance with a pH of 5 is [an acid/a base/neutral].

9. As a train approaches, its sound changes. This can be explained by

   A. convection
   B. refraction
   C. the Doppler Effect
   D. momentum

10. The equation for power is

   A. power = work + time
   B. power = work × time
   C. power = work ÷ time
   D. power = time ÷ work

ANSWERS TO QUICK QUIZZES

QUICK QUIZ 1

Page 39

1.

J	Cell membrane	A.	control center of the cell, contains DNA
H	Centrioles	B.	synthesizes proteins to be exported out of the cell
G	Golgi apparatus	C.	site of protein synthesis
K	Lysosomes	D.	site of cellular respiration and energy production
B	Rough ER	E.	makes lipids and detoxifies enzymes
C	Ribosomes	F.	stores waste and other substances
I	Nucleolus	G.	sorts and packages membrane and secreted proteins
F	Vacuole	H.	related to the formation of spindle during mitosis
E	Smooth ER	I.	site of ribosome synthesis in the nucleus
D	Mitochondria	J.	barrier that controls what enters and leaves the cell
A	Nucleus	K.	digest foreign substances and worn organelles

2. The order from largest to smallest is:

Kingdom

Phylum

Class

Order

Family

Genus

Species

3. photosynthesis

4. **D** tundra

5.

	A	A
A	AA	Aa
a	Aa	aa

The probability that the parents produce offspring with attached earlobes is 75%.

The probability that the parents produce offspring with unattached earlobes is 25%.

6. **C** Interphase   chromosomes replicate

    E Prophase   nuclear membrane breaks up, spindles form, centrioles move to opposite poles

    D Metaphase   chromosomes line up

    B Anaphase   chromatids split and chromosomes move to opposite poles

    A Telophase   nuclear membrane forms, cytokinesis occurs

7. The nervous system can be divided into two parts: <u>the central nervous system</u> and the <u>peripheral nervous system</u>. The brain and spinal cord are parts of the <u>central nervous system</u>. The peripheral nervous system can be divided into the <u>somatic nervous system</u> and <u>the autonomic nervous system</u>. The <u>somatic nervous system</u> controls voluntary actions. The autonomic nervous system controls involuntary actions. The autonomic system can be divided into the <u>sympathetic</u> and <u>parasympathetic nervous systems</u>.

8. **C** plants

9. C   Vitamin A   a lack of this may cause night blindness

    E   Vitamin B$_1$ a lack of this may cause rickets

    D   Vitamin B$_2$ a lack of this may cause weakness or skin infections

    F   Vitamin B$_{12}$ a lack of this may cause anemia

    H   Vitamin C   a lack of this may cause scurvy

    B   Vitamin D   a lack of this may cause rickets

    F   Vitamin E   a lack of this may cause anemia

    G   Vitamin K   a lack of this may cause excessive bleeding

10. False. Type O is the universal donor, not the universal recipient.

11. **C** moss

12. **A** I only

13. **B** it is a control system that has extremely rapid effects on the body

14. tracheophytes

15. **B** members of the same genus

16. **B** an omnivore

17. **D** zebra

18. The vas deferens is a large duct that conducts sperm from the testes to the urethra.

19. smooth, skeletal, and cardiac

20. **E** Both B and C

21. A. mouth, esophagus, stomach, small intestine, large intestine, rectum, anus

22. Ova travel from the (ovaries) through the (fallopian tubes) to the (uterus).

23. **B** XX

24. **C** alveolus

QUICK QUIZ 2
Page 52

1. **B** Igneous   starts as magma and then cools and hardens

   A Sedimentary   composed of mall pieces of rock, minerals, and organic material that have been compressed and cemented together

   C Metamorphic   changes from one type of rock into another, due to extreme heat, pressure, or chemical processes

2.

   A   cold front
   B   stationary front
   C   occluded front

3. **B** Precambrian, Paleozoic, Mesozoic, Cenozoic

4. **B** Neritic Zone

5. **D** Troposphere, Stratosphere, Mesosphere, Thermosphere

6. It takes the earth <u>365 days/1 year</u> to revolve around the sun. It takes the earth <u>24 hours/1 day</u> to rotate once.

7. **D** I, II, III, and IV

8. A <u>lunar eclipse</u> occurs when the earth casts a shadow on the moon. A <u>solar eclipse</u> occurs when the moon casts a shadow on the earth.

9. False (this statement describes an asteroid, not a meteoroid).

10.

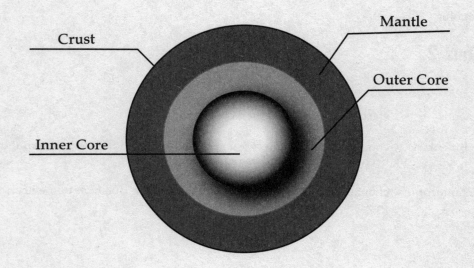

QUICK QUIZ 3

Page 61

1. Energy that is stored in an object as a result of its position, shape, or state is called <u>potential</u> energy. Energy that a moving object has is called <u>kinetic</u> energy.

2. False

3. An atom is made up of: <u>protons</u>, <u>neutrons</u>, and <u>electrons</u>.

4.

E	Isotope	two atoms of the same element with an unequal number of neutrons
G	Molecule	the smallest unit of a chemical
F	Ion	an atom with a charge, either positive or negative
B	Atom	the smallest unit of a particular element
A	Proton	found in the nucleus, positively charged
C	Neutron	found in the nucleus, not charged
D	Electron	found outside the nucleus, negatively charged

5. 1 meter = <u>100</u> centimeters = <u>1000</u> millimeters

   1 kilometer = <u>1000</u> meters

   1 kilogram = <u>1000</u> grams

   1 liter = <u>1000</u> milliliters

6. **B** II and III only

7. **B** II only

8. A substance with a pH of 9 is (a base). A substance with a pH of 7 is (neutral). A substance with a pH of 5 is (an acid).

9. **C** The Doppler Effect

10. **C** power = work ÷ time

3

MATH

INTRODUCTION TO THE MATH SECTIONS

The three ASVAB math sections—Arithmetic Reasoning, Mathematical Comprehension, and Numerical Operations—test your understanding of basic arithmetic, algebra, and geometry. Each section has its own style, but the concepts tested are similar. In this chapter we will review everything you need to know to do well on all three sections. The key to improving in math, however, is practice. Make sure to learn the concepts and then use the practice materials provided.

Study Tips for the Math Sections

- Learn the definitions to all of the terms we introduce; you will need them!

- When you're taking the test, use the scrap paper provided to work out the problems. Trying to solve problems in your head only leads to mistakes.

- Draw pictures to help clarify the problem.

- Break the question up into Bite Size Pieces.

- After you get an answer, double-check your work.

- Use Ballparking when appropriate.

MATH TERMINOLOGY

Before we begin our review, it is important that you know the definitions to some math terms that you will see.

Term	Definitions	Examples
Average (or "Mean")	The midway point in a series of numbers.	The average of 10 and 20 is 15.
Denominator	The bottom number in a fraction.	In the fraction $\frac{1}{3}$, the 3 is the denominator.
Difference	The result of subtraction.	The difference of $5 - 3$ is 2.
Dividend	The number being divided into.	The dividend in $10 \div 5$ is 10.
Divisor	The number you are dividing by.	The divisor in $10 \div 5$ is 5.
Even	Any integer that is divisible by 2.	2, 4, 6, 14, 20, 34, 100...
Exponent	A small raised number next to a big number that indicates how many times to multiply the big number by.	The 2 is the exponent in 3^2.
Improper Fraction	A fraction with a larger numerator than denominator.	$\frac{10}{4}$
Integer	A number that doesn't contain a fraction or a decimal.	$-5, -4, 0, 4, 5...$
Mixed Number	A number that contains both an integer and a fraction.	$6\frac{1}{4}$
Negative Number	Any number less than zero.	$-7, -0.25...$
Numerator	The top number in a fraction.	In the fraction $\frac{1}{3}$, the 1 is the numerator.
Odd	A number not divisible by 2.	$-3, -1, 1, 3, 5, 11...$
Positive Number	Any number greater than zero.	1, 4, , 0.25...
Prime Number	A number divisible only by 1 and itself. 1 is not considered a prime number. All prime numbers are odd except for 2.	2, 3, 5, 7, 11, 13...
Product	The result of multiplication.	The product of 2×2 is 4.
Quotient	The result of division.	The quotient of $10 \div 5$ is 2.
Ratio	A relationship between two quantities.	1:2, 4:5, 9:10
Sum	The result of addition.	The sum of $5 + 5$ is 10.
Square Root	A factor of a number that, when squared, equals that number.	$\sqrt{9} = 3$
Whole Number	All the positive integers and zero.	0, 1, 2, 3, 4, 12, 400...

THE NUMBER LINE

Zero

Negatives   Positives

A number line allows you to see the relationship between numbers.

- Zero is a neutral number. It is neither positive nor negative.

- Positive numbers are numbers greater than zero. They lie to the right of zero on the number line.

- Negative numbers are numbers less than zero. They lie to the left of zero on the number line.

Number lines can be useful when adding and subtracting negative numbers.

1. $-5 + 4 = ?$

When you are adding a positive number, go right on the number line.

Start at -5 and count 4 to the right. That takes you to -1. That's the answer!

2. $-2 + -3 = ?$

When you are adding a negative number, go left on the number line.

Start at -2 and count 3 to the left. That takes you to -5. That's the answer!

3. $5 - 4 = ?$

When you are subtracting a positive number, go left on the number line.

Start at 5 and count to the left 4. That takes you to 1. That's the answer!

4. $5 - -1 = ?$

Subtracting a negative number is just like adding a positive number. Change both negative signs to one positive sign.

5. $5 + 1 = ?$

Start at 5 and move 1 to the right, since we are now adding. That takes you to 6. That's the answer!

MULTIPLICATION AND DIVISION

You need to know your multiplication table for the ASVAB.

X	1	2	3	4	5	6	7	8	9	10
1	1	2	3	4	5	6	7	8	9	10
2	2	4	6	8	10	12	14	16	18	20
3	3	6	9	12	15	18	21	24	27	30
4	4	8	12	16	20	24	28	32	36	40
5	5	10	15	20	25	30	35	40	45	50
6	6	12	18	24	30	36	42	48	54	60
7	7	14	21	28	35	42	49	56	63	70
8	8	16	24	32	40	48	56	64	72	80
9	9	18	27	36	45	54	63	72	81	90
10	10	20	30	40	50	60	70	80	90	100

There's no way around it: Memorizing this table is essential to doing multiplication problems. But there are a few tricks to help you out. Do you notice any patterns in the table? Look at the 9s column. $9 \times 1 = 9$, $9 \times 2 = 18$, $9 \times 3 = 27$, and so forth. When you multiply 9 by any number from 1 to 10 you always get an answer whose digits add up to 9. For example, look at $9 \times 4 = 36$. The digits of the product, 36, add up to 9: $3 + 6 = 9$. Or take $9 \times 8 = 72$. The digits of the product, 72, also add up to 9: $7 + 2 = 9$. And so on. Another trick you can use with the 9s is to look at the number you are multiplying the 9 by. The first number in the product will be one less than that number. For example, look at $9 \times 4 = 36$ again. We are multiplying 9 by 4 so the product will start with a 3. This works whenever you are multiplying by a number between 2 and 9.

Another pattern you can use works with the 10s column. Do you see the pattern in the table above? Whenever you multiply 10 by a number, all you have to do is add a zero to that number. For example, $2 \times 10 = 20$ and $9 \times 10 = 90$.

RULES FOR MULTIPLYING

Here are some more rules to remember when you're multiplying:

- Positive number × Positive number = Positive number

$$2 \times 4 = 8 \quad [2, 4, \text{ and } 8 \text{ are all positive}]$$

- Negative number × Negative number = Positive number

$$-2 \times -4 = 8 \quad [-2 \text{ and } -4 \text{ are negative, and } 8 \text{ is positive}]$$

- Positive number × Negative number = Negative number

$$2 \times -4 = -8 \quad [2 \text{ is positive}, -4 \text{ is negative, and } -8 \text{ is negative}]$$

Factorials

A factorial is just another way of asking you to multiply. You can see factorial questions written in two ways:

5 factorial or 5!

When you see either of these, do this:

$$1 \times 2 \times 3 \times 4 \times 5 =$$

Then multiply out what you've got:

$$1 \times 2 = 2 \times 3 = 6 \times 4 = 24 \times 5 = 120$$

DIVISION

Division is the opposite of multiplication. Division can be expressed in the following ways:

$$10 \div 5 \quad \text{or} \quad 5\overline{)10} \quad \text{or} \quad 10/5 \text{ (which is the same as } \frac{10}{5})$$

- If you see the ÷ sign between two numbers, the number before the ÷ is being divided by the number that comes after the ÷.

- If you see the $\overline{)}$ sign, the number on the outside is being divided into the number on the inside.

- If you see numbers in this form, 10/5 or $\frac{10}{5}$, the number on top is being divided by the number on the bottom.

The number that you are dividing by is called the **divisor,** and the number you are dividing into is the **dividend**. In this example:

$$10 \div 5 = 2$$

10 is the dividend and 5 is the divisor. The result, 2, is called the **quotient**. You can check your division by multiplying the quotient by the divisor. If you've divided correctly, the product of the quotient and the divisor should be equal to the dividend. To check the example above we would multiply the quotient 2 by the divisor 5:

$$2 \times 5 = 10$$

We ended up with the dividend, 10, so our division was correct. This is another reason why it's so important you know your multiplication tables well!

Let's look at another example:

$$10 \div 3 =$$

In the example above, the divisor doesn't divide into the dividend an even number of times. So we are going to have a **remainder**. A remainder is what is left over after you divide. In this example, 3 divides into 10 three times for a total of 9, with 1 left over. In other words, the remainder is 1. Let's check our work:

$$3 \times 3 = 9 \text{ plus our remainder of } 1$$
$$9 + 1 = 10$$

Note: The remainder in a division problem will always be smaller than the divisor. Think about it like this: if you divided 25 shirts among 5 friends and gave each friend 4 shirts, then you would have 5 shirts remaining.

$$\begin{array}{r} 5r5 \\ 2\overline{)10} \end{array}$$

If you have 5 as a remainder, you have enough to give everybody 1 more shirt. That means you can make the quotient bigger. If you ever have a remainder larger than the quotient, go back and make the quotient bigger.

Long Division

Sometimes you will be asked to divide large numbers. When this happens, it is best to write your division like this:

$$34\overline{)578}$$

34 is the divisor and 578 is the dividend.

At first glance this looks like a really hard division problem. But you can break it up into smaller, easier to handle pieces. First, figure out how many times 34 divides into 57. Well 34 x 2 = 68, so we know that 34 goes into 57 once. Place a 1 above the 7 like this:

$$\begin{array}{r} 1 \\ 34\overline{)578} \end{array}$$

The next step is to multiply the 1 by 34, which gives us 34. Write that below the 57 and subtract the 34 from the 57. You get 23.

$$\begin{array}{r} 1 \\ 34\overline{)578} \\ -34 \\ \hline 23 \end{array}$$

Drop the next digit of 578 down, which is the 8.

$$
34{\overline{\smash{)}578}} \\
\underline{-34} \\
238
$$

The next step is to divide 238 by 34. You probably don't know off the top of your head how many times 34 divides into 238. That's okay—I don't know either. Let's think about this a little. We know that $34 \times 10 = 340$ because whenever you multiply by 10 you just add a zero to the end of the number. 340 is greater than 238, so our number will be less than 10, but how much less than 10? We also know that there are approximately three 30s in every 100, and there are a little more than two 100s in 238. So our number will be more than 6, for instance 7. Let's try 7 and see what happens.

$$
34{\overline{\smash{)}578}} \\
\underline{-34} \\
238 \\
\underline{-238} \\
0
$$

$7 \times 34 = 238$, so there is nothing left over. You also don't have any digits left over to use in 578, so you're done. If you wanted to check your answer, you could multiply 34 by 17:

$$34 \times 17 = 578$$

Division with Negative Numbers

Dividing with negative numbers is the same as multiplying with negative numbers. Keep these rules in mind:

Positive number ÷ positive number = positive number

$$4 \div 2 = 2$$

Negative number ÷ negative number = positive number

$$-4 \div -2 = 2$$

Positive number ÷ negative number = negative number

$$4 \div -2 = -2$$

ORDER OF OPERATIONS

Sometimes you will see math problems that ask you to perform more than one operation to a series of numbers, such as this: $13 - 2 \times (8 + 4)$. When this happens, you need to know which operations to do first. That order is summarized by the acronym PEMDAS and the mnemonic device **Please Excuse My Dear Aunt Sally**.

Parentheses
Exponents
Multiplication
Division
Addition
Subtraction

Here's an example:

$$10 - (6 - 5) - 2(3 + 3) + 3 =$$

Start by doing the operations in the parenthesis.

$$10 - (1) - 2(6) + 3 =$$

There are no exponents, so next multiply and divide.

$$10 - (1) - 12 + 3 =$$

Finish by adding and subtracting in the order the operations are presented, from left to right.

$$10 - 1 - 12 + 3 =$$
$$9 - 12 + 3 =$$
$$-3 + 3 = 0$$

Quick Tip!

Use the following mnemonic to help you remember the order of operations:

Please Excuse My Dear Aunt Sally

QUICK QUIZ 1

You can check your answers at the end of the chapter.

1. $18 - 5 \times (2 + 3) =$ _____

2. $(2 \times 3 \times 4) \div (10 - 6) =$ _____

3. $2(2 - 1) + 3(3 - 1) =$ _____

FRACTIONS

Fractions are a very important topic for the ASVAB—you'll see many questions involving them. Fractions are a way of representing numbers that lie between integers on the number line.

$-2\frac{1}{2}$ -2 $-1\frac{1}{2}$ -1 $-\frac{1}{2}$ 0 $\frac{1}{2}$ 1 $1\frac{1}{2}$ 2 $2\frac{1}{2}$

Fill in the following numbers on the number line below.

$1\frac{1}{2}$, -2, 3, $-\frac{1}{2}$, -5, 5, $4\frac{1}{2}$, $\frac{1}{3}$, $-3\frac{2}{3}$

0

By using zero as a starting point, you can determine where all of the numbers should go. When completed, the number line should look like this:

-5 $-3\frac{2}{3}$ -2 $-\frac{1}{2}$ 0 $\frac{1}{3}$ $1\frac{1}{2}$ 3 $4\frac{1}{2}$ 5

Fractions can be thought of as $\dfrac{\text{Part}}{\text{Whole}}$

REDUCING FRACTIONS

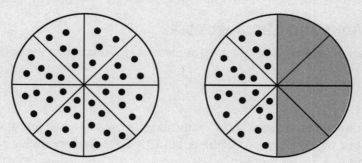

Imagine you had a pizza with 8 slices. You eat 4 pieces of the pizza. What fraction of the pizza did you eat?

You ate $\frac{4}{8}$ of the pizza. What is half of 8? It's 4. That means you ate exactly half of the pizza, or $\frac{1}{2}$ of the pizza.

Changing the fraction from $\dfrac{4}{8}$ to $\dfrac{1}{2}$ is called *reducing* the fraction. To reduce a fraction to its lowest terms, just divide the numerator and denominator by the same number until you can't divide anymore. Let's reduce $\dfrac{20}{100}$.

$$\dfrac{20}{100} \div \dfrac{2}{2} = \dfrac{10}{50}$$

We reduced $\dfrac{20}{100}$ to $\dfrac{10}{50}$ by dividing the numerator and denominator by 2. Can the fraction $\dfrac{10}{50}$ be reduced any further? Yes! There is a number that divides evenly into both 10 and 50. That number is 10.

$$\dfrac{10}{50} \div \dfrac{10}{10} = \dfrac{1}{5}$$

The fraction $\dfrac{1}{5}$ is reduced to its lowest form because there are no numbers that will divide evenly into 1 and 5. Note that, when you're reducing a fraction, you have to use numbers that divide evenly into both the numerator and denominator. For example, when reducing the fraction $\dfrac{4}{9}$, you cannot divide the two digits by the number 2, because 2 does not divide evenly into 9, though it does divide evenly into 4. $9 \div 2 = 4$ remainder 1, or 4.5. In fact, there are no numbers that divide evenly into both 4 and 9. Therefore, $\dfrac{4}{9}$ cannot be reduced any further. It has already been reduced to its lowest form.

> **Quick Tip!**
>
> When reducing fractions, always use the same number on the top and bottom!
> Try using small numbers like 2, 3, and 5.

IMPROPER FRACTIONS AND MIXED NUMBERS

Improper fractions are fractions where the top (numerator) is bigger than the bottom (denominator). For example:

$$\dfrac{12}{8}$$

If this improper fraction represented how many slices of pizza we had left, it would indicate that we have more than one whole pizza. To figure out exactly how much pizza we have we can convert the improper fraction to a mixed number.

$$\dfrac{12}{8} = 1\dfrac{4}{8} \text{ or } 1\dfrac{1}{2}$$

To convert an improper fraction to a mixed number, follow these steps:

1. Divide the denominator into the numerator. (8 divides into 12 one time)

2. Put the remainder over the denominator. (4 remains, so put it over the 8)

3. Reduce the fraction to lowest terms. ($\dfrac{4}{8}$ reduces to $\dfrac{1}{2}$)

ADDING, SUBTRACTING, AND COMPARING FRACTIONS

If you want to add, subtract, or compare the sizes of fractions, the denominators of the fractions you're working with **must** be the same.

$$\frac{7}{10} + \frac{2}{10} = \frac{9}{10} \quad \text{YES!}$$

$$\frac{4}{5} + \frac{2}{3} \neq \frac{6}{8} \quad \text{NO!}$$

If you are given two fractions with different denominators and are asked to add, subtract or compare them, you must first find a common denominator. Here's how:

The Bow tie

$$\frac{2}{\textcircled{7}} + \frac{3}{\textcircled{4}} = \qquad \text{Different denominators}$$

$$\frac{2}{7} + \frac{3}{4} = \frac{}{28} \qquad \text{Multiply the denominators.}$$

$$\overset{\textcircled{8}}{\underset{}{\frac{2}{7}}} \overset{\textcircled{21}}{\underset{}{\frac{3}{4}}} = \frac{}{28} \qquad \text{Multiply across the equation.}$$

$$\frac{8}{21} + \frac{21}{28} = \frac{29}{28} \qquad \text{Put your new numerators above the new denominators and add!}$$

It works the same for subtraction:

$$\overset{\textcircled{8}}{\underset{}{\frac{2}{7}}} \overset{\textcircled{21}}{\underset{}{\frac{3}{4}}} = \frac{8}{28} - \frac{21}{28} = \frac{13}{28}$$

If you're asked to compare fractions, use the Bow tie to see which one is bigger.

$$\frac{2}{5} \text{ or } \frac{3}{7}$$

$$\frac{2}{5} \underset{}{\overset{}{\times}} \frac{3}{7} = \frac{14}{35} \text{ or } \frac{15}{35} \qquad \frac{3}{7} \text{ is bigger.}$$

Adding and Subtracting Mixed Numbers

To add or subtract mixed numbers, you can either change them into improper fractions:

$$3\frac{2}{7} + 2\frac{4}{7} = \frac{23}{7} + \frac{18}{7} = \frac{41}{7} = 5\frac{6}{7}$$

Or you can work them straight through, starting with the fractions:

$$
\begin{array}{r}
3\frac{2}{7} \\
+2\frac{4}{7} \\
\hline
\frac{6}{7} \\
+5 \\
\hline
5\frac{6}{7}
\end{array}
$$

If the fractions do not have the same denominators, you can change them into improper fractions and use the Bow tie:

$$4\frac{2}{5} + 6\frac{1}{4} = \frac{22}{5} + \frac{25}{4} = \frac{}{20} + \frac{}{20} = \frac{88}{20} + \frac{125}{20} = \frac{213}{20} = 10\frac{13}{20}$$

Or you can work them straight through, starting with the fractions. You just have to find the least common denominator (LCD) of the two fractions:

$$
\begin{array}{r}
4\ \frac{2}{5} \\
+\ 6\ \frac{1}{4} \\
\hline
4\ \frac{8}{20} \\
+\ 6\ \frac{5}{20} \\
\hline
10\frac{13}{20}
\end{array}
$$

The procedure for subtracting fractions is exactly the same.

MULTIPLYING FRACTIONS

Multiplying fractions is an easier process than adding or subtracting them. Just multiply the numerators and denominators straight across.

$$\frac{4}{5} \times \frac{2}{3} = \frac{8}{15}$$

If you have mixed numbers, be sure to change them to improper fractions before you multiply.

DIVIDING FRACTIONS

To divide fractions, you multiply by the second fraction's reciprocal. In other words, turn the second fraction upside down (that is, put its denominator over its numerator), and then multiply:

$$\frac{4}{5} \div \frac{2}{3} = \frac{4}{5} \times \frac{3}{2} = \frac{12}{10} = \frac{6}{5} = 1\frac{1}{5}$$

COMPLEX FRACTIONS

A complex fraction has a fraction as its numerator or denominator. To simplify these, remember that the fraction bar is really a dividing bar:

$$\frac{\frac{2}{3}}{5} = \frac{2}{3} \div 5 = \frac{2}{3} \times \frac{1}{5} = \frac{2}{15}$$

That's all there is to fractions. Try the following drill to test your understanding of fractions before you move on. Fractions are important on the ASVAB. You will see lots of them.

QUICK QUIZ 2

You can check your answers at the end of the chapter.

Solve.

1. $\dfrac{6}{7} + \dfrac{2}{5} = \underline{\hspace{1cm}}$

2. $5\dfrac{2}{3} + 2\dfrac{1}{3} = \underline{\hspace{1cm}}$

3. $\dfrac{4}{7} + \dfrac{3}{4} = \underline{\hspace{1cm}}$

4. $9\dfrac{7}{8} - 6\dfrac{1}{8} = \underline{\hspace{1cm}}$

5. $\dfrac{4}{9} - \dfrac{1}{6} = \underline{\hspace{1cm}}$

Compare: Which is bigger?

6. $\dfrac{8}{9}$ or $\dfrac{9}{10}$ $\underline{\hspace{1cm}}$

7. $\dfrac{3}{24}$ or $\dfrac{4}{25}$ $\underline{\hspace{1cm}}$

8. $-\dfrac{1}{10}$ or $-\dfrac{1}{100}$ $\underline{\hspace{1cm}}$

Multiply.

9. $\dfrac{2}{3} \times \dfrac{3}{4} =$ _____

10. $\dfrac{1}{4} \times \dfrac{7}{8} =$ _____

11. $\dfrac{15}{16} \times -\dfrac{1}{2} =$ _____

Divide.

12. $\dfrac{1}{2} \div \dfrac{3}{8} =$ _____

13. $\dfrac{20}{21} \div \dfrac{2}{3} =$ _____

Solve.

14. $\dfrac{\frac{2}{5}}{\frac{2}{3}} =$ _____

15. $\dfrac{\frac{10}{9}}{11} =$ _____

16. $23 - 4(12 - 8) - -5 + 9 =$ _____

DECIMALS

Think back to the pizza example for a moment. Out of 8 pieces of pizza, 4 had been eaten. That left $\dfrac{1}{2}$ a pizza. This can also be written using decimals.

$$\dfrac{1}{2} = 0.5$$

To find the decimal for a fraction, just remember that a fraction bar is just division in disguise.

$\dfrac{1}{2}$ is the same as $1 \div 2$, or $2\overline{)1}$. When you do the division, you get $2\overline{)1.0}^{.5}$.

You can convert any fraction to a decimal by dividing the numerator by the denominator.

$$\dfrac{11}{2} = 11 \div 2 = 2\overline{)11.0}^{5.5}$$

Where you put the decimal point is very important. Each spot before and after the decimal point has a different meaning.

$.3 = \dfrac{3}{10}$, because the 3 is in the tenths spot.

$5.75 = 5\dfrac{75}{100}$, because the 5 is in the ones spot, the 7 is in the tenths spot, and the 5 is in the hundredths spot.

ADDING AND SUBTRACTING DECIMALS

When you add and subtract decimals, you have to make sure the decimal points are lined up. For example:

$$7.92 + 34.9 + .097 + 6.37 =$$

Line up the numbers like this:

$$
\begin{array}{r}
7.92 \\
34.9 \\
.097 \\
+6.37 \\
\hline
49.287
\end{array}
$$

MULTIPLYING AND DIVIDING DECIMALS

You multiply and divide decimals just as you would whole numbers. The important thing to remember is that the number of decimal places in your answer will be equal to the sum of the numbers after the decimals in each of the numbers being multiplied. For example, if you were multiplying 3.283 by .097, it would look like this:

$$
\begin{array}{r}
3.283 \\
\times .097 \\
\hline
22981 \\
285470 \\
\hline
.308451
\end{array}
$$

There are six numbers after the decimal in the numbers being multiplied, so there are six numbers after the decimal in the answer.

When you divide a decimal by a whole number, you treat it just like division of whole numbers. The decimal point in the answer should be in the same place as the decimal point in the dividend (the number you're dividing into). For example, if you were dividing 16.1 by 35, it would look like this:

$$
\begin{array}{r}
.46 \\
35\overline{)16.1} \\
14\ 0 \\
\hline
210 \\
210 \\
\hline
0
\end{array}
$$

When dividing a decimal by a decimal, you have to eliminate the decimal in the divisor by shifting it to the right of the divisor's last digit—but when you do that, you also have to compensate by shifting the decimal in the dividend the same number of places to the right. For example, if you were dividing 15.5 by .31, it would look like this:

$$
.31\overline{)15.5} = 31\overline{)1550}
$$

$$
\begin{array}{r}
50 \\
31\overline{)1550} \\
155 \\
\hline
0
\end{array}
$$

QUICK QUIZ 3

Think you got all that? Take this short Decimal Quiz and find out! You can check your answers at the end of the chapter.

1. $25.3 + 14.7 =$

2. $122.5307 - 36.753 =$

3. $5.2 \times 10.3 =$

4. $2.5 \times 2.5 =$

5. $110.4 \div 9.2 =$

6. $69.2 \div 17.3 =$

7. $7.74 \div .43 =$

MULTIPLYING AND DIVIDING BY POWERS OF TEN

In this case, a "power of ten" is simply a multiple of 10—10, 100, 1000, 10,000, etc. To multiply decimals by powers of 10, just move the decimal point to the right as many spaces as there are zeros in the power of 10.

In other words, if you're multiplying a decimal by 10, you move the decimal point to the right one space. If you're multiplying a decimal by 100, you move the decimal point to the right two spaces. For example:

$$24.7 \times 100 = 2470$$
$$.385 \times 10 = 3.85$$

When you divide a decimal by a power of 10, you move the decimal place to the left as many spaces as there are zeros in the power of 10.

In other words, if you're dividing a decimal by 10, you move the decimal point to the left one space. If you're dividing a decimal by 100, you move the decimal point to the left two spaces. For example:

$$24.7 \div 100 = .247$$
$$.953 \div 10 = .0953$$

ROUNDING NUMBERS

Sometimes you may be asked to round off numbers. The general rule for rounding numbers is this:

If the last digit of the number is less than 5, **round down** (14.4 is rounded off to 14).
If the last digit is greater than or equal to 5, **round up** (14.6 is rounded off to 15).

For example:
24.3 rounded to the nearest whole number is 24.
0.76 rounded to the nearest tenth is 0.8.
–0.22 rounded to the nearest tenth is –0.2.

EXPONENTS AND SQUARE ROOTS

An exponent tells you how many times to multiply a number by itself. For example:

$$3^2 = 3 \times 3 = 9$$
$$2^3 = 2 \times 2 \times 2 = 8$$

The number that an exponent is "attached" to is called a base.

RULES FOR EXPONENTS WITH THE SAME BASE:

- To **multiply**, add the exponents: $x^2 \times x^5 = x^{2+5} = x^7$

- To **divide**, subtract the exponents: $x^6 \div x^3 = x^{6-3} = x^3$

- To **raise the power**, multiply the exponents: $\left(x^4\right)^3 = x^{4 \times 3} = x^{12}$

You cannot add or subtract different exponents, so $x^6 + x^3$ is just $x^6 + x^3$. You can't reduce $x^6 + x^3$ any further.

RULES FOR EXPONENTS WITH DIFFERENT BASES

You can't do anything. Don't try to add, subtract, multiply, divide, or cancel.

EXPONENTS AND PARENTHESES

Exponents carry over all parts within the parentheses:

$$2(3a^3)^2 = 2(9a^6)$$

SQUARE ROOTS

The sign $\sqrt{}$ indicates the positive square root of a number. The square root of x, or $\sqrt{x}$, is the number that, when multiplied by itself, equals x. For example, the square root of 25 is 5, or $\sqrt{25} = 5$. That's because $5 \times 5 = 25$. The square root of 9 is 3, and the square root of 36 is 6.

There are two rules you need to know regarding square roots.

1. $\sqrt{x}\sqrt{y} = \sqrt{xy}$.

    For example, $\sqrt{3}\sqrt{12} = \sqrt{36} = 6$

2. $\sqrt{\dfrac{x}{y}} = \dfrac{\sqrt{x}}{\sqrt{y}}$.

    For example, $\sqrt{\dfrac{5}{4}} = \dfrac{\sqrt{5}}{\sqrt{4}} = \dfrac{\sqrt{5}}{2}$

Note that rule 1 also works in reverse:

$$\sqrt{50} = \sqrt{25} \times \sqrt{2} = 5\sqrt{2}$$

SEQUENCES

A sequence is a list of numbers in a certain order. Each number in a sequence is called a **term**.

When the difference between any two consecutive terms in a sequence is the same, the sequence is called an **arithmetic sequence**. The difference is called the **common difference**.

2, 4, 6, 8, 10 ... is an arithmetic sequence with a common difference of 2.

If the consecutive terms of a sequence are formed by multiplying by a constant factor, it's a **geometric sequence**, and the factor is called a **common ratio**.

2, 4, 8, 16, 32 ... is a geometric sequence with a common ratio of 2.

If the sequence is neither arithmetic or geometric, it is a **miscellaneous sequence**. There can still be a pattern, just not a common difference or ratio.

If the terms in a sequence get bigger, they are **ascending**; if they get smaller, they are **descending**.

To find missing terms in a sequence, first determine what type of sequence you're dealing with: Subtract the first term from the second, and the second from the third (or vice versa, if the sequence is descending). If the results are the same, it's an arithmetic sequence. If not, try dividing the second term by the first, and the third by the second (or vice versa, if the sequence is descending). If the results are the same, it's a geometric sequence. If the sequence is miscellaneous, look for a pattern.

For example, let's look at the sequence 1, 2, 5, 10, 17. The terms here are getting bigger, so the sequence is ascending. This means we want to subtract the first term from the second, and the second from the third. The difference between the first and second terms is one, the difference between the second and third terms is 3. The results are also different if we try dividing 2 by 1 (which equals 2) and 5 by 2 (which equals 2.5). So the sequence is miscellaneous, and therefore we need to find the pattern. If we keep subtracting the terms from each other, we will see that the difference between the terms follows the first positive odd numbers in the number line: 1, 3, 5, and 7. Since we've identified the pattern, we can now predict that the next number in the sequence will be 26, because 17 (the last number given in the sequence) + 9 (the next odd number) = 26.

QUICK QUIZ 4

Take this short quiz before moving on. You can check your answers at the end of the chapter.

1. $135.7 \times 10 =$ _____

2. $.314 \times 100 =$ _____

3. $58.47 \div 100 =$ _____

4. $1.76 \div 10 =$ _____

5. Round 99.6 to the nearest whole number. _____

6. Round 12.12 to the nearest tenth. _12.1_

7. $5^2 =$ _____

8. $3^3 =$ _____

9. $2^2 \times 2^3 =$ _____

10. $7^4 \div 7^2 =$ _____

11. $\sqrt{2} \sqrt{32} =$ _____

12. $\sqrt{\dfrac{81}{9}} =$ _____

13. Identify the next three terms in the following sequence: 24, 21, 18, 15, 12, __9__, __6__, __3__.

MISCELLANEOUS ARITHMETIC QUESTIONS

UNITS OF MEASURE

In addition to the math skills being tested, the ASVAB also tests your knowledge of basic units of measurement. Make sure you know all the measurements listed below.

- 1 foot = 12 inches
- 1 yard = 3 feet
- 1 hour = 60 minutes
- 1 day = 24 hours
- 1 year = 365 days
- 1 year = 52 weeks
- 1 dollar = 100 cents = 10 dimes = 4 quarters
- 1 gallon = 8 pints
- 1 gallon = 4 quarts
- 1 pound = 16 ounces

CALCULATING CHANGES IN PERCENTAGE

A common type of question on the ASVAB asks you to figure out the percent change in the price of something.

For example:

A $40 book went on sale for $35. What was the percentage by which the book was discounted?

A. 5%
B. 10%
C. 12.5%
D. 15%

To calculate the percent change, use the following formula:

$$\text{percent increase or decrease} = \frac{\text{difference}}{\text{original amount}}$$

So, for this question, we would just plug in the numbers to find the change:

$$\text{percent decrease} = \frac{5}{40} = .125 \text{ or } 12.5\%$$

The answer is C.

RATIOS

A ratio gives information about the relative amounts of things. For example, a banana split may be made up of 1 part banana, 3 parts ice cream, 2 parts toppings, and 1 part whipped cream. Therefore, the ratio of banana to ice cream to toppings to whipped cream is 1:3:2:1. This means that for every one part of banana there is three parts ice cream. For every two parts of toppings there is one part of whipped cream and so on. Let's look at a ratio question now:

> The ratio of red to blue marbles in a bowl is 7:8. There are 30 marbles total. How many red and blue marbles are there?
>
> A.   7 red and 8 blue
> B.   8 red and 7 blue
> C.   10 red and 12 blue
> D.   14 red and 16 blue

Whenever you see a ratio question, plug the information into a **ratio box**.

Red	Blue	Total
7	8	
		30

Put the information about the ratio in the top line and the total number in the bottom line. Then, add the numbers from the original ratio and put the sum on the top line in the "Total" category.

Red	Blue	Total
7	8	15
		30

Let's look at the "Total" category. What number multiplied by 15 equals 30? Multiply 15 by 2 and you get 30. So, write "× 2" in the second row. Your ratio table now looks like this:

Red	Blue	Total
7	8	15
×2	×2	×2
		30

Now all you need to do is multiply the 7 and the 8 by 2 to find the answer. That gives us 14 red marbles and 16 blue marbles. The answer is D.

PROPORTIONS

A proportion is a way of comparing ratios with equal values. Proportions are usually used to figure out how big or small something will be in comparable circumstances. For example, if a 3-foot-high flagpole casts a shadow of 2 feet, then a 6-foot-high flagpole will cast a shadow of 4 feet.

$$\frac{\text{flagpole}}{\text{shadow}} = \frac{3}{2} = \frac{6}{4}$$

Another way to write this proportion is 3:2 :: 6:4. The four dots in the middle are the proportion sign. The numbers on the outside, 3 and 4, are called the extremes. The numbers on the inside are called the means. The product of the extremes will equal the product of the means. Let's multiply them out and see for ourselves:

$$3 \times 4 = 12 \text{ and } 2 \times 6 = 12$$

How does this help you? It provides you with a way to figure out a missing number in a proportion. For example:

If 10 nails cost 4 cents, how much do 50 nails cost?

The question is giving us the proportion 10:4 :: 50:?. We need to complete the proportion 50:?. It's simple using what we just learned.

$$4 \times 50 = 200 \text{ so } 10 \times \text{?} = 200$$

Remember that multiplication is the opposite of division, so you can find the missing value by division:

$$200 \div 10 = 20$$

50 nails cost 20 cents.

This method also works if you write the proportion the other way. Just make sure you keep the categories the same on the top and bottom.

$$\frac{\text{nails}}{\text{cents}} = \frac{10}{4} = \frac{50}{?}$$

In this case, the extremes are diagonal from each other, so you need to cross-multiply—in other words, multiply the top number from the first fraction times the bottom number in the other fraction, and the top number in the second fraction times the bottom number in the first fraction.

$$\frac{10}{4} = \frac{50}{?} \qquad 4 \times 50 = 200 \text{ and } 10 \times \text{?} = 200, \text{ so } \text{?} = 20 \text{ cents}$$

PROBABILITY

Sometimes you may be asked to find the probability of a certain event. For example:

A pet store has 14 kittens. Three of the kittens are black, 3 are calico, 4 are white, and 4 are black and white. If 1 kitten is selected at random, what is the probability that it will be a calico kitten?

A. $\dfrac{3}{14}$

B. $\dfrac{3}{10}$

C. $\dfrac{11}{14}$

D. $\dfrac{1}{5}$

In this case, we need to figure out how likely it is that we'd get a calico kitten if we picked one randomly out of the bunch. There are 14 different kittens, which gives us fourteen different possible choices. Out of all 14 kittens, 3 of them are calico. Therefore, we would have a 3 out of 14 chance, or a $\dfrac{3}{14}$ chance, of choosing a calico kitten if we chose one at random.

AVERAGES

To find the average of a set of numbers, just add up the numbers and divide the sum by the number of numbers in the set.

What is the average of 3, 5, and 10?

$$3 + 5 + 10 = 18$$

Since there are three numbers in the set, we next divide 18 by 3.

$$18 \div 3 = 6$$

The average of 3, 5, and 10 is 6.

Sometimes the ASVAB will make things trickier by not giving you a list of numbers. But you can still do the problem. To find any average, all you need are two out of three things: the sum of the numbers, the number of things in the set, and the average. To find any one of these things, you need to know the other two. The ASVAB will always give you two of these things and then ask you to find the third. The easiest way to solve average problems is to use the **Average Pie.**

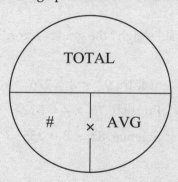

Let's look at an example:

The average of 3 numbers is 22, and the smallest of these numbers is 2. The other two numbers are equal. What are they?

A. 22
B. 32
C. 40
D. 64

In this problem, you have the average (22) and the number of items in the set (3). Plug those numbers into the average pie. It will look like this:

Now we need to find the total. It's 3 × 22 = 66. We know that one of the numbers in the set is 2. Subtract 2 from 66 and we are left with 64. The remaining two numbers must be equal to each other, so we just divide 64 by 2. That gives us 32. The answer is B.

Weighted Averages

Sometimes one item in a set may be more important than another. In this case, we say the items are "weighted" differently. When this happens, you need to take the weight of each item into consideration when finding the average. For example:

Winnie received a 92 in Math, a 78 in English, and an 85 in Science. Suppose the subjects have the following weights: Math 3, English 4, and Science 3. What is Winnie's average?

A. 72
B. 78
C. 84.1
D. 93.25

To find the average, we must first "weigh" the grades accordingly. To do this, just multiply the grade by the weight for that class.

Math: 92 × 3 = 276

English: 78 × 4 = 312

Science: 85 × 3 = 255

Then, add the products together. This is your "Total" for the average pie.

$$274 + 312 + 255 = 841$$

You find the number of items in the set by adding the weights together.

$$3 + 4 + 3 = 10$$

You now have two of the spots in the average pie filled in and can find the third.

The average is 841 ÷ 10 = 84.1.
The answer is B.

QUICK QUIZ 5

Try the following problems before moving on. You can check your answers at the end of the chapter.

1. Curtis earns $600 every month except for December and January, when he takes a vacation and earns no income. What is his average monthly income for the entire year?

   A. $500
   B. $484
   C. $300
   D. $275

2. In a bowl there are 5 red sticks, 4 blue sticks, 7 yellow sticks, and 9 white sticks. If 1 stick is to be drawn at random, what is the probability it will be red?

   A. $\dfrac{1}{10}$

   B. $\dfrac{1}{5}$

   C. $\dfrac{5}{10}$

   D. $\dfrac{5}{12}$

3. At a coed camp, the ratio of girls to boys is 5:3. If the camp's enrollment is 160, how many of the children are boys?

    A.   20

    B.   60

    C.   100

    D.   120

4. Ken received a 72 in Math, a 64 in Science, and an 80 in Art. If the subjects have the following weights: Math 3, Science 4, and Art 3, what is Ken's average?

    A.   70.5

    B.   71.2

    C.   79.2

    D.   80.0

5. A store owner buys a pound of grapes for 80 cents and sells it for a dollar. What percent of the original price of grapes is the store owner's profit?

    A.   10%

    B.   20%

    C.   25%

    D.   40%

6. Fill in the blanks

    1 foot = __12__ inches

    1 yard = __3__ feet

    1 hour = __60__ minutes

    1 day = __24__ hours

    1 year = __365__ days

    1 year = __52__ weeks

    1 dollar = __100__ cents = __10__ dimes = __4__ quarters

    1 gallon = __8__ pints

    1 gallon = __4__ quarts

    1 pound = __16__ ounces

ALGEBRA

You won't need to know much algebra for the ASVAB, but you do have to know the basics. Most of the algebra questions on the ASVAB test your ability to solve for a variable or factor. Before we begin our review, let's define a few terms you should know.

ALGEBRA TERMINOLOGY

- **Algebra**: Math that uses letters to represent numbers.
- **Coefficient**: The number multiplied by a variable in a term.
- **Expression**: A bunch of numbers and variables being added or subtracted.
- **Equation**: Two expressions set equal to each other.
- **Factor**: The factors of a number are the numbers that when multiplied together, equal that number.
- **Formula**: An expression representing a set relationship among the terms.
- **Inequality**: An expression where one side is set greater than, or both greater than or equal to, the other side.
- **Simultaneous equations**: Separate equations in which each term has only one variable. Both equations have the same two distinct variables.
- **Term**: A number or variable or both combined by multiplication or division.
- **Variable**: A letter used to represent a number.

SOLVING FOR X

One of the most common types of algebra questions on the ASVAB is one where you are asked to solve for a variable (usually x). You will be given an equation like this:

$$8x - 4 = 12 + x$$

Your job is to figure out what x equals. To do this, you must first **isolate the variable** (x) on one side of the equation.

$$8x - 4 = 12 + x$$
$$\underline{-x = -x} \quad \text{Subtract } x \text{ from both sides.}$$
$$7x - 4 = 12$$
$$\underline{+4 = +4} \quad \text{Add 4 to both sides.}$$
$$7x = 16$$

$$\frac{7x}{7} = \frac{16}{7} \quad \text{Divide both sides by 7.}$$

$$x = \frac{16}{7}$$

Isolating the Variable

To isolate a variable, you must do the opposite of what the equation does *on both sides* of the equation. For example, if the equation subtracts 4 from one side, you must add four to both sides. If it multiplies by 7 on one side, you must divide by 7 on both sides. The cardinal rule is this: **Whatever you do to one side, you must do to the other side**. Let's look at an example:

$$3x = 27$$

To isolate the variable, the coefficient 3 needs to be moved. To move something from one side of the equation to the other you need to perform the opposite operation on both sides of the equation. In this example, the 3 is being multiplied by x, so you need to divide by 3. Again, the most important thing to remember is that whatever you do to one side of the equation you must do to the other side.

$$\frac{3x}{3} = \frac{27}{3}$$

The 3s on the left side divide out and on the right side, $27 \div 3 = 9$.

$$x = 9$$

Let's look at another example:

$$t - 5 = 20$$

To isolate the variable t, we need to perform the opposite operation on both sides. The coefficient 5 is being subtracted, so we need to add 5 to both sides.

$$t - 5 + 5 = 20 + 5$$
$$t = 25$$

Another way you might see algebra on the ASVAB is when they provide you with the values of the variables. For example:

Solve the equation. $x = 3$ and $z = -2$

$$x^2 + 4z + 15 =$$

To answer this question, just plug in the values they provided and solve.

$$3^2 + 4(-2) + 15 =$$
$$9 + (-8) + 15 =$$
$$1 + 15 = 16$$

FACTORING

The factors of a number are the numbers that when multiplied together, equal that number. For example, the factors of 6 are (1,6) and (2,3). The factors of 12 are (1,12), (2,6), and (3,4).

You can also identify the factors of algebraic expressions. To factor expressions find a common factor of all the terms in the expression. For example:

$$6x^2y + 3xy^2$$

The first thing you want to look at is the coefficients, 6 and 3. Do they have any common factors? Yes, 3 is a common factor of both of them. Divide the 3 out of each and put the remaining terms in parenthesis.

$$3(2x^2y + xy^2)$$

Now you want to factor out the variables. Let's look at them one at a time. First, let's factor out the x's. We have x^2 and x. We can factor an x out of both terms. Move it out of the parenthesis.

$$3x(2xy + y^2)$$

Now look at the y's. We have y and y^2. We can factor a y out of both terms. Move it out of the parenthesis.

$$3xy(2x + y)$$

The expression is completely factored now. If you multiply it out again, you will see that you end up with the same expression you started with.

$$3xy(2x + y) = 6x^2y + 3xy^2$$

You may also be asked to factor an expression that looks like this:

$$x^2 + 2x = 15$$

To factor this expression, the first thing you need to do is move the 15 to the other side. To do this, just subtract 15 from both sides.

$$x^2 + 2x -15 = 0$$

Next, figure out what the factors of the last term (15) are. They are:

$$(1,15) \text{ and } (3,5)$$

Which pair of factors, when either added or subtracted, will give you the middle term from the expression (2)? The pair (1,15) definitely won't. If you add them you get 16. If you subtract, you get 14 or –14. What about (3,5)? If you add them you get 8. If you subtract, you end up with 2 or –2. That's what we're looking for. So we know the factors for this expression are 3 and 5. Since the middle term is 2 and not –2 we know that we need a positive 5 and a negative 3, because $5 - 3 = 2$. The factored form of the expression looks like this:

$$(x + 5)(x - 3)$$

To check your work, you can use FOIL. FOIL tells you what order to multiply the terms of the factors in.

First
Outer
Inner
Last

First multiply the first terms in the factors together: $x \times x = x^2$.
Next multiply the outer terms together: $x \times -3 = -3x$.
Then multiply the inner terms together: $5 \times x = 5x$.
Finally, multiply the last terms together: $5 \times -3 = -15$.

$$(x + 5)(x - 3) = x^2 - 3x + 5x -15 = x^2 + 2x - 15$$

Let's look at another example. Pay attention to where the minus sign appears.

$$r^2 - 9r + 20$$

First, identify the factors of the third term: (1,20), (2,10), and (4,5). Which of these pairs combines to form –9? (4,5) do. But we need them both to be negative, so the factors will look like this:

$$(r - 4)(r - 5)$$

Multiply to check your work. Remember, when you multiply two negative numbers, the result is a positive number.

$$(r - 4)(r - 5) = r^2 - 9r + 20$$

It's important to pay attention to the sign in the expression being factored. Here are some helpful generalizations:

- When the second term of the expression is being subtracted and the third tem is being added, both factors will be negative.

$$r^2 - 9r + 20 = (r - 4)(r - 5)$$

- When the second term is being added and the third term is being subtracted, one of the factors will be positive and one will be negative.

$$x^2 + 2x - 15 = (x + 5)(x - 3)$$

- When both the second and third terms of the expression are being added, both factors are positive.

$$x^2 + 8x + 16 = (x + 4)(x + 4)$$

SIMULTANEOUS EQUATIONS

Sometimes you will be given two equations and asked to solve for a variable. For example:

If $2x + 3y = 12$ and $3x - 3y = -2$, what is the value of x?

When given simultaneous equations, stack them up, and either add or subtract. The goal is to get rid of the extra variable. Here it's the y. By adding these two equations together, we will eliminate the y. Then, we can solve for x.

$$\begin{array}{r} 2x + 3y = 12 \\ + 3x - 3y = -2 \\ \hline 5x + 0y = 10 \\ 5x = 10 \\ x = 2 \end{array}$$

If we had subtracted, we'd have gotten $-x + 6y = 14$, which wouldn't help us out at all. If you choose the wrong operation, no big deal, just try the other one.

Let's look at a slightly harder example now:

If $2x + 3y = 7$ and $3x + 2y = 8$, what is the value of x?

At first glance this problem may not seem any harder. But when you look more closely you'll see that neither of the variables cancels out by adding or subtracting. That is because the coefficients of the terms are different. To solve this problem we are going to have to make the coefficients of one of the variables equal. Let's do it with the y terms.

To make the coefficients of the y terms equal, we need to multiply one or both of the equations. It's sort of like finding a common factor.

$$2(2x + 3y = 7)$$
$$3(3x + 2y = 8)$$

By multiplying the equations by 3 and 2 respectively, we will end up with $6y$ in each equation. That will allow us to eliminate the ys and solve for x.

$$4x + 6y = 14$$
$$9x + 6y = 24$$

Now subtract the equations to eliminate the y terms.

$$4x + 6y = 14$$
$$-9x + 6y = 24$$
$$\pm 5x + 0y = -10$$
$$\pm 5x = -10$$
$$x = \pm 2$$

Sometimes the ASVAB likes to be a little tricky. Instead of giving you the two equations you need to add or subtract with, they give you one of them and the result. For example:

If you add $4a - 6b + 2c$ to a polynomial, you get $12a + 3b - 8c$. What is the polynomial?

The question is giving you the sum (result of addition). To find the answer, do the opposite. In this case, that means subtract.

$$12a + 3b - 8c$$
$$-4a + 6b + 2c$$
$$8a + 9b - 10c$$

The answer to the question will be $8a + 9b - 10c$. You can check your answer by doing what the question says. In other words add the polynomial they give you to the polynomial you found.

$$8a + 9b - 10c$$
$$-4a + 6b + 2c$$
$$12a + 3b - 8c$$

If you end up with the right result, you have the right answer.
Another way the ASVAB likes to test you with questions like this:

Given the formulas $t = \dfrac{r}{s}$ and $p = tr - s$, which formula expresses the value of p without using r?

The key to solving this problem is in the words *without using r*. What do you think you should do? If you said solve for r, you're right! Solve for r by isolating it and then you can plug the value of it into the equation for p.

$$t = \frac{r}{s} \text{ so } r = \frac{t}{s}$$

Now you can replace the r in the equation $p = tr - s$ with its value $\dfrac{t}{s}$.

$$p = t\frac{t}{s} - s \text{ or } p = \frac{t^2}{ts} - s = \frac{t}{s} - s. \text{ So, } p = \frac{t}{s} - s, \text{ and that's the answer!}$$

QUICK QUIZ 6

Practice factoring and solving simultaneous equations below. You can check your answers at the end of the chapter.

1. $11x + 4 = -x + 16$
2. $3(x + 2) = 4(2 + x)$
3. Factor: $x^2 - 4x - 21$
4. $a^2 + 10a + 25 = 0$
5. If $3x + 3y = 4$ and $2x - 3y = 1$, what is the value of x?

INEQUALITIES

Inequalities are just like equations, with one special exception. If you multiply or divide by a negative number, you must flip the inequality sign.

$$2x > 16$$

Divide both sides by 2. This gives you

$$x > 8$$

What if the equation looked like this?

$$-2x > 16$$

You would divide both sides by –2 and flip the inequality sign around.

$$x < -8$$

What if it looked like this?

$$x - 5 > 3x + 1$$

We are solving for x, so we need to isolate it on one side. First, let's move the x over by subtracting x on both sides.

$$x - x - 5 > 3x + 1 - x$$
$$-5 > 2x + 1$$

Now move the 1 over by subtracting 1 from both sides

$$-5 - 1 > 2x + 1 - 1$$
$$-6 > 2x$$

Move the 2 by dividing both sides by 2.

$$\frac{-6}{2} > \frac{2x}{2}$$

$$-3 > x \text{ or } x < -3$$

SPECIAL FORMULAS

There are a couple of special formulas the ASVAB likes to test. For both of the formulas, it is simply a matter of Plugging In the information the question provides and solving for the missing variable.

Motion

The formula for motion is: Distance = rate × time

Jackson drove 200 miles in 4 hours. What was his rate of travel?

A.   50
B.   80
C.   204
D.   800

The distance in this problem is 200. The time is 4 hours, and the problem asks you to find the rate. Just plug in the numbers and solve!

$$200 = \text{rate} \times 4$$

$$\frac{200}{4} = \text{rate}$$

$$\text{rate} = 50$$

The answer is A.

Interest

The formula used on the ASVAB to determine interest is:

I = prt
I = interest
p = amount of money invested (principal)
r = annual interest rate
t = time

How long must Cherie invest $500 at 7% to earn $350 in interest?

A.   5 years
B.   10 years
C.   12 years
D.   15 years

The problem gives us the principal, interest rate, and interest. We need to find the time. Plug everything in and solve.

$$350 = 500 \; .07 \times t$$

$$\frac{350}{500} = .07t$$

$$\frac{0.7}{0.7} = t$$

$$t = 10$$

The answer is B.

QUICK QUIZ 7

Try the following problems on your own. You can check your answers at the end of the chapter.

1. $-9m - 12 > 11 - 3m$

2. $10 + x < 14 - 3x$

3. $4x - 5 > 2x + 1$

4. If Bonzo rode his bicycle 30 miles in 5 hours, how long would it take him to ride 12 miles at the same rate?

   A. 2 hours
   B. 2.5 hours
   C. 5 hours
   D. 12 hours

5. If Jen puts $1,000 in a savings account with an annual interest rate of 5%, how much interest will she earn in two years?

   A. $50
   B. $75
   C. $100
   D. $150

6. Rob drove for 6.5 hours at a speed of 45 miles per hour. How far did he travel?

   A. 153 miles
   B. 292.5 miles
   C. 300 miles
   D. 450 miles

GEOMETRY

For the ASVAB, you will only need to know a few geometric definitions and equations. Let's start with a terminology review.

GEOMETRY TERMINOLOGY

- **π**: Also known as "Pi", and pronounced "Pie". π is a number approximately equal to 3.14. It is the ratio of the circumference of a circle to the circle's diameter.

- **Area**: the space covered within the outline of a figure.

- **Circumference**: the perimeter of a circle.

- **Cube**: a three-dimensional box in which all edges and faces are equal.

- **Decagon**: a ten-sided polygon.

- **Diameter**: any line from one side of a circle to the other side through the center of the circle.

- **Equilateral triangle**: a triangle in which all sides and all angles are equal.

- **Face**: a side of a three-dimensional shape.

- **Hypotenuse**: the side of a right triangle that is opposite the right angle.

- **Octagon**: an eight-sided polygon.

- **Parallel lines**: lines that run infinitely, never meet, and are always the same distance apart; the symbol for this is $\parallel$.

- **Pentagon**: a five-sided polygon.

- **Perimeter**: the outline measurement of a figure.

- **Polygon**: a closed plane figure of three or more sides (such as a triangle, rectangle, or quadrilateral).

- **Radius**: any line from the center of a circle to any point on the edge of the circle; symbolized by r.

- **Right Triangle**: a triangle in which one of the angles measures 90 degrees.

- **Pythagorean theorem**: $a^2 + b^2 = c^2$, where a, b, and c are the lengths of the three sides of a right triangle. In other words, the sum of the squares of the lengths of the two smaller legs of a right triangle will add up to the square of the length of the hypotenuse.

- **Supplementary angles**: angles that together add up to 180.

- **Triangle**: a three-sided polygon.

- **Vertical angles**: opposite angles formed by the intersection of two lines.

- **Volume**: the amount of three-dimensional space a three-dimensional object takes up.

GEOMETRY: LINES AND ANGLES

There are 360 degrees in a circle.

There are 180 degrees in a straight line.

A right angle (or quarter circle) has 90 degrees.

Two angles that form a straight line add up to 180 degrees.

When two lines cross, the vertical angles are equal.

There are 180 degrees in a triangle: $a° + b° + c° = 180°$.

Fred's Theorem

Fred's Theorem is just a name we made up for some rules you need to remember. Here it is: These three things are always true when a line crosses two parallel lines:

- Two kinds of angles are created: big ones and small ones.

- All the big angles are equal to each other; all the small angles are equal to each other.

- Any big angle plus any small angle equals 180 degrees.

TRIANGLES

There are a few different types of triangles that you need to know about.
Right triangles have a right (or 90°) angle.

If you know the lengths of two sides of a right triangle you can use the **Pythagorean theorem** to find the third. The Pythagorean theorem states that $a^2 + b^2 = c^2$, where a, b, and c are the lengths of the three sides of a right triangle. In other words, the sum of the squares of the lengths of the two smaller legs of a right triangle will add up to the square of the length of the hypotenuse.

In the formula, *a* and *b* always denote the length of the legs of the triangle, and *c* the length of the hypotenuse.

If $a = 4$ and $b = 3$, then $4^2 + 3^2 = 25$. Therefore, $c^2 = 25$ and so $c = 5$
If $a = 5$ and $c = 13$, then $5^2 + b^2 = 13^2$. So $25 + b^2 = 169$ and therefore $b^2 = 144$ and $b = 12$

Isosceles triangles have 2 equal sides and 2 equal angles.

Equilateral triangles have 3 equal sides and 3 equal angles.

Similar triangles have equal angles and proportional sides.

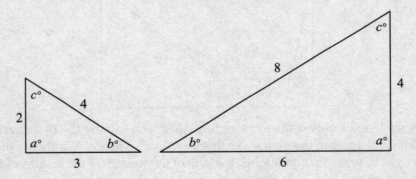

Finding the Area of a Triangle

To find the area of a triangle, use the equation:

$$\text{Area} = \frac{1}{2}\text{base} \times \text{height}$$

Let's look at an example:

A = _____

The base = 8 and height = 6, so the equation is Area = $\frac{1}{2}$(8)(6) = $\frac{1}{2}$48 = 24.

Finding the Perimeter of a Triangle

To find the perimeter of a triangle, just add up the lengths of all the sides.

In this example, the sides are 4, 5, and 6. So the perimeter is 4 + 5 + 6 = 15.

CIRCLES

Circles are perfectly round shapes. All circles have three parts that you need to know about: the radius, the diameter, and the circumference.

The **radius** is a line drawn from the center of the circle to any point on the edge of the circle. It is usually denoted by r.

The **diameter** is a line drawn from one side of the circle to the other side, which crosses through the center of the circle. It is equal to two times the radius and can be found with the formula: diameter = $2r$.

The **circumference** of a circle is the perimeter of the circle. You can find the circumference of a circle using this formula: circumference = $2\pi r$.

You are probably wondering what the π is. This symbol stands for "pi." π is the ratio of a circle's circumference to its diameter. π is the same for all circles—it's a number approximately equal to 3.14. When solving problems that use π, the ASVAB will tell you what value to use. Sometimes you can just leave the π as it is. In other words, you don't always have to plug in a numerical value for π, because the answer will be something like 9π or 12π.

You also need to know how to find the area of a circle. The formula for that is: Area = πr^2. Now that we know the basics, let's look at some circles!

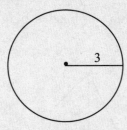

In the above circle, the radius r has been provided. $r = 3$. Therefore,

- Diameter = 6
- Area = 9π
- Circumference = 6π

The diameter of the circle is 10. What is the radius and circumference?
Let's start with the radius, since we need to know that to find the circumference.

The diameter is two times the length of the radius, so the radius is $\dfrac{10}{2} = 5$.

Now let's find the circumference:

$$\text{Circumference} = \pi r^2 = \pi 5^2 = 25\pi$$

QUADRILATERALS

A quadrilateral is a four-sided figure. The measures of its four angles always add up to 360 degrees. There are a few different quadrilaterals you may be asked about.

Parallelograms are quadrilaterals with two pairs of opposite sides that are parallel, and two pairs of opposite angles that are equal.

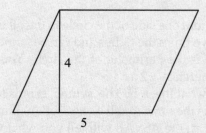

A **rectangle** is a parallelogram with four right angles and equal opposite sides.

5

9

A **square** is a parallelogram with all equal sides and four right angles.

3

A **trapezoid** is a parallelogram with exactly one pair of parallel opposite sides.

Finding the Area of a Quadrilateral

The formula for finding the area enclosed by a quadrilateral depends on the type of quadrilateral you are working with.

For a rectangle, use: Area = length × width

For a square, use: Area = side × side, or side^2

For a parallelogram or trapezoid use: Area = base × height

The first quadrilateral above is a square, so we use the formula:
Area = side^2. In this case, Area = 4^2 = 16

The second quadrilateral is a rectangle, so we use the formula:
Area = length × width. Area = 10 × 15 = 150

The third quadrilateral is a parallelogram, so we use the formula:
Area = base × height. Area = 6 × 4 = 24

Finding the Perimeter of a Quadrilateral

To find the perimeter of a quadrilateral, just add up all the sides.

The quadrilateral shown above is a rectangle with a length of 8 and a height of 3. To find the perimeter, add up all the sides of the rectangle.

$$\text{Perimeter} = 8 + 8 + 3 + 3 = 22$$

Remember, although the drawing only gave us two sides, we need to add all four sides.

Finding the Volume of a Box

To find the volume of a box, which is a three-dimensional rectangle, use this formula:

$$\text{Volume} = \text{length} \times \text{width} \times \text{height}$$

In the figure above, length = 8, width = 4, and height = 3. So the formula is
Volume = 8 × 4 × 3 = 96

Finding the Surface Area of a Box

The surface area of a box is the sum of the areas of all its sides.

In the figure above, we are given the length, width, and height of the box. To find the surface area, we just find the area of each side and then add them together.

Front side = 4 × 6 = 24
Back side = 4 × 6 = 24
Top side = 4 × 6 = 24
Bottom side = 4 × 6 = 24
Left side = 4 × 3 = 12
Right side = 4 × 3 =12
The surface area is 24 + 24 + 24 + 24 + 12 + 12 = 120

QUICK QUIZ 8

That's all the geometry you need to know. Memorize the formulas and then take the quick quiz. You can check your answers at the end of the chapter.

1. A circular swimming pool has a circumference of 12π. What is the radius of the pool?

    A. 3
    B. 6
    C. 24
    D. 30

2. If one of the angles in a right triangle measures 20 degrees, what are the measurements of the other two angles?

    A. 20 degrees, 140 degrees
    B. 40 degrees, 120 degrees
    C. 70 degrees, 90 degrees
    D. 80 degrees, 90 degrees

3.

    A line crosses two parallel lines, creating angle a, which measures 50 degrees. How many degrees does angle b have?

    A. 50 degrees
    B. 90 degrees
    C. 130 degrees
    D. 180 degrees

4. Mrs. Stewart baked two apple pies. One had a radius of 4 inches, the other a radius of 5 inches. Find the difference in the areas of the two pies.

    A. 1 square inch
    B. 9 square inches
    C. 9π square inches
    D. 41π square inches

5. If a triangle has an area of 21 and a base of 7, what is its height?

    A. 4
    B. 6
    C. 7
    D. 8

6. The length of a rectangle is 2 less than 3 times the width. If the perimeter is 20 mm, what is the length?

    A. 3 mm
    B. 7 mm
    C. 9 mm
    D. 10 mm

7. A box has a length of 5 inches, a width of 3 inches, and a height of 4 inches. What is the volume of the box?

    A. 12 cu in.
    B. 60 cu in.
    C. 120 cu in.
    D. 600 cu in.

8. What is the surface area of a cube with a volume of 27 cubic inches?

    A. 18 square inches
    B. 27 square inches
    C. 54 square inches
    D. 81 square inches

9. The perimeter of a triangle is 25 inches. If two of the sides are 8 inches and 10 inches, what is the length of the third side?

    A. 5 inches
    B. 7 inches
    C. 12 inches
    D. 18 inches

MATH TECHNIQUES

We've now covered all the math you need to know for the ASVAB. The next thing we are going to talk about is how to make the questions easier to answer.

WORD PROBLEMS

The questions in the Arithmetic Reasoning section are usually presented as word problems. For example:

> Admission to the zoo costs $8.00 for adults and $5.00 for children. If the Brown family, which consists of two adults and three children, goes to the zoo and pays with two $20.00 bills, how much change will they receive?
>
> A. $5.00
> B. $9.00
> C. $23.00
> D. $31.00

All you need to know to answer this question is how to multiply, add, and subtract. Sound easy enough? The tricky part is being able to figure out what to multiply, add, and subtract. That is where Bite Size Pieces comes into play...

Bite Size Pieces

Bite Size Pieces is a technique that helps you take a long, complicated word problem and break it into smaller, easier to handle, pieces. Let's take the above example step by step:

Step 1: The first thing to do is to identify what we're being asked to do. In this question, we need to figure out how much change the Brown family will receive from two $20.00 bills, or $40.00.

Step 2: The next thing is break to the problem into smaller parts. First, let's figure out how much it's going to cost for the two adults to get into the zoo:

$$\$8.00 \text{ per adult} \times 2 \text{ adults} = \$16.00$$

Next, let's figure out how much it's going to cost for the children to get in:

$$\$5.00 \text{ per child} \times 3 \text{ children} = \$15.00$$

Now let's figure out the total cost for the Brown family to get in:

$$\$16.00 + \$15.00 = \$31.00$$

Step 3: Remember, the question is asking us how much change the family will receive from $40.00. So as for the last step, we subtract the cost of admission from the $40.00.

$$\$40.00 - \$31.00 = \$9.00$$

And that's our answer, B!

Let's try another example:

Greg works 30 hours a week at the gas station for $6.45 an hour and 15 hours a week at the coffee shop for $8.00 an hour. Helen works 35 hours a week at the stationary store for $7.50 an hour. What is the difference in the amount of money Helen and Greg make in two weeks?

A. $51.00
B. $102.00
C. $238.00
D. $576.00

Step 1: Identify what the problem is asking. This word problem is asking us to figure out the difference between what Greg makes in two weeks and what Helen makes in two weeks.

Step 2: Break the problem into Bite Size Pieces. Since we need to figure out the difference in their incomes, the first thing we need to do is figure out how much each one makes. The problem told us how many hours they work each week and how much they are paid per hour. Let's start there.

Greg

Greg has two jobs, so we need to figure out how much he makes each week at both jobs.

Gas station: 30 hours per week × $6.45 an hour = $193.50 per week
Coffee shop: 15 hours per week × $8.00 an hour = $120.00 per week

Then we add the two numbers together to figure out how much money he makes in total each week:

$193.50 + $120.00 = $313.50

Then we multiply that sum by 2 to figure out how much he makes in two weeks:

$313.50 × 2 = $627.00

Helen

Helen works only one job, so figuring out her pay will be easier for us.

Stationary store: 35 hours per week × $7.50 an hour = $262.50 per week
Multiply by 2 to find out how much Helen makes in two weeks:

$262.50 × 2 =$525.00

Step 3: Refer back to the problem to make sure you're answering the right question. The question is asking us what the difference is between Greg and Helen's pay. To figure this out we just subtract:

$627.00 – $525.00 = $102.00

That's answer choice B.

BALLPARKING

Ballparking is a technique that helps you eliminate bad answer choices before you've even worked the problem. For example:

> On a test of 50 questions, Gertrude answered 47 correctly. If Gertrude answered every question, what percentage did she answer incorrectly?
>
> A. 97%
> B. 47%
> C. 6%
> D. 3%

Without even doing the math involved, we can eliminate two answers. We know that she answered 47 out of 50 correctly, which means she got right almost all of the questions—in other words, she did pretty well on the test. Based on that, we can immediately rule out answers (A) and (B), because they are way too high. If she got almost all the questions right, it would be impossible for her to have gotten 97% or 47% of the answers *wrong*. That leaves us with (C) and (D). Even if we didn't know how to answer this problem, we could still guess and still have a 50/50 shot of getting it right. But we can do the math that will get us the answer for sure:

$$\frac{47}{50} = 50\overline{)47}^{\,0.94}$$

$$100\% - 94\% = 6\%$$

So the answer is C.

Let's look at another example:

> A circle is inscribed in square PQRS. What is the area of the shaded region?
>
> A. $16 - 6\pi$
> B. $16 - 4\pi$
> C. $16 - 2\pi$
> D. 16π

This is a really tough question, but by ballparking we can make it easier. Let's start by looking at the picture. How much of the square do you think is shaded? Half? Three-quarters? Less than half? In fact, about one-quarter of the square is shaded.

Next, let's do a little math. The length of one side of the square is 4 so the area of the square is 4 × 4 or 16. The area is 16 and the amount of the shaded area is about one-fourth of the square.

One-fourth of the square is $\frac{16}{4}$ or 4. So we need an answer choice that is about 4.

Now let's look at the answers:

Let's say π is about 3. Plug 3 into the answers and see what you end up with.

A. $16 - 6\pi$ $16 - 6(3) = 16 - 18 = -2$
B. $16 - 4\pi$ $16 - 4(3) = 16 - 12 = 4$
C. $16 - 2\pi$ $16 - 2(3) = 16 - 6 = 10$
D. 16π $16 \times 3 = 48$

Based on our work, the answer is B. That happens to be correct.

DRAW IT!

A lot of the geometry questions in the Mathematics Knowledge section give you a description of a figure but don't actually provide a drawing. When this happens, it helps to draw the picture yourself.

The area of a triangle is 30. If the height is 5, what is the base?

A. 10
B. 12
C. 30
D. 40

It might help if we drew the triangle described in the problem.

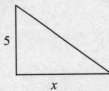

Don't worry too much about what the triangle looks like. All that matters is that the height is 5. We have labeled the base x just to keep track of it. Now let's plug everything into the equation for the area of a triangle and solve for x.

$$\text{Area} = \frac{1}{2} \text{ base} \times \text{height}$$

$$30 = \frac{1}{2}(x)(5)$$

$$30 = \frac{1}{2}5x$$

$$60 = 5x$$

$$x = 12$$

The base of the triangle is 12, so the answer is B.

The last example was pretty straightforward. Let's look at a tougher one to see how drawing the picture can really help.

A small street is intersected by a highway. The southwest corner of the intersection is an angle of 65 degrees. What is the size of the angle of the northwest corner?

A.   65 degrees

B.   90 degrees

C.   115 degrees

D.   180 degrees

Let's draw the intersection described in the problem to make things a little clearer.

By looking at our diagram, we can see that there are four angles, or corners of the street, that we can label. The problem gives us the size of the southwest angle, which is 65 degrees. Recall from our geometry review that adjacent angles add up to 180 degrees. Based on that, we know that the adjacent angle, the southeast corner, is 115 degrees. Also recall that opposite angles are equal. So, we know that the northwest corner, which is opposite the southeast corner, also equals 115 degrees. The answer is C.

PLUGGING IN

Plugging In is a problem-solving technique that works when the answers contain variables, or when the question asks you for a specific amount. When Plugging In, use numbers that will be easy to work with, like 2, 4, or 10. Do not plug in zero or one, or numbers that appear in the question. If you have two variables to plug in for, use two different numbers. Here's an example:

Clare is C years old and is six years younger than Alan. In terms of C, how many years old will Alan be in 3 years?

A.   C − 6

B.   C − 3

C.   C + 3

D.   C + 9

What did you think when you read this problem? If you're like most people, you probably didn't know what to think. At first glance this problem looks really hard. But if you know how to handle it, this problem is actually quite simple.

Whenever a problem has a variable like C in the answers, you should use Plugging In to find the answer. To plug in for the example above, we just want to pick a number that we can substitute for C. It's best to choose a number that's easy to work with. Let's use 10.

Claire is C years old and is six years younger than Alan. In terms of C, how many years old will Alan be in 3 years? If Claire is 10 years old, that makes Alan 16 years old. In three years he will be 19 years old. That is our target number. The next step is to plug in 10 into the answer choices. The answer that equals our target number 19 is the correct answer.

(A) $10 - 6 = 4$. No, we are looking for 19. This is not the answer.

(B) $10 - 3 = 7$. No, not the answer.

(C) $10 + 3 = 13$. Still not the answer.

(D) $10 + 9 = 19$. Yes, this is the answer.

Let's look at another example:

A mechanic buys a set of tools. He gives half of the tools to one coworker and five of them to another. If the mechanic now has nine tools left, how many tools did he buy originally?

A.   14

B.   20

C.   28

D.   36

In this example, the problem does not give us a variable. Instead, it asks us to find a specific amount. The specific amount is our target number. The easiest way to solve this problem is to plug in the answers. The answer that leaves us with the target number of 9 is the answer.

Let's start by Plugging In B, 20. If the mechanic buys 20 tools, and gives half to a coworker, that leaves him with ten tools. Then he gives five tools to another coworker. He now has 5 tools left. This isn't our target number, so this isn't the correct answer. Eliminate B.

Now we know that 20 is too low. Let's try a higher number, like answer C, 28. The mechanic buys 28 tools and gives half to a coworker, leaving him with 14 tools. He then give five to another coworker, leaving him with nine. That's the target number, so the answer is C. We don't even have to check the others, since we already have the right one.

ANSWERS TO QUICK QUIZZES

QUICK QUIZ 1

Page 76
1. -7
2. 6
3. 8

QUICK QUIZ 2

Page 81

1. $\dfrac{6}{7} + \dfrac{2}{5} = \dfrac{30}{35} + \dfrac{14}{35} = \dfrac{44}{35} = 1\dfrac{9}{35}$

2. $5\dfrac{2}{3} + 2\dfrac{1}{3} = \dfrac{17}{3} + \dfrac{7}{3} = \dfrac{24}{3} = 8$

3. $\dfrac{4}{7} + \dfrac{3}{4} = \dfrac{16}{28} + \dfrac{21}{28} = \dfrac{37}{28} = 1\dfrac{9}{28}$

4. $9\dfrac{7}{8} - 6\dfrac{1}{8} = 3\dfrac{6}{8} = 3\dfrac{3}{4}$

5. $\dfrac{4}{9} - \dfrac{1}{6} = \dfrac{24}{54} - \dfrac{9}{54} = \dfrac{15}{54} = \dfrac{5}{18}$

6. $\dfrac{9}{10}$

7. $\dfrac{4}{25}$

8. $-\dfrac{1}{100}$

9. $\dfrac{2}{3} \times \dfrac{3}{4} = \dfrac{6}{12} = \dfrac{1}{2}$

10. $\dfrac{1}{4} \times \dfrac{7}{8} = \dfrac{7}{32}$

11. $\dfrac{15}{16} \times -\dfrac{1}{2} = -\dfrac{15}{32}$

12. $\dfrac{1}{2} \div \dfrac{3}{8} = \dfrac{1}{2} \times \dfrac{8}{3} = \dfrac{8}{6} = 1\dfrac{1}{3}$

13. $\dfrac{20}{21} \div \dfrac{2}{3} = \dfrac{20}{21} \times \dfrac{3}{2} = \dfrac{60}{42} = 1\dfrac{18}{42} = 1\dfrac{3}{7}$

14. $\dfrac{\frac{2}{5}}{\frac{2}{3}} = \dfrac{2}{5} \div \dfrac{2}{3} = \dfrac{2}{5} \times \dfrac{3}{2} = \dfrac{6}{10} = \dfrac{3}{5}$

15. $\dfrac{\dfrac{10}{9}}{11} = \dfrac{10}{1} \div \dfrac{9}{11} = \dfrac{10}{1} \times \dfrac{11}{9} = \dfrac{110}{9}$

16. $23 - 4(12\text{-}8) - -5 + 9 = 23 - 4(4) + 5 + 9 = 23 - 16 + 5 + 9 = 21$

QUICK QUIZ 3

Page 84
1. 40
2. 85.7777
3. 53.56
4. 6.25
5. 12
6. 4
7. 18

QUICK QUIZ 4

Page 87
1. 1357
2. 31.4
3. 0.5847
4. 0.176
5. 100
6. 12.1
7. 25
8. 27
9. $4 \times 8 = 32$
10. $2401 \div 49 = 49$
11. $\sqrt{64} = 8$
12. $\dfrac{\sqrt{81}}{\sqrt{9}} = \dfrac{9}{3} = 3$
13. 9, 6, 3

QUICK QUIZ 5

Page 93

1. **A**
2. **B**
3. **B**
4. **B**
5. **C**
6. 12 inches
    3 feet
    60 minutes
    24 hours
    365 days
    52 weeks
    100 cents = 10 dimes = 4 quarters
    8 pints
    4 quarts
    16 ounces

QUICK QUIZ 6

Page 100

1. $12x = 12$
    $x = 1$
2. $3x + 6 = 8 + 4x$
    $x = -2$
3. $(x - 7)(x + 3)$
4. $(a + 5)(a + 5)$

5. $$\begin{array}{r} 3x + 3y = 4 \\ +2x - 3y = 19 \\ \hline ? \end{array}$$

    $5x = 23,$

    $x = \dfrac{23}{5}$

Quick Quiz 7

Page 102

1. $-6m > 23$

   $m < -\dfrac{23}{6}$

2. $4x < 4$
   $x < 1$

3. $2x > 6$
   $x > 3$

4. **A**
5. **C**
6. **B**

Quick Quiz 8

Page 111

1. B
2. C
3. C
4. C
5. B
6. B
7. B
8. C
9. B

4

WORD KNOWLEDGE

INTRODUCTION TO THE WORD KNOWLEDGE TEST

The Word Knowledge test consists of 35 questions designed to test your vocabulary. But since you're given only 11 minutes to complete the section, it's more like a speed-reading test than a vocabulary test. Luckily, most of the words being tested aren't too difficult. In fact, you probably know most of them already. And those you don't know, we will help you to learn. You should try to learn every word in our "Hit Parade" of vocabulary words, at the end of the chapter

IMPROVING YOUR VOCABULARY

There are several techniques you can use to learn new words, so let's get started!

FLASH CARDS

One of the best ways to learn new words is to use flash cards. You can make your own flash cards out of 3" × 5" index cards. On one side of the card, write down the word you're trying to learn. On the other side of the card, write the definition. Then you can quiz yourself on the words, or practice with a friend. You can even carry the cards around with you and practice when you have spare time.

THE IMAGE APPROACH

The image approach involves letting each new word suggest a wild image to you, then using that image to help you remember the word. For example, the word enfranchise means "to give the right to vote." First, let's use the word in a sentence.

"Women did not become enfranchised in the United States until 1920, when the Nineteenth Amendment to the Constitution guaranteed them the right to vote in state and federal elections."

Now we need to come up with an image that will help us remember the definition. "Franchise" might suggest to you a McDonald's franchise: you could remember the new word by imagining people lined up to vote at a McDonald's. If you remember the image, chances are you'll remember the word. The weirder and more vivid the image you create, the more memorable it will be.

MNEMONICS

A mnemonic is a verbal trick that helps you remember something. Once again, the funnier or the stranger you make your mnemonic, the more likely you are to remember it. Here's an example:

"Swarm" means a large crowd, often of insects. Our mnemonic for this word might be "Swinging ARMs". Think about it—if a swarm of bees were chasing you, you'd probably be swinging your arms. By remembering that image, and the phrase "Swinging ARMs," you can easily remember the definition of the word "swarm."

Here's another example: "Cower" means to hide in fear. Our mnemonic will be "COW fEaR." Picture someone scared of cows and cowering in the corner to avoid them.

As you make up your own mnemonics, write them down (3" × 5" cards are great for these). Although you may not always be able to think of a clever mnemonic for every Hit Parade word, sometimes you'll end up learning the word just by spending enough time trying to make up a mnemonic.

Look It Up

Well-written general-interest publications—newspapers and news magazines, for example—are good sources for new vocabulary words. You should start to read them on a regular basis. When you come across a new word, write it down, look it up in the dictionary, and make a new flash card for it. And most important, you need to:

Use It

It's not enough to just look up a word in the dictionary. Make it a part of your life. Use it whenever you can in everyday life. A powerful vocabulary requires lots of exercise.

QUICK QUIZ 1

You can check your answers at the end of the chapter.

1. What are five ways to improve your vocabulary?

   _____

   _____

   _____

   _____

   _____

2. Try coming up with mnemonics for the following words.

   Chaos: noun; complete confusion
   _____

   Provoke: verb; to cause a feeling or reaction; to push into action
   _____

   Jeer: verb; to taunt or ridicule
   _____

   Aloof: adjective; keeping apart from others
   _____

   Abundance: noun; a great amount
   _____

THE QUESTIONS

Now that you are on your way to a better vocabulary, it's time to discuss the types of questions you will see on the ASVAB. The questions come in two forms. The first form gives you a sentence with a word underlined. Your job is to choose the answer choice that could replace the underlined word in the sentence without changing the meaning of the sentence. For example:

1. He was <u>inconsolable</u> when his team lost.

   A. happy
   B. freezing
   C. sad
   D. rushed

We call these "Vocabulary in Context" questions, because the word being tested is given in the context of a sentence. Usually the sentence provides valuable clues that can help you find the answer. Let's look at our example from above. We know that the team lost, which is a bad thing. So inconsolable probably means something negative. We can get rid of answer A. Of the remaining answers, C—sad, makes the most sense in the context of the sentence. Let's look at another example:

2. He was very upset over the unexpected death of his <u>benefactor</u>.

   A. dictator
   B. supervisor
   C. sponsor
   D. partner

The sentence tells us that he was very upset over the benefactor's death. So the benefactor is probably someone he likes. If we didn't know the definition of benefactor, we could use this information to eliminate at least a couple of the answers. We could safely eliminate answers A and B, which would leave us with C and D. At this point, if we guessed, we'd have a 50-50 chance—and that's without even knowing the definition. The correct answer is C, sponsor. If you didn't know this, make a flash card for "benefactor."

The second form of question is a straightforward definition question. It gives you a word and asks you to choose the answer choice that is most similar in meaning. For example:

3. <u>Chuckle</u> most nearly means

   A. throw
   B. laugh
   C. consider
   D. change

Unfortunately, these types of questions don't provide any clues. But there are a couple of techniques you can use to make finding the answer easier.

PROCESS OF ELIMINATION

Process of Elimination is a very important tool on the Word Knowledge test. It helps you avoid careless mistakes and improves your chances of choosing the correct answer. Always write the answers choices out on your scrap paper and cross them off as you eliminate answers.

WHICH SIDE OF THE FENCE?

This is another useful technique. Imagine you are taking the Word Knowledge test. You are moving through the questions quickly and confidently because you know every word on the test. Then, suddenly, you come to a word you can't define. You've heard the word before, but you just can't remember the definition. Don't panic! "Which side of the fence?" is designed for exactly this situation. First, try to recall where you heard the word before. That may help you remember its meaning. Next, try to determine whether the word has a positive or negative connotation. If you know it means something positive, eliminate all negative answer choices. If it's negative, eliminate all the positive choice. Once you've eliminated everything you can, guess from the remaining answers and move on.

THE THREE CATEGORIES

With both types of questions, the first thing you need to do is identify what type of word is being tested. By this we mean assign it into one of three categories: Words You Know, Words You "Sort of" Know, and Words You Don't Know. The strategy is a little different for each type of word.

Words You Know

These are words you can define accurately. If you can't give a definition of a word that's pretty close to what a dictionary would say, then it's not a word you know.

Strategy: When a question asks you about a Word You Know, define the word in your head. Then look through the answer choices carefully, crossing off answers you know are wrong. If you don't know a word in the answers, don't eliminate it—it could still be the right choice. Choose the one closest in meaning to your definition.

Words You "Sort of" Know

These are words you've seen before, or heard, or maybe even used yourself, but can't define accurately.

Strategy: Check the answer choices to see if there's any choice you can eliminate based on your "sort of" knowledge. If you know the word is positive, eliminate any negative words in the answer choices. If you know the word is negative, eliminate any positive words in the answer choices. Again, if you don't know a word in the answers, don't eliminate it. Use context if available, and guess from the remaining answers.

Note: whenever you're practicing and you encounter a Word You "Sort of" Know, look it up in the dictionary and make a flash card for it. Turn it into a Word You Know!

Words You Don't Know

You probably won't see too many words on the test that look totally foreign to you. But if you do...

Strategy: Eliminate any answer choices you can based on context. Then guess from the remaining answers. Never leave a question blank!

THE HIT PARADE

Obviously, you want as many words as possible to fall into the Words You Know category. But you're probably wondering, what words do I need to know? Well, we can't tell you exactly which words will be tested on the ASVAB, but we can give you a good idea of the types of words that will be there by providing you with a list. We call this list the Hit Parade. The words here are similar to the vocabulary the ASVAB tests. In fact, some of them may even appear on the ASVAB. If you're wondering how you will do on the Word Knowledge test, take a look at the Hit Parade. If you know most of the words on the list, you're in pretty good shape. If you don't know a lot of the words, then start studying!

In the Hit Parade, a "*v.*" after the word means that the word is a verb; "*adj.*" means it's an adjective; "*n.*" means it's a noun; and "*adv.*" means it's an adverb.

abandon *v.*
To forsake or desert.

abolish *adj.*
To do away with.

absurd *adj.*
Ridiculously unreasonable.

abundant *adj.*
Marked by great plenty (as of resources).

accessible *adj.*
Able to be reached or used.

accidental *adj.*
Happening by chance or unexpectedly.

accurate *adj.*
Conforming exactly to truth or to a standard.

accuse *v.*
To charge with a fault; to blame.

adapt *v.*
To adjust or make usable.

address *v.*
To make a spoken or written communication to.

admire *v.*
To regard with approval, respect, or satisfaction.

admission *n.*
Permission to enter.

adore *v.*
To regard with the utmost esteem and affection.

analysis	*n.* The process of looking at something carefully and methodically.
anticipate	*v.* To feel or realize beforehand; to look forward to.
anxious	*adj.* Mentally upset over possible misfortune or danger, etc; worried.
apologize	*v.* To express regret, acknowledge faults, or make excuses for.
apparel	*n.* Clothing; something that covers or adorns.
application	*n.* Something that is being used or applied.
assume	*v.* To take for granted as true.
authority	*n.* Power to influence or command thought, opinion, or behavior.
awe	*n.* An emotion combining fear and wonder.
basic	*adj.* Of or relating to essential structure, function, or facts.
behavior	*n.* The manner of conducting oneself.
benefactor	*n.* Someone who takes care of or gives money to another person.
bias	*n.* A preference or inclination; prejudice.
bizarre	*adj.* Very strange; unusual.
boast	*v.* To speak of or assert with excessive pride.
brilliant	*adj.* Distinguished by unusual mental keenness or alertness.
budget	*n.* A sum of money allocated for a particular purpose.
chaos	*n.* Disorder.

characterize *v.*
To describe the qualities of.

cite *v.*
To quote or refer to a person's speech or writing.

cling *v.*
To hold or hold on tightly or tenaciously.

colleague *n.*
A co-worker.

command *v.*
To give orders to; to have at your disposal.

commodity *n.*
Something bought or sold.

compel *v.*
To force.

competition *n.*
A contest between opponents.

compromise *n.*
An agreement that partially satisfies each side.

compromise *v.*
To give up something in order to reach an agreement.

conceive *v.*
To imagine.

conclusive *adj.*
Putting an end to any uncertainty or doubt; final.

conform *v.*
To act in accordance with prevailing standards or customs.

conquer *v.*
To defeat an opponent.

consciousness *n.*
The state of being aware and awake.

consequence *n.*
A result.

consideration *n.*
Careful thought.

contradiction *n.*
A situation in which two things do not make sense together.

contrary *adj.*
Opposite; disagreeing.

controversial   *adj.*
Causing debate or argument.

conventional   *adj.*
Following accepted customs; normal.

convey   *v.*
To express.

cordial   *adj.*
Hearty; sincere; warm; affectionate.

corruption   *n.*
Dishonesty; immoral behavior.

crisis   *n.*
An unstable or crucial time or state of affairs in which a decisive change is impending.

critical   *adj.*
Tending to call attention to flaws.

crude   *adj.*
Raw; rude.

cult   *n.*
A religion considered to be extreme.

cultivate   *v.*
To help something to grow.

curiosity   *n.*
Desire to know.

current   *adj.*
Up-to-date; at the moment.

cynical   *adj.*
Distrustful of people's motives.

deceive   *v.*
To cause someone to believe an untruth.

deduction   *n.*
Something that is inferred from something else; something removed or taken away.

deliberate   *v.*
To think deeply about.

deliberate   *adj.*
Carefully considered and intended.

demolish   *v.*
To throw or pull down; to raze; to destroy the fabric of; to pull to pieces; to ruin.

deny
v.
To disclaim connection with or responsibility for.

depict
v.
To represent by or as if by a picture; to describe.

despair
n.
Utter loss of hope.

detached
adj.
Set apart from others.

determined
adj.
Committed; certain.

devastated
adj.
Made uninhabitable; ravaged; ruined; wasted.

devious
adj.
Characterized by insincerity or deceit; evasive; deviating from a straight course.

devise
v.
To imagine or create.

diligent
adj.
Careful and steady in application to one's work or duties.

diminish
v.
To decrease in size, extent, or range; to lessen the authority, dignity, or reputation of.

discouraged
adj.
Made less hopeful or enthusiastic.

dismiss
v.
To reject serious consideration of.

disprove
v.
To overthrow by argument, evidence, or proof.

disrupt
v.
To throw into disorder.

distant
adj.
Separated in space or by time.

distaste
n.
A feeling of intense dislike.

distinguish
v.
To perceive a difference in.

disturb
v.
To interfere with.

dominant   *adj.*
Most powerful.

draft   *n.*
A version of a letter or essay.

effect   *n.*
An outward sign.

effective   *adj.*
Producing a decided, decisive, or desired effect.

enact   *v.*
To order by virtue of superior authority.

enclosed   *adj.*
Closed in or surrounded or included within.

encounter   *n.*
A meeting, especially between hostile parties.

encourage   *v.*
To inspire with courage, spirit, or hope.

endurance   *n.*
The power to withstand hardship or stress; a state of surviving; remaining alive.

endure   *v.*
To undergo (as a hardship) especially without giving in.

enhance   *v.*
To make better or stronger.

enthusiasm   *n.*
A feeling of excitement.

essential   *adj.*
Of the utmost importance; necessary.

establish   *v.*
To bring into existence.

esteem   *n.*
Respect or admiration.

esteem   *v.*
To respect or admire.

evident   *adj.*
Obvious; easily seen or understood.

exasperation   *n.*
The state of being annoyed or irritated.

excavation   *n.*
Digging.

exhibit   *v.*
To show publicly.

extent   *n.*
The range over which something extends; scope.

extraordinary   *adj.*
Going beyond what is usual, regular, or customary.

faculty   *n.*
Teachers at a school; members of a learned profession.

fascinating   *adj.*
Extremely interesting or charming.

fatigue   *n.*
Temporary loss of strength and energy resulting from hard physical or mental work; a lack of vitality.

feasible   *adj.*
Capable of being accomplished; possible.

fine   *n.*
A sum imposed as punishment for an offense.

flaw   *n.*
An imperfection or fault.

force   *n.*
Strength or energy exerted or brought to bear; cause of motion or change; active power.

forge   *v.*
To make or imitate falsely, especially with intent to defraud.

forge   *v.*
To advance (alternate definition).

fragile   *adj.*
Easily broken.

fraud   *n.*
Intentional deception resulting in injury to another person; deliberate trickery intended to gain an advantage.

frustration   *n.*
A feeling of annoyance at being hindered or criticized.

fundamental   *adj.*
A leading or primary principle, rule, law, or article, which serves as the groundwork of a system; essential part.

funding   *n.*
Financial resources provided to make some project possible.

generalization   *n.*
A statement or judgment about a group based on a few examples.

generate   *v.*
To create.

generous   *adj.*
Willing to give and share unstintingly.

graceful   *adj.*
Characterized by beauty of movement, style, form, etc.; suggesting taste, ease, and wealth; elegant.

gracious   *adj.*
Doing or producing good; exhibiting courtesy and politeness.

harmony   *n.*
Compatibility in opinion and action.

harsh   *adj.*
Very strict; unkind or cruel.

hazardous   *adj.*
Involving risk or danger.

headstrong   *adj.*
Bold; stubborn.

hesitate   *v.*
To pause or hold back in uncertainty or unwillingness.

hilarious   *adj.*
Marked by or causing boisterous merriment or convulsive laughter.

honor   *v.*
To regard or treat with esteem or respect; to revere.

humanity   *n.*
The quality of being humane; kindness.

ideal   *n.*
A standard of perfection, beauty, or excellence.

ignorance   *n.*
Lack of knowledge or education.

ignorant   *adj.*
Lacking knowledge or comprehension.

illumination   *n.*
Lighting.

immediate   *adj.*
Direct; without anything in between.

implement   *n.*
Tool.

imply   *v.*
To lead someone to believe something without directly stating it.

impolite   *adj.*
Not polite; not of polished manners; wanting in good manners; discourteous; uncivil; rude.

impractical   *adj.*
Not usable or effective.

impulse   *n.*
Force or urge.

inaccurate   *adj.*
Not according to truth; inexact; incorrect; erroneous.

inadvisable   *adj.*
Not recommended.

inconsequential   *adj.*
Unimportant.

inconsistency   *n.* Discordance in respect to sentiment or action.

inconsistent   *adj.*
Not agreeing with another fact or claim.

independent   *adj.*
Free; not subject to control by others; not relying on others; not subordinate.

indignation   *n.*
Moral outrage.

infer   *v.*
To conclude or figure out.

influence   *n.*
Ability to persuade or affect.

influential   *adj.*
Having influence or power.

inhibit   *v.*
To check; to hold back; to restrain; to hinder; to discourage from free or spontaneous activity.

innocent   *adj.*
Free from evil or guilt; lacking intent or capacity to injure.

insecure	*adj.* Not firm or firmly fixed; lacking self-confidence or assurance.
insightful	*adj.* Exhibiting clear and deep perception.
interpretation	*n.* A particular adaptation or version of a work, method, or style; an explanation of something not immediately obvious.
irrelevant	*adj.* Having no connection to a subject.
irresponsible	*adj.* Showing lack of care for consequences.
labor	*n.* Work; effort.
lack	*v.* To be deficient or missing something.
legend	*n.* A story about mythical or supernatural beings or events; a brief description accompanying an illustration.
loyalty	*n.* The quality of being unswerving in allegiance.
majority	*n.* The quality or state of being greater.
mass	*n.* A large quantity, amount, or number.
mercy	*n.* Kindness; forgiveness.
mere	*adj.* Only; nothing more than.
misleading	*adj.* Deceptive.
modest	*adj.* Marked by simplicity.
modify	*v.* To make partial changes in; to make different.
moral	*n.* The significance of a story or event.
moral	*adj.* Relating to principles of right and wrong in behavior.

morose	*adj.* Sad and dreary.
mythical	*adj.* Fictional; unreal.
narcissistic	*adj.* Having an inflated idea of one's own importance.
narrate	*v.* To give a detailed account of.
nostalgic	*adj.* Longing for familiar things or persons, or for a period of time or an occurrence that has passed.
novel	*n.* A book that tells a fictional story.
obedience	*n.* Compliance with that which is required by authority; subjection to rightful restraint or control.
obscure	*adj.* Not clearly understood or expressed.
obsessive	*adj.* Characterized by obsession; excessive, often to an unreasonable degree.
obstacle	*n.* Something that stands in the way and must be circumvented or surmounted.
opponent	*n.* One that takes an opposite position.
optimistic	*adj.* Anticipating the best possible outcome.
organic	*adj.* Derived from living organisms.
origin	*n.* The first existence or beginning of anything; the point at which something begins or from which it derives.
original	*adj.* Preceding all others in time or being as first made or performed.
outcast	*n.* A person who is rejected (from society or home).
outcome	*n.* Something that follows as a result or consequence.

outdated	*adj.* Old-fashioned.
overdue	*adj.* Delayed beyond the proper time of arrival or payment.
overlook	*v.* To fail to see.
overthrow	*v.* To cause the downfall of.
overwhelm	*v.* To overcome by superior force or numbers.
overwhelming	*adj.* Tending to overpower in thought or feeling.
passion	*n.* Extreme feeling or emotion; an irrational but irresistible motive for a belief or action.
passive	*adj.* Not active.
patience	*n.* Calm endurance of hardship, provocation, pain, delay, etc.
patron	*n.* One who uses wealth or influence to help a cause.
penalize	*v.* To inflict a penalty or punishment on.
perceive	*v.* To attain awareness or understanding of; to become aware of through the senses.
perceptive	*adj.* Having the ability to understand; keen in discernment.
perseverance	*n.* The act of not quitting.
persist	*v.* To continue.
persuasive	*adj.* Able to move people to act or believe.
pessimist	*n.* One who emphasizes adverse aspects, conditions, and possibilities.
phenomenon	*n.* An observable fact or event.

pictorial
adj.
Consisting of pictures.

pilfer
v.
To steal (a small amount).

pitiful
adj.
Eliciting compassion.

pity
v.
To feel pity or compassion for; to have sympathy with.

plastic
adj.
Easily bendable.

playwright
n.
Someone who writes plays.

pledge
n.
A binding commitment to do or give or refrain from something.

poll
v.
To obtain and analyze information or opinions from people.

poll
n.
A survey of people's opinions.

ponder
v.
To consider carefully; think deeply.

portrait
n.
A picture or painting of a person.

potential
n.
Ability.

practical
adj.
Concerned with actual use or practice.

precious
adj.
Highly esteemed or cherished.

precisely
adv.
In a manner or measure or to a degree or number that strictly conforms to a fact or condition.

predominant
adj.
Having superior numbers, strength, or importance.

predict
v.
To declare or indicate in advance.

predictable
adj.
Possible to foretell.

primarily   *adv.*
Most importantly.

principle   *n.*
A rule or guide.

prohibit   *v.*
To forbid by authority.

prominence   *n.*
The state of being noticeable.

prose   *n.*
Words in sentences and paragraphs, as opposed to poetry.

prosperity   *n.*
The state of being successful; economic well-being.

quarrel   *n.*
A usually verbal conflict between antagonists.

quest   *n.*
A long search.

radiant   *adj.*
Filled with happiness; emitting light or heat.

reaction   *n.*
The act or process or an instance of responding; a response.

refute   *v.*
To disprove.

relatively   *adv.*
In comparison to something else.

repulsive   *adj.*
Tending to repel or drive off; disgusting.

resentment   *n.*
Deep hatred.

resolution   *n.*
Something settled or resolved; the outcome of a decision.

revolution   *n.*
A political overthrow.

rile   *v.*
To irritate or stir up.

skeptical   *adj.*
Doubtful; disbelieving.

standard   *adj.*
Common or ordinary.

| standard | *n.* |
| | A common feature or rule used to judge. |

| strive | *v.* |
| | To try very hard. |

| stupor | *n.* |
| | Mental confusion; daze. |

| subtle | *adj.* |
| | Hard to detect; not obvious. |

| sufficient | *adj.* |
| | Enough. |

| sympathy | *n.* |
| | Compassion. |

| terminate | *v.* |
| | To bring to an end or stop. |

| tolerance | *n.* |
| | Ability to endure pain or hardship; respecting the beliefs or practices of others. |

| transparent | *adj.* |
| | Clear; see-through. |

| turmoil | *n.* |
| | A state or condition of extreme confusion, agitation, or commotion. |

| undermine | *v.* |
| | To remove support from; to weaken. |

| unscrupulous | *adj.* |
| | Without honor or morals. |

| validity | *n.* |
| | Truth; correctness. |

| values | *n.* |
| | Beliefs of a person or social group. |

| vend | *v.* |
| | To sell; to offer (an idea). |

| verify | *v.* |
| | To test the truth of. |

| vital | *adj.* |
| | Important, necessary. |

| vivid | *adj.* |
| | Bright or lively. |

ANSWERS TO QUICK QUIZZES

QUICK QUIZ 1
Page 125

1. Flash cards, the image approach, mnemonics, look it up, and use it.

2. "Chaos" means complete confusion. Your mnemonic might be anything that helps you remember the definition. Here's ours: Stay Lost.

    "Provoke" means to cause a feeling or reaction; to push into action. Our mnemonic: Poke.

    "Jeer" means to taunt or ridicule. Our mnemonic: Jerks.

    "Aloof" means keeping apart from others. Our mnemonic: ALone on the rOOF.

    "Abundance" means a great amount. Our mnemonic: A BUNch in attenDANCE.

5

PARAGRAPH
COMPREHENSION

INTRODUCTION TO THE PARAGRAPH COMPREHENSION TEST

The Paragraph Comprehension test has 15 questions that you must answer in 13 minutes. The questions are intended to test your ability to comprehend written material. The answer to every question can be found in the passages. You will never need any outside information to answer a question on this test.

THE PASSAGES

The passages vary in length from a couple of sentences to several paragraphs. The length of the passage tends to correspond to the number of questions that accompany it. Shorter passages usually have only one question, while longer passages can have several questions. The passages cover a wide variety of topics. You could see anything from art to business to science to history.

The passages differ from the reading most people are used to, in that they're specifically designed to relay information in a small amount of text. So if you read the ASVAB passages like you read a book or newspaper, you are going to have a hard time on this section. That's because you normally read with the goal of remembering everything. On the ASVAB, trying to remember everything is not necessary and can actually hurt your score.

If this advice seems strange, think about it this way: Your goal in the test is to answer the questions correctly. You won't get any points for reading the passage thoroughly if you don't answer the questions correctly. So the majority of your time should be spent on the questions and answers, not on reading the passages. Slow down and make sure you check each answer choice carefully. When you choose an answer, you should be able to point to the place in the passage that supports your answer. Use the passage to help you find the correct answer, but don't get caught up in it and waste time memorizing things you won't need. Remember, you can always go back to the passage later if you need to.

Think of the ASVAB as an open-book test. In a way it is—the questions and the passages are right in front of you. All you need to do is find the answers in the passages. The hard part is the time limit. We've devised a system to help you improve your accuracy while saving time. The best part of our system is that it will work for every question and every passage you see.

THE THREE-STEP SYSTEM

Since you're given only 13 minutes for the whole section, which is less than one minute per question, you won't have time to fully comprehend everything. That's why you need a system in place to tackle every question and passage on this test. Our system has three simple steps:

1. Read the Questions for a Passage

2. Skim the Passage

3. Use Process of Elimination

STEP 1: READ THE QUESTIONS

The first thing you should always do is read all the questions for a particular passage. By reading the questions *before* you read the passage, you'll know what to be on the look out for when you do read the passage.

You will see a variety of questions on this test. All questions can be assigned to one of two categories: specific or general.

Specific questions

Specific questions ask you for a detail from the passage. You don't need to understand the entire passage to answer this question, just the part of the passage that is specifically answering the question. There are four main types of specific questions. Here are the types, with some examples of each:

1. Fact

   - According to the author/passage...

   - The author states that...

   - Which of the following question is answered by the passage?

   - All of the following are mentioned EXCEPT...

2. Definition in context

   - What does the passage mean by X?

   - X probably represents/means...

3. Specific interpretation

   - It can be inferred from paragraph X...

   - The most likely interpretation of X is...

4. Purpose

   - The author uses X in order to...

   - Why does the author say X?

The questions above range from flat-out requests for information found in the passage to questions that require some interpretation of what you find in the passage.

When you encounter specific questions, you want to recognize and jot down any words that will help you find the answer in the passage. We call these **lead words**. They include names, places, and phrases that will be easy to find in the passage. If the passage asks for a detail from the passage, write down something to remind you of the detail. For example, if the question states, "The word lunar most nearly means," write down the word "lunar." This will help you remember what's important as you work through the passage. Let's look at a few questions with the lead words underlined.

   - According to the passage, people suffering from <u>high cholesterol</u> are more at risk for...

   - In the author's view, the phrase "<u>modern art</u>" means art that...

   - The passage best supports the statement that <u>underage drinking</u> is...

When looking for the lead words in a question, keep in mind that you want them to be specific to the question at hand. Let's look at the first question above. We wouldn't want to choose "people" because that's a common word that might appear in several parts of a passage. "High cholesterol" is a good choice because it's much more specific.

Some specific questions don't have lead words. You will have to find the relevant part of the passage without their help. That's one reason why reading the questions first is so helpful. If you read the questions first, you will recognize relevant parts of the passage as you skim through the passage later. That makes it easier to find the answers.

QUICK QUIZ 1

Practice finding the lead words in specific questions. Underline the lead words in the following questions. Answers can be found at the end of the chapter.

1. The stars are considered luminous because

2. According to the passage, an opaque object

3. The passage best supports the idea that elementary schools

4. The planet Jupiter differs from all other planets in the solar system in that it

5. According to the passage, Pygmy Marmosets are commonly found in

6. According to the passage, anthropologists study

General Questions

The other type of question you will see asks you about a large part of the passage or the whole passage. We call these **general questions.** There are four types:

1. Main idea
   - Which of the following best expresses the main point?
   - The passage is primarily about…
   - The main idea of the passage is…
   - The best title for this passage would be…

2. Tone/attitude
   - The author's tone is…
   - The attitude of the author is one of…

3. General interpretation
   - The author would most likely agree with…
   - This passage deals with X by…
   - The passage implies that…
   - Which of the following words best describes the passage?
   - It can be inferred from the passage that…
   - The style of the passage is most like…
   - What is the author's opinion of X?

4. Purpose
   - The purpose of the passage is…
   - The author wrote this passage in order to…

All of these questions require that you know the main idea of the passage, but the ones at the beginning of the list are more straightforward. The ones at the end of the list require you to interpret a little more.

When reading these general questions, use your scrap paper to jot down what you're on the look-out for. For example, if the question asks for the main point of the passage, write down "main point" or m.p. for short.

QUICK QUIZ 2

Identify each of the following questions as specific or general. The answers can be found at the end of the chapter. Then, identify what type of specific or general question it is. For example:

The woman probably mentions "blizzards" in order to…

This is a specific purpose question.

1. The passage primarily concerns:
   _____

2. The last sentence of paragraph 1 implies that:
   _____

3. According to the passage, television has become a medium whose main goal is:

   _____

4. The author's reference to "talking hair-dos" is a reference to:
   _____

5. According to the passage, which of the following was an artist?

   I. Brancusi
   II. Cox
   III. Hughes

   _____

6. The author of the passage can most reasonably be described as:
   _____

Step 2: Skim the Passage

After you've read the questions for a passage, skim through the passage. Note that you should *skim* the passage and not read it. As we've already stated, you don't get any points for good, thorough reading. The purpose of skimming the passage is to get a general idea of what the passage is about, not to memorize it. Remember, the majority of the passage will have nothing to do with the questions. As you skim, keep on the lookout for the lead words that you've already jotted down. When you find them, read carefully a few lines above and a few lines below. The answer to a question should be close by.

If the passage is long or particularly difficult, it may help to take some short and simple notes on your scrap paper. Don't write a book report about the passage, just a few words to help you remember.

Step 3: Process of Elimination (POE)

This is where you should spend the majority of your time. Write the letters A, B, C, and D on your scrap paper and cross them off as you eliminate each answer choice. Always refer back to the passage when crossing off an answer. When you settle on one answer, you should be able to support that answer with something in the passage.

Answering a specific question

To answer a specific question, you should always reread the relevant part of the passage. Remember, this is an open-book test. Use that to your advantage! You don't want to reread the entire passage, of course, just the part the question is focusing on.

Answering a general question

To answer a general question, you need to know the main point of the passage. Before you look at the answer choices, spend a few seconds trying to state the passage's main point in your own words. Then use Process of Elimination to get rid of answers that either don't answer the question or answer it incorrectly.

- For **main idea** questions, eliminate answers that are too narrow or too broad. The correct answer will cover the entire passage without claiming more than the passage actually says.

- For a **tone/attitude** question, first determine if the author was for, against, or neutral on the subject. Use that to eliminate as many answers as you can. For example, if the author was in favor of the subject he or she was discussing, eliminate any negative answers. Then, determine the degree of the author's tone. Was the tone mild or strong? Be wary of answers that go further than the passage does.

- For **general interpretation** questions, choose the answer that comes closest to what the passage says. For questions asking for an "inference," look for an answer that paraphrases the passage.

- For **general purpose** questions, ask yourself why the author wrote the passage. Keep in mind the tone of the passage as you answer this question.

Eliminating answer choices

Process of Elimination is one of the most important tools you can use throughout any standardized test. You should train yourself to automatically eliminate any answer that you know is wrong. Sometimes you can find the correct answer to a question just by eliminating answers that you know are wrong. Remember, it doesn't matter how you get to the correct answer, as long as you get there!

In order to effectively use POE in the Paragraph Comprehension test, you must be able to recognize incorrect answers. Luckily, there are a few types of wrong answer choices that you will see over and over again. Let's look at them, so you will be able to recognize and eliminate them!

- **Extremes:** Be on the look out for extreme statements in the answer choices. The passages on the ASVAB are rarely extreme in tone, so the answers shouldn't be either. If you see extreme words—such as "all," "none," "every," and "must"—in an answer be suspicious. It's probably wrong. Of course, if the passage is extreme in tone, the answer might be extreme too.

- **Correct But Irrelevant; True But Not Stated:** Some incorrect answers are, in a sense, absolutely true. They just don't answer the question that's being asked. Make sure the answer you choose is not only correct, but also answers the question.

- **Direct Opposite:** Sometimes you will be given the exact opposite of what you're looking for. If you're not careful, you might choose that answer instead of the correct one. When you see two answer choices that directly contradict each other, it is very likely that one of them is the correct answer.

- **Out of Scope:** You need to be particularly careful with general questions to avoid answers that are out of scope. You don't want an answer that is too broad or too narrow. Keep in mind that the correct answer choice must be limited to what's in the passage, but must cover all of it.

I, II, III Questions

Questions with Roman numerals are time-consuming and more difficult than other questions. But though they take more work than other questions, with careful use of POE, they can be answered. Here's an example:

8. According to the passage, which of the following is true?

   I. The sky is blue.

   II. Nothing rhymes with "orange."

   III. Smoking cigarettes increases lung capacity.

   A. I only
   B. I and II only
   C. I and III only
   D. II and III only

The best way to tackle these questions is with careful POE. First, determine whether the first statement was stated in the passage. If it was, eliminate every answer that doesn't include statement I. If it wasn't, eliminate every answer that *does* include statement I. If you still have more than one answer remaining, do the same for the next statement. Let's try this with the question above.

Let's assume the passage says that the sky is blue and nothing rhymes with orange. Therefore, we should eliminate answers that don't include statement I. That gets rid of D. We also want to eliminate any answers that don't include statement II, which gets rid of C and A. That leaves us with B.

EXCEPT/LEAST/NOT Questions

This is another type of confusing question. The test writers are asking you to look for the answer that is false. Again, with careful POE, this question type is doable. For example:

9. All of the following can be inferred from the passage EXCEPT:

   A.   Americans are patriotic.
   B.   Americans have great ingenuity.
   C.   Americans love war.
   D.   Americans are brave in times of war.

Let's assume that the passage says every one of these statements except for C. Now read through the answers, writing "T" for true on your scrap paper next to the answer choices that are stated in the passage and "F" for false next to the one that isn't. Your answer is the one with the "F" next to it.

What do I keep?

In general, correct answers are likely to be:

- paraphrases of the words in the passage.
- traditional and conservative in their outlook.
- moderate, using words like "may," "can," and "often."

One last tip

If you've eliminated all but two answers choices, don't get stuck and waste time. Keep the main idea in the back of your mind and step back.

- Reread the question.
- Look at what makes the two answers different.
- Go back to the passage.
- Which answer is worse? Eliminate it.

Staring at the answers won't make the correct one jump out at you; it will only waste time!

PUTTING IT ALL TOGETHER

Let's work through the following passage. Remember to use the three-step technique:

Step 1: Read the Questions: Read all seven questions and jot down on scrap paper a list of the things you need to look out for in the passage.

Step 2: Skim the Passage: Skim the passage, looking for the things you listed on your scrap paper. As you work through the passage, jot down notes. If you find the answer to a question, you can even write down where you found it, to save time later.

Step 3: POE: Refer back to the passage as you cross off incorrect answer choices. When you've chosen your answer, make sure the passage supports it.

Questions 1 – 7 are based on the following passage.

Contrary to popular belief, the first European known to lay eyes on America was not Christopher Columbus or Amerigo Vespucci but a little-known Viking by the name of Bjarni Herjolfsson. In the summer of 986, Bjarni sailed from Norway to Iceland, heading for the Viking settlement where his father Heriulf resided.

When he arrived in Iceland, Bjarni discovered that his father had already sold his land and estates and set out for the latest Viking settlement on the subarctic island called Greenland. Discovered by a notorious murderer and criminal named Eric the Red, Greenland lay at the limit of the known world. Dismayed, Bjarni set out for this new colony.

Because the Vikings traveled without chart or compass, it was not uncommon for them to lose their way in the unpredictable northern seas. Beset by fog, the crew lost their bearings. When the fog finally cleared, they found themselves before a land that was level and covered with woods.

They traveled farther up the coast, finding more flat, wooded country. Further north, the landscape revealed glaciers and rocky mountains. Though Bjarni realized this was an unknown land, he was no intrepid explorer. Rather, he was a practical man who had simply set out to find his father. Refusing his crew's request to go ashore, he promptly turned his bow back out to sea. After four days' sailing, Bjarni landed at Herjolfsnes on the southwestern tip of Greenland, the exact place he had been seeking all along.

1. This passage is primarily about

    A.   the Vikings and their civilization.
    B.   the waves of Viking immigration.
    C.   the sailing techniques of Bjarni Herjolfsson.
    D.   one Viking's glimpse of the new world.

2. It can be inferred from the passage that prior to Bjarni Herjolfsson's voyage, Greenland

    A.   was covered in grass and shrubs.
    B.   was overrun with Vikings.
    C.   was populated by criminals.
    D.   was as far west as the Vikings had traveled.

3. What was the author's purpose in writing this passage?

    A.   to turn the reader against Italian adventurers
    B.   to show his disdain for Eric the Red
    C.   to demonstrate the Vikings' nautical skills
    D.   to correct a common misconception about the European discovery of America

4. According to the passage, Bjarni Herjolfsson left Norway to

    A. found a new colony.

    B. open trading lanes.

    C. visit his relations.

    D. settle in Greenland.

5. Bjarni's reaction upon landing in Iceland can best be described as

    A. disappointed.

    B. satisfied.

    C. amused.

    D. indifferent.

6. "The crew lost their bearings," in the third paragraph, probably means that

    A. the ship was damaged beyond repair.

    B. the crew became disoriented.

    C. the crew decided to mutiny.

    D. the crew went insane.

7. With which of the following statements about Viking explorers would the author most probably agree?

    A. Greenland and Iceland were the Vikings' final discoveries.

    B. Viking explorers were cruel and savage.

    C. The Vikings' most startling discovery was an accidental one.

    D. All Viking explorers were fearless.

Here's how to crack it

During step 1, you should have made a short list of what you're looking for on your scrap paper. That list might look something like this:

> about?
> before voyage
> author's purpose
> Norway
> Iceland
> crew lost bearings...
> author agree?

During step 2 you should have skimmed the passage looking for its main point—in other words, what the passage was about (question 1). While doing this, you may have recognized some of the words from the questions. If you did, that's great! If not, you'll still have the chance to find them in the next step.

Most of your time should be spent in step 3, and that's where we will spend most of our discussion.

1. This passage is primarily about

   A. the Vikings and their civilization.
   B. the waves of Viking immigration.
   C. sailing techniques of Bjarni Herjolfsson.
   D. one Viking's glimpse of the new world.

   This is a general purpose question, so think about why the author wrote the passage. Use POE to answer the question. We can get rid of A because the passage doesn't really talk about Viking civilization. It also never mentions Viking immigration (B) or Bjarni's sailing techniques (C), so that leaves us with D.

2. It can be inferred from the passage that prior to Bjarni Herjolfsson's voyage, Greenland

   A. was covered in grass and shrubs.
   B. was overrun with Vikings.
   C. was populated by criminals.
   D. was as far west as the Vikings had traveled.

   This is a specific question, so you should have referred back to the part of the passage that discusses Bjarni right before he left for his voyage. This part is located at the end of paragraph one. By reading a few lines before and a few lines after, you can see that answers A, B, and C are never stated. What we do know is that "Greenland lay at the limit of the known world," which D paraphrases.

3. What was the author's purpose in writing this passage?

   A. to turn the reader against Italian adventurers
   B. to show his disdain for Eric the Red
   C. to demonstrate the Vikings' nautical skills
   D. to correct a common misconception about the European discovery of America

   Before trying to find the answer to this question, think about the tone of the passage. Did the author exhibit an opinion at any time? Not really, so it's unlikely that answers A and B could be correct. The passage doesn't really talk their nautical skills either, so the answer is D.

4. According to the passage, Bjarni Herjolfsson left Norway to

   A. found a new colony.
   B. open trading lanes.
   C. visit his relations.
   D. settle in Greenland.

   This is a specific question and the lead word is Norway. So, find the place in the passage that discusses Norway. It's in the first paragraph. By reading a few lines before and after, we see that he went to Norway to visit his father. That gives us C as the answer.

5. Bjarni's reaction upon landing in Iceland can best be described as

    A.   disappointed.

    B.   satisfied.

    C.   amused.

    D.   indifferent.

This is another specific question, and the lead word is Iceland. In the paragraph in the passage that mentions Iceland, we see that Bjarni was "dismayed." The best answer is A, disappointed.

6. "The crew lost their bearings," in the third paragraph, probably means that

    A.   the ship was damaged beyond repair.

    B.   the crew became disoriented.

    C.   the crew decided to mutiny.

    D.   the crew went insane.

This specific question tells you exactly where to go for the answer. By referring back to paragraph 3, you see that the passage is describing how common it was for the Vikings to get lost. Answer B goes best with this.

7. With which of the following statements about Viking explorers would the author most probably agree?

    A.   Greenland and Iceland were the Vikings' final discoveries.

    B.   Viking explorers were cruel and savage.

    C.   The Vikings' most startling discovery was an accidental one.

    D.   All Viking explorers were fearless.

This is a general interpretation question, so we are looking for the answer that comes closest to saying something that the passage says. The passage never says whether Greenland and Iceland were the Vikings' final discoveries and never even hints at it, so we can cross off A. Answer choice B is extreme and never stated, so we can cross that off too. C sounds reasonable, so leave it in. D is also extreme and unfounded, so the answer is C.

QUICK QUIZ 3

Here's a quiz on our techniques. Fill in the blanks, and check your answers at the end of the chapter.

    1. What should you do when answering a main idea question?

    _____

    2. What should you do when answering a tone/attitude question?

    _____

3. What should you do when answering a general interpretation question?

   _____

4. What should you do when answering a general purpose question?

   _____

5. When you're using POE to get rid of answers choices, what types of answers should you keep?

   _____

6. What should you do when you've got the answer choices down to two?

   _____

PACING IN PARAGRAPH COMPREHENSION

One of the biggest hurdles to overcome in the Paragraph Comprehension test is the time limit. The ASVAB doesn't give you very much time to read all those passages and answer the questions. So, it's important to remember that *every question is worth one point.*

That's right. You don't earn extra points for the harder questions. So don't spend too much time on one question. The worst thing you can do on this section is get hung up on one question. If you get stuck on a question, use POE to get rid of as many wrong answers as possible, then guess from the remainder and move on.

LETTER OF THE DAY

Don't forget, in the ASVAB there's no penalty for guessing. That means it's always to your benefit to answer every question. That doesn't mean you need to read every passage and work every question. It just means that you should record an answer for every question. Keep track of the time with your own watch. When time is almost up, let's say one minute or so, pick your favorite letter, A, B, C, or D, and choose it for any questions you haven't gotten to.

TECHNIQUES FOR THE PAPER TEST

If you are taking the ASVAB on paper, try to do the questions in an order that works for you. If you see a passage that looks difficult, skip it. You can always come back to it later. Why spend four minutes answering a question worth one point when you can spend two minutes on an easier question worth the same amount?

If you're confronted with a long passage with several questions, answer the specific questions first. Not only are they usually simpler, but by answering them first you learn more about the passage. That makes the general questions easier when you get to them.

QUICK QUIZ 4

Well that's it, everything you need to know about the Paragraph Comprehension test. Not so bad, was it? Practice everything you've learned on the following questions. Answers can be found at the end of the chapter.

1. The force of lunar activity is not as strong as earth's own gravitational pull, which keeps our bodies and our homes from being pulled off the ground, through the sky, and into space toward the moon. The lunar force is strong enough, however, to exert a certain gravitational pull as the moon passes over the earth's surface. This pull causes the water level to rise (as the water is literally pulled ever-so-slightly toward the moon) in those parts of the ocean that are exposed to the moon and its gravitational forces. When the water level in one part of the ocean rises, it must naturally fall in another, and this is what causes tides to change, dramatically at times, along any given piece of coastline.

   The author's primary purpose in writing this paragraph is to

   A. prove the existence of water on the moon.

   B. refute claims that tides are caused by the moon.

   C. explain the main cause of the ocean's tides.

   D. argue that humans should not interfere with the processes of nature.

2. Florence Nightingale began a school in London, England, to set the standards for nursing. She was able to do this because she had already established a reputation with her work with soldiers during the Crimean War. She carried a lamp above her head as she walked among the wounded men, thereby earning the nickname "the lady with the lamp." It was this great lady who lit the way for nursing to become the respected profession it is today.

   The primary reason that Florence Nightingale was able to open a school for nursing was that

   A. she was already famous for her work in the war.

   B. her family was willing to finance her work.

   C. she had cared for many wealthy sick people herself.

   D. she worked endless hours every night.

3. There are many types of microscopes, from the simple optical microscope to the electron microscope. While a simple, inexpensive optical microscope may magnify an object from about fifty times its size to about one to two thousand times its size, the expensive electron microscope can magnify an object by up to about 250,000 times. The electron microscope works not with glass lenses, but with magnetic lenses as well. These lenses use electrons instead of light to produce an image. Just as a ray of light bends as it passes through a curved lens, streams of electrons bend as they pass by a magnetic lens. Very small objects do not affect light at all, but they do affect electrons. Because of that, an electron microscope can distinguish objects that are very small and very close together.

   The passage implies that the greatest advantage of the electron microscope is

   A. its expense.

   B. its versatility.

   C. its use of magnets.

   D. its greater ability to magnify.

4. A black hole starts out as a star. A star burns hydrogen, and this process, called fusion, releases energy. The energy released outward works against the star's own gravity, pulling inward and preventing the star from collapsing. After millions of years of burning hydrogen, the star eventually runs out of fuel. At this point, the star's own gravity and weight cause it to start contracting. If the star is small and not very heavy, it will shrink a little and become a white dwarf. If the star is bigger and heavier, it will collapse very quickly in an explosion. If the matter that remains is not too much heavier than our sun, it will eventually become a very dense neutron star. However, if the matter that remains is more than 1.7 times the mass of our sun, there will not be enough outward pressure to resist the force of gravity, and the collapse will continue. The result is a black hole.

A collapsing star will become a neutron star if

A. it is less than 1.7 times the mass of our sun.

B. it still has fuel to use for fusion.

C. it is more than 1.7 times the mass of our sun.

D. it shrinks slowly for a short time.

5. An Eskimo navigating in polar darkness and whiteouts makes use of many clues to find his way. When traveling on ice in the fog, the Eskimo uses the voices of seabirds against the cliffs and the sound of the surf at the edge of the ice. When he begins to travel over open terrain, he marks the angle of the wind and aligns the fur of his parka with the breeze. He notes the trend of any cracks in the ice as he crosses them. Sea ice cracks can reveal the presence of a cape or headland invisible in the distance, or they may confirm one's arrival at a known area. Constant attention to such details, memories of the way the land looks, and stories told by other travelers are used together with the movements of animals, to keep the traveler on course. The most dependable sources of direction for most Eskimos are the behavior of the wind and ocean currents, and such subtle clues as the flow of a river.

All of the following are mentioned as techniques Eskimos use for navigation EXCEPT:

A. consulting with elders of the Eskimo community

B. examining cracks in the ice along the route

C. learning from the experiences of earlier travelers

D. using the angle of the wind to judge direction

6. As the name implies, the electric eel has the ability to generate a strong electric field. When it comes time to feed, the eel relies on its electrical system for hunting. Because small animals have a different electrical "signature" than do plants or rocks, the electric eel effectively has a kind of radar that allows it to find fish. When the eel finds its prey, it delivers a strong electric current, which can instantly kill smaller animals, such as fish. The force of the charge is often strong enough to kill or stun even larger animals. How does the eel avoid hurting itself? The eel has evolved a kind of insulation that protects its nervous system. This insulation acts as a buffer against the electricity that it generates.

It can be inferred from the paragraph that the electricity is dangerous because it

A. damages the nervous system.

B. interferes with breathing.

C. deprives animals of food.

D. causes animals to bleed.

7. Most people know that the ancient Egyptians mummified their dead. But few people know the details of how or why a mummy was made. The point of mummification was to remove all of the parts of the body that could decompose, to insure that the remaining parts lasted forever. This was important to the Egyptians, who believed that parts of a person's soul needed a body to live in. If the body were to rot and disappear, the soul would be left homeless for eternity. To prevent the body from rotting, all the water had to be removed and all the bacteria had to be killed.

According to the paragraph, the Egyptians mummified their dead in order to insure that

A. the dead person would be protected from wolves.

B. the dead person's soul would have a home.

C. nobody would rob the dead person's grave.

D. the dead person's organs were not lost.

8. Julius Caesar was perhaps the most important political leader of all time. It was his military and political genius that created the Roman Empire, a civilization so large and powerful that no other western government could be considered its equal until the 1700s. Caesar's historical influence was so great that the German and Russian words for emperor (Kaiser and Czar) are derived from his name.

The author gives us the German and Russian words for emperor to demonstrate

A. the similarities between the German and Russian languages.

B. how words can change over time.

C. the importance of Julius Caesar in western history.

D. that Julius Caesar spoke German and Russian.

9. The initial American policy toward both World Wars was to stay out of them. The U.S. remained neutral at the beginning of both wars until certain events (the sinking of the Lusitania and the Zimmerman Telegram in World War I, and the bombing of Pearl Harbor in World War II) caused them to get involved.

Based on the above paragraph, all of the following are true EXCEPT:

A. Pearl Harbor was bombed during World War II.

B. Initially, the U.S. did not want to enter either World War.

C. The U.S. heavily supported the Allies at the beginning of World War II.

D. The sinking of the Lusitania was one reason the U.S. entered World War I.

10. In a preliminary test-tube laboratory study, a scientist found elevated growth rates in cancer cells exposed to low doses of microwave radiation. These results are only preliminary because, first of all, there has been no controlled study of the effects of microwaves on human beings. Second, this study was only of short duration, raising the possibility that the dangers of long-term exposure have not yet been assessed.

According to the information presented, the cancer cells' increased growth in the laboratory experiment is most probably due to

A. the sterile conditions of the laboratory.

B. the cancer cells' natural reproductive rate.

C. a short-term growth spurt that might mean nothing.

D. exposure to microwave radiation.

11. When I was eighteen I wanted something to do. I had tried teaching for two years and hated it; I had tried sewing and could not earn my bread that way, at the cost of health; I tried storywriting and got five dollars for stories that now bring a hundred; I had thought seriously of going up on the stage, but certain highly respectable relatives were so shocked at the mere idea that I relinquished my dramatic aspirations.

The author implies that writing is a job that is

A. profitable.

B. rewarding.

C. miserable.

D. unprofitable.

12. The first "horseless carriages" of the 1880s may have been worthy of a snicker or two, but not the cars of today. The progress that has been made over the last one hundred years has been phenomenal. In fact, much progress was made even in the first twenty years—in 1903 cars could travel at 70 mph. The major change from the old cars to today is the expense. Whereas cars were once a luxury that only the very wealthy could afford, today, people of all income levels own cars.

The "progress" mentioned in line 2 most likely refers to

A. the ability of a car to move forward.

B. technological advancement.

C. research.

D. the cost of the car.

13. Born as Gertrude Margaret Zelle in the Netherlands in 1876, Mata Hari was probably the most famous spy of all time. During World War I, she was a beautiful dancer who worked in Paris. Mata Hari was her stage name.

Many believe that Mata Hari was a double agent, someone who spies for two countries at the same time. It was thought that she spied for Germany by stealing secrets from the French, and for the French by stealing secrets from the Germans. She charmed military men with her great beauty. Mata Hari was arrested and executed by the French in 1917.

What is the primary purpose of the passage?

A. To discuss the moral ramifications of spying

B. To help uncover the reasons Mata Hari turned to spying

C. To discuss the life of Mata Hari

D. To demonstrate Mata Hari's great beauty

14. The native inhabitants of the Americas arrived from Asia more than 20,000 years ago. Many were skilled hunters, farmers, and fishers. They belonged to numerous tribes. Some of the most famous Native American tribes are the Sioux, the Cheyenne, the Iroquois, and the Apache. These tribes settled and developed organized societies. The European settlers who arrived in America many years later often fought the Native Americans for land. Geronimo was the last great Native American chief to organize rebellions against the settlers. He led raids across the southwest and into Mexico. Although he was eventually captured, he later became a celebrity.

The passage names all of the following as skills of the Native Americans EXCEPT

A. farming.

B. hunting.

C. fishing.

D. gathering.

Questions 15–19 are based on the following passage.

Marie Sklodowska was born November 7, 1867 in Warsaw, Poland. She grew up in a family that valued education, and as a young woman she studied at the Sorbonne in Paris, France. There she met Pierre Curie, a physics teacher at the University of Paris. The two quickly married and began conducting research on radioactive substances. Together they discovered two highly radioactive elements, radium and polonium. In 1903 they were awarded the Nobel Prize for physics for their work. They shared the award with another French scientist, Antoine Henri Bacquerel, who had discovered natural radioactivity. In 1906 Pierre was killed when he was run over by a car.

In 1911 Marie won the Nobel Prize for chemistry for her work in isolating radium and studying its chemical properties. In 1914 she helped found the Radium Institute in Paris and was its first director. When World War I broke out, she believed that x-rays would help doctors locate bullets in soldiers. Since it was dangerous to move wounded soldiers, she invented portable x-ray machines and trained 150 women to operate them. On July 4, 1934, Marie Curie died at the age of 67. The cause of death was leukemia. It is believed that exposure to high levels of radiation due to her research caused the cancer. After her death the Radium Institute was renamed the Curie Institute in her honor.

15. What did Pierre and Marie Curie win the Nobel Prize in physics for?

    A.   Inventing the x-ray machine
    B.   Discovering radium and polonium
    C.   Founding the Radium Institute
    D.   Training x-ray technicians

16. Why did Marie Curie invent portable x-ray machines?

    A.   So she could study radium in its natural environment.
    B.   In order to win another Nobel Prize.
    C.   To locate bullets in wounded soldiers without moving the soldiers.
    D.   Because x-ray machines were very expensive and by making them portable, several
         laboratories at the Radium Institute could share one machine.

17. Why was the Radium Institute renamed the Curie Institute?

    A.   As a tribute to Marie Curie for her great advances in the fields of chemistry and physics.
    B.   In honor of Pierre Curie, who had originally conceived of the idea for the institute.
    C.   Because Marie Curie left a large sum of money to the institute in her will.
    D.   Because Pierre Curie was killed on its grounds.

18. Who discovered natural radioactivity?

    A.   Pierre Curie
    B.   Marie Curie
    C.   Scientists at the Radium Institute
    D.   Antoine Henri Bacquerel

19. The author of this passage probably believes that Marie Curie was

    A. a gifted scientist.
    B. given more credit than she deserved.
    C. unworthy of the 2 Nobel prizes she won.
    D. uninterested in biology and other life sciences.

ANSWERS TO QUICK QUIZZES

Quick Quiz 1
Page 148

1. The stars are considered <u>luminous</u> because
2. According to the passage, an <u>opaque</u> object
3. The passage best supports the idea that <u>elementary schools</u>
4. The planet <u>Jupiter</u> differs from all other planets in the solar system in that it
5. According to the passage, <u>Pygmy Marmosets</u> are commonly found in
6. According to the passage, <u>anthropologists</u> study

Quick Quiz 2
Page 149

1. The passage primarily concerns:
   General main idea

2. The last sentence of paragraph 1 implies that:
   Specific interpretation

3. According to the passage, television has become a medium whose main goal is:
   Specific fact

4. The author's reference to "talking hair-do's" is a reference to:
   Specific interpretation

5. According to the passage, which of the following was an artist?

   I.   Brancusi

   II. Cox

   III. Hughes

   Specific fact

6. The author of the passage can most reasonably be described as:
   General interpretation

Quick Quiz 3

Page 156

1. Eliminate answers that are too broad or too narrow. The correct answer should cover the entire passage without claiming more than the passage actually says

2. Determine whether the author was for, against, or neutral on the subject and eliminate what answer choices you can. Then ask yourself about the degree of the author's tone, i.e., whether it was mild or strong.

3. Choose the answer that comes closest to what the passage says. Look for a paraphrase.

4. First ask why the author wrote the passage. Keep the author's tone in mind.

5. Paraphrases of the passage, and answers that use moderate wording like can, may, and often.

6. Reread the question, look at what makes the two answers different, refer back to the passage, and eliminate the worse answer. Whatever you do, don't just sit and stare at the answers!

Quick Quiz 4

Page 158

1. **C** The passage never mentions water on the moon, so eliminate A. B is the exact opposite of what the passage says, so eliminate it. D is never mentioned, so the answer is C.

2. **A** The answer to this specific question is located in lines 2–3, "she had already established a reputation for her work with soldiers during the Crimean War." Answer A paraphrases that.

3. **D** A isn't an advantage of the electron microscope, B isn't stated, C is true but not an advantage, and so the answer is D.

4. **A** Use the lead words "neutron star" to find the answer. By reading a few lines before and a few lines after, you can see that A is the answer.

5. **A** Use POE to eliminate answers that are stated in the passage. That gets rid of B, C, and D.

6. **A** The passage states, "The eel has evolved a kind of insulation that protects its nervous system." Based on this we can infer that electricity is dangerous to the nervous system.

7. **B** The passage states that if the body was not preserved, "the soul would be left homeless for eternity." Also, the passage never mentions A, C, or D.

8. **C** The passage is describing what an important political figure Caesar was, and answer C goes best with that.

9. **C** Use POE to get rid of answers that are mentioned in the passage. That gets rid of A, B, and D.

10. **D** The answer to this question is stated plainly in the first sentence. If you read the question first it should have been obvious. The rest of the passage is there to waste time and confuse you.

11. **D** The passage says "I tried storywriting and got five dollars for stories that now bring a hundred," implying that the author didn't make much money.

12. **B** The sentence is discussing the technological advancement from the first "horseless carriages" to the cars of today.

13. **C** The passage never discusses the morality of spying or the reasons why Mata Hari spied, so eliminate A and B. Though the passage does mention her great beauty, this is not the main purpose of the passage, so eliminate D. The answer is C.

14. **D** This is an EXCEPT question. By crossing off the answers that are mentioned in the passage, we are left with D.

15. **B** The answer can be found in line 5 of the passage. The other choices can be eliminated: The passage never says who invented the x-ray machine (A), Pierre was dead before the Radium Institute was founded (C), and D occurred after they won the Nobel prize.

16. **C** The passage states "Since it was dangerous to move wounded soldiers, she invented portable x-ray machines."

17. **A** The answer can be found in the last sentence of the passage.

18. **D** The lead words "natural radioactivity" take you right to the answer, Antoine Henri Bacquerel.

19. **A** The entire passage describes Marie Curie's achievements, so it's unlikely that the author would think she was given more credit than she deserved (B), or unworthy of the 2 Nobel prizes (C). D is never mentioned, so the answer is A.

6

Auto and Shop Information

INTRODUCTION TO AUTO AND SHOP INFORMATION

You won't need detailed knowledge and years working as a mechanic to do well on the Automobile and Shop section of the ASVAB. This section gives you 11 minutes to answer 25 questions, half of which are related to automobile systems (mainly simple problem diagnosis) and the other half to identifying and choosing the right shop tool for a particular job. The questions range in difficulty throughout the section, so if you are taking the paper version of the test, it is best to simply start at the beginning of the section you do best on and work straight through without spending too much time on any one question. Of course, you will have the opportunity to see what kinds of questions you do better on later in this chapter. But first we need to go into a brief review of the concepts you'll need to know.

SHOP SECTION

There are three basic types of questions that you will find in the Shop section. The first kind is Tool Identification. Tool Identification questions will ask you either to identify a tool either from its picture or from its purpose. For example:

1. The tool shown above is a

    A.   Flathead screwdriver
    B.   Philips screwdriver
    C.   Chisel
    D.   Allen wrench

The second type of question is called Tool Part Definition. This type will either give you a term and ask you to choose the correct definition from a list of four, or give you the definition of a term referring to a part of a tool and ask you to select the proper term. For example:

2. The end of the saw that is located the farthest from the handle is called the

    A.   Heel
    B.   Knee
    C.   Toe
    D.   Bight

The third type of question, Shop Methods, will ask about proper methods and processes used in the shop. For example, you might be asked about how to cut wood, how to harden metals and why some bolts have to be tightened down with a certain amount of torque.

BASIC TOOL REVIEW

Everyone can recognize a saw or a hammer, but the ASVAB, as in the first example above, is also going to ask you to differentiate between various types of similar tools. When reviewing this section, be sure to pay attention to the differences between the individual tools within each type and how they are each used.

Measuring Tools

Tape Measure

The ability to measure objects is essential in order to be able to construct anything. To complete quick measurements that do not require a high degree of accuracy, a rule or tape is often used. Measuring tapes and rules are both marked off in regular intervals, normally feet and inches, or meters and centimeters. Rules are designed to give accurate measurements quickly. They are generally marked down to 1/64th of an inch, indicating that they are accurate to about 1/32nd of an inch, or about one millimeter. Rules are shorter and thicker than measuring tapes. Their rigidity prevents them from shrinking and expanding as the temperature changes and allows a more accurate measurement over shorter distances. Measuring tape generally expands or contracts a little bit in extreme temperatures.

> Measuring tape is normally calibrated to measure exactly as its markings indicate when the temperature of the tape is 70 degrees Fahrenheit.

However, measuring tapes are preferred for measuring long distances, as they generally come in lengths from five feet to several hundred feet. The tape is usually made out of a thin steel strip that is curved slightly upward to give it support when extended. Many tape measures designed to give more precise measurements at longer distances include a table that shows how far the tape will stretch on a hot day or shrink on a cold day.

Slide Caliper

Calipers are measuring tools used to measure diameters of pipes and tubes. All calipers have two points set an adjustable distance from each other. The two points are set inside of a pipe or hole or outside of a rod and secured so that they touch the object being measured. There are several variations on this basic idea:

Simple calipers look a little like a pair of legs. If the points, or the feet, are turned outward, then the calipers are used to measure the inside diameter of pipes and holes. If the points are turned inward, then the calipers are used to measure the outer diameter of the pipe or rod. After the calipers have been secured at the set distance, they are taken out, and the distance between the points is measured with a rule.

A **slide caliper** has a rule built into the caliper. One of the points is fixed to the rule and the other one slides along the rule. The distance between the two points is then measured directly off of the rule, or from a gauge that is connected directly to the rule. If a special type of scale called a vernier scale is used, then the caliper is called a **vernier caliper**. This type of caliper is accurate down to as little as 0.001 inch.

Micrometer

If accuracy in small measurements is important, a **micrometer** can be used. This tool has two small surfaces connected to a sliding rule, similar to a slide caliper. The moveable surface is connected to an arm that allows the surface to go around an object. The rule is normally connected to a vernier scale or a digital gauge and has excellent resolution.

There are several other types of measurement tools that you should be familiar with. At times, it is important to know what direction is straight down from a hook or other object and what point lies directly beneath it. The **plumb line** uses the effects of gravity to determine where this point is. A plumb line is a string attached to a round weight, called a plumb bob. The plumb bob has a ring to which you can attach a string at one end and a pointer at the other end. The plumb bob is dangled from the hook (or other object) above by the string. Gravity will pull the plumb bob straight down and the pointer on the plumb bob will point to the spot directly underneath the hook. This system is not very technically advanced, but it works well.

Carpenter's Level

A **carpenter's level** is used to tell when a surface, such as a table, is level to the ground or a wall is standing straight up and down. A level uses the idea that a bubble will always rise to the highest point of a liquid. Therefore, within the level, a bubble is set in a transparent tube of liquid, and the tube is marked so that when the level is completely horizontal, the bubble rests between the two marks on the tube. If one side is too high, the bubble will rest to the other side of the tube. Levels can also tell you whether an object's edge is straight up and down or not. Some levels features digital readouts that show the grade of the tilt of a surface

Thickness gauges are used to determine how much space there is between two surfaces that are close together. Thickness gauges are normally found in a set that consists of several thin calibrated plates or wires. The plates are slid into the gap between the two objects until one of the plates fits snugly. The thickness of that particular plate is the same as the gap between the two objects. One example of a thickness gauge is the wire gauge used to check the separation between the two points of a spark plug.

Capenter's Square

Squares look like a giant, metal letter "L" and help carpenters and machinists know when two objects or surfaces are at right angles to each other.

Hammers

Hammers are one of the most well known tools. Several types of hammers are shown below.

Carpenter's Hammer   Mallet   Ball Peen Hammer

The main differences in the hammers come from the differences in the parts labeled above. Parts of tools are generally named either for what the tool does or for a body part. For hammers, we refer to the "head," "neck," and "face." The **head** of the hammer is always the heavy part of the hammer, and the **face** is the flat part, used for striking something. The head is connected to the handle at the **neck**. The only part of the hammer that does not have to do with part of the head is the **claw**, which, not surprisingly, looks like a claw.

The first hammer shown above is a **carpenter's hammer**. It is used for driving nails into wood with the head or for pulling them out with the claw. The claw on this type of hammer is generally two pronged.

The second hammer is a **mallet**. Mallets generally have a soft double-sided head, made of rubber or plastic, and no claw. The soft head of the mallet will not leave a mark or a dent in what is strikes, so a mallet is used for shaping metal or striking something that a hard-headed hammer would damage. Mallets are also used to hit the back of chisels, punches, or other tools, so as not to damage the tool. Whenever a tool must be struck as part of a process, a mallet should be used.

The third hammer above is a **ball peen hammer**, used mainly by machinists and metalworkers. These hammers have a peen in place of a claw. The peen can be shaped in many different ways; its purpose is to allow the machinist to get the hammer into hard-to-reach places or to strike small things. Most peen hammers are named after the shape of the peen. Machinists' hammers can also have soft heads, so as not to mar the surface that is to be struck.

Screwdrivers

A screwdriver is a device designed to either tighten or loosen screws in both wood and metal objects. A screwdriver works by increasing the amount of **torque** applied to a screw so that you can turn it far more easily than if you simply used your fingers. You'll need to be able to distinguish between the basic types of screwdrivers and to understand why each type is used. The screwdriver has three parts: the **handle**, which you hold; the **blade**, which fits into the top of the screw; and the **shank**, which connects the handle and the blade. The only difference between the two types of screwdrivers is the shape of the blade of the screwdriver.

Flathead Screwdriver   Phillips Head Screwdriver

Flathead Screw   Phillips Head Screw

The first picture above is a **standard** or **flathead** screwdriver. These screwdrivers come in a wide variety of lengths, widths and thickness of blades. They are to be used to drive a simple slotted screws only, usually into wood, and not as a chisel or pry bar.

In order to allow the screwdriver to stay in the slot easier and to transfer more torque to the screw to prevent slipping, a **Phillips head** screw and screwdriver was developed. The Phillips head screw looks like it has an imprinted "plus" sign on the top of the screw instead of a simple slot. The Phillips head screwdriver fits into this plus sign snuggly. This type of screw is found in many applications, because it is easy to work with.

Wrenches

Wrenches are used to turn nuts, bolts, pipes, and other types of fasteners. They work in the same fundamental way that screwdrivers work, by using torque or mechanical advantage to turn the fastener. All wrenches are in some way able to "grip" a fastener and turn it. There are many types of wrenches and each one has its own particular use. Outlined here are the 10 most common types their uses.

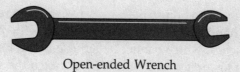

Open-ended Wrench

Open-ended wrenches have jaws that cannot be adjusted. They come in different sizes, to be used for different-sized bolts or fasteners. Generally, you slip the wrench around the sides of the bolt head and then turn the bolt. This is the simplest type of wrench. However, if a wrench is the wrong size, then it can't be used.

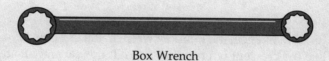

Box Wrench

Box wrenches are similar to open ended wrenches in that you have to choose one of the correct size to be used on a particular bolt. What's different about a box wrench is that the jaws are completely closed, in order to fit snugly around the head of the bolt. This wrench can't slip sideways off a bolt, making it easy to affix to the bolt head. Box wrenches, like open-ended wrenches, come in a wide array of sizes.

Socket wrenches are similar to box wrenches in that the socket completely surrounds the nut or bolt head. The socket comes in an array of specific sizes and can be attached to a handle or ratchet unit easily. One end of the socket looks like the jaws of a box wrench, and the other end has a square hole that attaches to one of three sizes of drives on the handles. The handles come in a wide variety of shapes, lengths, and sizes, allowing access to hard-to-reach places. This wrench is relatively cheap, is easy use, and versatile.

Crescent Wrench

A **crescent wrench** allows you to adjust the gap between the wrench's open jaws by turning a screw adjuster located in the handle. This wrench can be used with many sizes of bolts, as opposed to open-ended and box wrenches, which cannot be adjusted. The top jaw on crescent wrenches is fixed to the handle, while the lower jaw can be moved to match the size of the nut or bolt.

Monkey Wrench

Another type of adjustable wrench, the **monkey wrench**, is a close relative of the crescent wrench. The monkey wrench, like the crescent wrench, has a fixed top jaw and an adjustable lower jaw. But monkey wrenches are generally a little stronger, with bigger jaws, and are used for more heavy-duty jobs.

The purpose of the **pipe wrench** is to turn pipes in order to attach them to other pipes. The pipe wrench is also an adjustable open-jaw wrench. This wrench has the lower jaw fixed to the handle and a movable upper jaw. The jaws are set at a slight angle to each other, to allow better gripping of pipes and tubes. This is generally a heavy wrench, larger than the other kinds of wrenches.

It is often important to know how tight a bolt is when you're tightening it down. If the bolt or nut is tightened too much, the bolt can strip, or lose its shape. If it's not tightened enough, it can sometimes loosen even more and fall off. To avoid this, a wrench was developed to measure how hard you're turning the bolt in terms of the amount of torque placed on the bolt. A **torque wrench** is generally a long bar or handle attached to pointer and a scale. As you tighten a bolt, the wrench will bend slightly and the pointer will point to a number on a scale signifying the amount of torque that you are exerting on the bolt. These wrenches often fit sockets, so that they can be interchanged with the right wrench size.

A different type of wrench is used to turn large-diameter pipes and other shafts. The **strap wrench** uses a webbing strap, much like a seatbelt, that wraps tightly around the pipe. You can then turn the pipe by applying a force to the handle of the wrench. The friction between the strap and the shaft keeps the handle fixed to the shaft so that they will turn together. It is often difficult to use this type of wrench on a wet or lubricated shaft. **Chain wrenches** are similar to strap wrenches but feature a chain instead of a strap. This type of wrench is used when a strap wrench will slip or when the surface of the shaft does not need to be smooth. The chain wrench will mark the surface on which it is used.

Allen Wrench

Allen wrenches are hexagon-shaped bars bent about one third of the way down the shaft. These wrenches fit into machine screws that have a hexagonal hole in the head. Allen wrenches and Allen screws are used for many of the same applications that screws and screwdrivers are used for, but provide even more force to turn the screw without stripping the head.

Pliers

Pliers   Needle Nose Pliers   Vise Grips

Pliers are great tools to use to hold objects that would otherwise be difficult to grip. Pliers come in many different types but all have the same basic shape. They have **jaws** (like a wrench), a **handle**, a **joint** or **pivot point**, and a **nose**, located at the end of the jaws. Different types of pliers have different noses. The nose can be either straight or curved. It can also be either stubby and short, or long and thin, in which case the pliers are called **needle nose pliers**. Most pliers have a fixed pivot, limiting the size of the material that can be held. Some pliers have adjustable jaws, so that the tool can be used on objects of many different sizes. This special type of pliers is called **slip joint pliers**, because the joint can "slip" into different sizes.

Another type of pliers, called **vise grips**, allow the user to clamp down onto something and lock the jaws. Vise grips are great for holding onto something very tightly. A special lever in the tool allows it to release.

Vises and Clamps

Common Vise

Many shops also contain tools called vises that help to hold materials that are being cut, drilled, or glued. A **vise** is a heavy, solid iron or steel tool. One end of the vise is fixed and bolted to a table. The other end can be adjusted by tightening a lever attached to a worm gear; in this way, the jaws close upon an object. Vises must be heavy to be able to hold onto materials and keep them from moving even when they're under heavy pressure. The main jaws of a vise must be kept free from nicks and gouges, so that the objects can be held as tightly and evenly as possible.

C Clamp

Often times, an object can't fit into a vise because it is too big or awkward, so a clamp is used instead. The most common type of clamp is a **C clamp**, so called because it's shaped like the letter "C." The clamp has one side attached to the C and the other fixed to an adjustable screw. It's then simply put in place and tightened to hold an object. There are other types of clamps, but all have only two flat jaws connected by some type of screw to tighten them down.

Cutting tools — saws

There are dozens of types of tools used to cut materials in a shop. Each one has its own specialized use. We will start with the most widely known cutting tools and then discuss the ones used for shaping.

The most recognizable type of cutting tool is the **saw**. Most saws have a similar set of parts. The part of the saw that you hold on to is called the **handle**. The handle is connected in some way to the **blade**. The blade is the part of the saw that contains the **teeth**, which are responsible for actually cutting through the material. The end of the saw is called the **toe** and the part next to the handle is called the **heel**. Some or all of these parts will be different for each type of saw. One major difference is in the blade.

The blade on a saw has several major components. The cutting portion on a saw blade normally cuts only when the saw is pulled back or pushed forward—in other words, only in one direction. The teeth on the saw are bent slightly outward so that the slot being cut is slightly wider than the saw blade. The distance that the teeth are bent from the edge of the saw blade is called the **set** of the saw. The bigger the set, the more clearance there will be between the saw blade and the side of the cut slot. The total width of the slot that is cut is the same as the total width of the teeth, called the **kerf**. It is important to know the kerf of the saw when cutting something. One rule to keep in mind is the **Three Tooth Rule**: Three teeth must always be in contact with the material that is being cut. So if a thin material is being cut, a saw blade with teeth that are close together must be used.

Handsaw

For cutting wood, two major types of blades are used. **Ripsaws** are for cutting along the grain of the wood, and **crosscut saws** are for cutting across the grain of the wood. The difference between the saws is in the shape of their teeth. It's easy to remember that *cross*cut saws cut *across* the grain.

The saw shown above is a **handsaw**. The teeth on this saw can be arranged for ripping or for cross cutting. This is the saw most commonly used for cutting wood.

Backsaw

Backsaw and **dovetail** saws are used for cutting a straight line across the grain of the wood. The backsaw is reinforced with a strong metal back, so that the blade will not bend. Its teeth are for ripping. The handle is like that of the handsaw above. The dovetail saw is similar to the backsaw in that it has a strong backing, but its handle is shaped more like a file and the blade is much thinner. Sometimes, with these saws, a block of wood called a miter box is used to help keep the blade and the direction of the cut in a straight line.

Coping Saw

Hacksaw

The **coping saw** is used for cutting curves in wood. Its thin blade allows it to twist slightly in thin pieces of wood. The **compass saw** is used to cut intricate shapes in thicker pieces of wood. Its thicker blade gives it more support.

The **hack saw** looks similar to the coping saw except that its blade is much thicker and the arm that holds the blade is much stronger. The hacksaw is used for cutting metal. The arm of the saw extends and stretches the blade. The tension put on the blade helps it to remain stable when cutting. Various hack saw blades can be fit to the same saw; these blades come in a wide variety of teeth depths, number of teeth per inch along the blade, and kerfs.

Other cutting tools

Shears

Shears or **snips** look like scissors with a long handle and a short blade. They are used primarily for cutting very thin sheet metal. Cutting sheet metal with a saw is similar to trying to cut paper with a saw. It is much easier to use a scissor-like cutting tool on thin metal.

What do you use when you want to cut a pipe or piece of tubing? One option is a hacksaw. But a **pipe cutter** is a much better choice. A pipe cutter looks like a c clamp with several circular blades. The cutter is affixed around the pipe and then tightened. The pipe or tube is then rotated and the circular blades cut into the pipe. This method leaves a much cleaner and smoother surface than cutting with a hacksaw wood.

Wire Cutters

It is generally not advisable to use snips, shears, or scissors to cut electrical or other types of wire. This will damage the blades and wear down the tools. **Wire cutters** have a thicker and stronger blade, so they do not get damaged.

Bolt cutters are reinforced snips designed to cut through thicker pieces of hard metals, bolts, and rods. The handles on bolt cutters are very long and the cutting jaws very short, so that more leverage can be applied to cut thick bolts. These cutters generally also have a mechanism of levers near the jaws that help to transfer more force to the bolt. Bolt cutters should not be used as wire cutters.

Shaping Tools

Many times it is necessary to shape a tool after it has been cut to allow it to fit snugly with other parts. The tools discussed below are used to shape material in specific ways.

Plane

Planes are used to give wood a smooth surface and to remove small layers of wood. Planes are devices that allow the user to hold the tool and put pressure on the material, to shave part of it away. They can cut either with or across the grain of stock. Jackplanes, the most common type, have a slight convex curve to the blade.

Chisels

Chisels have been used throughout history to remove chips and pieces of wood and other material in order to make planks and other shapes. They're also used to help make and clean out grooves in wood. A chisel has a straight handle and a flat smooth blade. You hold the handle of the chisel in your hand and then strike the handle with a rubber mallet (not with a hammer). This process removes little chips of wood. Do not use a chisel as a paint scraper.

File

A **file** looks similar to a chisel but has a different blade. Files are used to remove layers of metal. The face of the file is covered with teeth, which can either be cut diagonally in either one direction in two directions, making the file either single cut or double cut files. Files that have more cuts per inch will leave a smoother surface on the material. The faces of files come in a variety of shapes, including square, flat, round, and triangular. At the heel of the file is a tang that's inserted into a universal handle. Files should never be struck with a hammer.

Grinder

Another type of tool used to remove material from a metal part is a grinder. A **grinder** is an abrasive wheel that spins at a high speed on an axle. Before operating a grinder, you should check the wheel to make sure it does not have cracks. If there are cracks, the wheel might explode while spinning. The metal part of the grinder is pressed into the wheel with medium force and moved slightly over the center of the wheel. The object to be ground should always be in contact with the lower part of the wheel, just above the wheel guard, so that if you lose control of the object it will be thrown to the ground instead of into the air.

Tap

Taps and **dies** are two special types of shaping tools used to make threads on objects. Taps are tools that look like a screw with the corners cut out and a handle at one end. They are used for making threads in metal holes so that a screw may be used in the hole. The tap is inserted into the hole, twisted about five times, and then pulled out to allow the shavings to be taken out of the hole; then it's inserted and twisted again an additional five times further than the previous time. This cycle repeats until the threads go far enough into the hole for the screw. A die is a block with what appears to be four connected holes going through it. The middle hole is threaded and the outer holes are smooth. The die is used for making threads on the outside of a tube or rod. It is placed over the rod and twisted so that the threads are cut just as with the tap.

Drills, Braces, and Bits

Drill   Brace

The best way to make a hole in a material using a hand tool is with a **bit** and a **drill** or **brace**. A drill is a device that turns a cutting tool at a very high rate of speed. Drills that use a manual crank are called braces. Braces are generally long enough to fit two hands on the shaft. The shaft is bent in several places to accommodate a handle that is off set from the main shaft and allows the user to turn the brace. Drills have a chuck that attaches to any one of a number of drill bits, which are the parts that actually come into contact with the material being drilled into.

Drill Bit

The drill bit that we are used to seeing is called a standard **twist drill bit**. It is used for drilling holes into metals and wood stock. The twist bit has two blades that are located inside the body of the bit. The cutting edges are straight and are separated by a portion of the tip of the drill bit that does not cut called the dead center. Consequently, if a large hole is being drilled, the dead center can sometimes be too large and the drill can't cut into the material. To avoid these problems, a smaller hole is first drilled into the material. Then the larger bit is used. The small hole removes the material that would have been encountered by the dead center so that the larger bit can enter the material. The twisted portion of the drill bit does not cut the hole. It is used to help to pull material out of the hole.

A **reamer** is a drill bit that is used to make an existing hole bigger. The cutting edges on a reamer are located on the outside edge of the body and not at the end. This allows the bit to cut out a hole of larger diameter than what already exists.

Sometimes a surface will need to be flat after it is screwed or bolted into place. In order to accomplish this, a **countersink screw** must be used. The hole that the screw goes into must be drilled with a countersink drill bit to accommodate the screw. The countersink drill bit is a cone-shaped bit that cuts out a cone at the top of a drilled hole to allow a screw to tighten so that its head is below the surface of the material.

Boring tools are often used to drill holes in wood. The boring tool has several parts that make it different from a twist drill. The tip of the boring tool is a threaded screw that grabs and pulls the bit into the material. The next part of the bit to come in contact with the material consists of two points that score the circumference of the circle that is to be cut. The blades on a boring tool are between the points and the threaded tip and are shaped like half moons. The cutting edges chip out the material within the scored circle. As the threaded tip pulls the boring tool further into the material, the twist moves material from the blades to the top of the hole.

Punch

Sometimes, before you start to drill in metals, you need to make a small indentation to allow the bit to drill in the right place. Without this indentation, the bit can jump and spin all over the surface of the metal and not drill the hole at the correct point. To make this small indentation, you can use a **punch**, which is a metal shaft that's flat on one end and sharp on the other. The punch point is placed on the center of the hole to be drilled and gently hit on the flat part with a rubber or plastic mallet. You then drill the hole at the spot by placing the center of the drill bit into the punch mark and starting the hole.

Punches can also be used to knock a pin out of a hole or to line up holes when assembling an object.

Welding

Welding is a method of bonding two pieces of metal or parts together permanently by melting the metal in a specific place on the pieces to be joined. The small area of melted metal is spongy and forms a bead. The welder uses a tool to push the bead of molten metal along the joint, adding a small amount of metal as needed to keep the joint strong. The parts are then normally cooled in oil or water, recrystalizing the metal and hardening it into one part.

Welding Torch

The tool that the welders use is called a **welding torch**. One of the most common types of torches is the **acetylene torch**. A pressurized tank feeds the gas to the end of the torch. The valves are opened and the torch lit with a spark. The flame is so bright that the welder must wear safety goggles. The welder then uses the flame to melt the metal and push the bead along the joint.

Another common type of welding is **arc welding**, which requires a tool connected to a voltage source. When the tool comes into contact with a metal object, it will conduct electricity. If the tool is pulled a small distance away from the metal object, an arc of electricity will form, heating up the metal and melting it at the arc point. The welder then joins the two pieces as with the acetylene torch. In some types of welding, the lead of the tool supplies the additional metal needed for the joint and is consumed by the welding process and incorporated into the joint.

Using POE

POE is the most powerful tool that you have to answer the questions on the exam. Even if you're unsure of the answer to a question on the Auto and Shop section, you can still use POE to give you a good chance of getting it right.

Sometimes you will be given a picture of a tool that you do not recognize or even have never seen before. Don't give up! Chances are that you are going to know some of the tools are that are listed below the picture in the answer choices. From your knowledge of what those tools look like, you can eliminate incorrect answers, and then you can guess from the answers you have left. This will greatly improve your odds of getting the question right.

AUTO SECTION

Now that we have reviewed the basic tools and shop procedures, we are going to discuss automobiles. About half of the auto questions on the ASVAB will be related to engine and automotive systems components, like carburetors, struts, and valves. The other half will involve the basic diagnosis of some given problem or condition in an automobile. Before we can diagnose problems, we need to understand the underlying principles and basic components of the automobile.

Automobiles can be broken down into several integrated systems that all work together but perform different functions. Many of the components from these systems overlap. But without each one of these systems working properly, it will not be long before the car is on the side of the road. Auto systems that you will need to know are:

- **Engine and Exhaust:** processes the fuel and turns the wheels

- **Cooling:** keeps the engine from overheating

- **Drive Train:** transports energy from the engine to the wheels

- **Steering:** allows the car to be turned from side to side

- **Braking:** allows the car to be stopped

- **Electrical:** ties into most of the other systems on the vehicle and allows the car to continue running

Automobile Systems Review

Engine and Exhaust

The basic idea behind an engine is that it harnesses the energy from burning fuels. An engine is a device that contains an explosion and uses the energy to turn a shaft. Where does the explosion come from? The explosion comes from igniting a mixture of fuel and air. The fuel is the benzene-based gasoline or diesel that you normally fill your car's gas tank with at the station. In order for anything to burn, it needs oxygen. In automobiles, oxygen is supplied from the air and mixed with the gasoline. The mixture is then ignited with a spark and explodes, releasing energy. When something burns or explodes, it does not disintegrate into oblivion; it leaves behind residues and gasses that must be removed. In the case of the automobile, this waste removal is done by the exhaust system.

The heart of the car is the engine, and the heart of the engine lies in the **cylinders**. A cylinder is basically a tube that is open at one end and closed off on the other, with the exception of two small holes to allow fuel and air to enter and exhaust gasses to exit. The closed side of the cylinder also has one end of the spark plug in it. The open side of the cylinder is "plugged" by another cylindrical object called the **piston**. The piston has a slightly smaller diameter than the cylinder to allow it to move up and down inside the cylinder easily. Two metal rings, called **piston rings**, wrap around the piston head and seal off the inside of the cylinder. The piston rings fit into small grooves in the piston and expand, so they always brush along the walls of the cylinder and create a tight seal. This seal helps to contain the explosion in the cylinder and use more of its energy. The piston is connected to the **piston rod**, a bar that extends out of the cylinder and attaches to the crankshaft. The piston rod is not connected to the center of the crankshaft; it is connected a little offset. In fact, no part of the crankshaft has a rod that passes all the way through the center. As the piston moves up and down, the **crankshaft** turns in a complete circle. This is much like watching someone pedaling a bicycle: The legs and knees are traveling up and down, but because the pedals are offset from the bicycle's crankshaft, the pedals and the person's feet will turn around in a circle. This motion is extremely important, because the turning of the crankshaft ultimately turns the wheels.

If the piston were the only thing attached to the crankshaft, the shaft would not turn smoothly but would jerk around in its circle. A heavy wheel, called the **flywheel**, is attached to the end of the crankshaft. Once it has started rotating, the flywheel is difficult to stop and helps the crankshaft and piston to move smoothly.

Cars do not run with a single cylinder and piston. Most cars have four-cylinder, six-cylinder or eight-cylinder engines. Most of the four cylinder engines are built with all of the cylinders lined up with the pistons entering from the bottom. This is called a "straight four" or "in-line" four-cylinder engine. However, most six and eight cylinder engines have the cylinders and pistons oriented to look like a letter "V" and are consequently called "V-6" or "V-8" engines.

So where does the initial up-and-down motion of the piston come from? Let's follow the fuel as it moves through the engine.

On older automobiles, the gasoline starts in the gas tank and is pumped by the fuel pump into the **carburetor**, which is responsible for mixing air and fuel together. The carburetor consists of a float tank to store fuel, an air intake valve, an air filter, and a series of tubing. The air enters through the filter, which removes dust and other impurities that could leave residue on the engine, ignite early in the combustion chamber, and decrease the life of the engine. The air then travels through a special tube called a venturi that looks like a pipe constricted in the middle. A tube coming from the fuel reservoir intersects the venturi at the smallest part. The air traveling by the small tube does two things: First, it sucks fuel into the air through the small tube; second, it mixes the fuel instantly and completely with the air. If the air and fuel do not mix completely, not all of the fuel will burn in the combustion chamber, leading to wasted fuel and increased pollutants. If there is too much fuel, the air/fuel mixture is said to be too rich, and the vehicle will not burn all of the fuel completely. If there is too little fuel, the mixture is called lean, and the engine will not get enough power. In order to get the mix just right, the carburetor uses about 15 pounds of air for every one pound of fuel.

A special valve called the **throttle valve** controls the amount of the fuel/air mixture that is sent to the engine. As the driver presses on the gas pedal, the valve opens and allows more of the mixture to enter the engine, giving a larger explosion and therefore more power.

That's how it's down on older vehicles. New cars have **fuel injectors**, instead of carburetors, to mix the air and fuel together and then inject this mixture into the engine. Fuel injectors perform basically the same function of the carburetor but allow more control over the exact mixture and the amount of fuel injected into the engine. These devices help reduce exhaust emissions by delivering the exact amount of fuel and air needed and improve the efficiency of the car.

Sometimes, gasoline in the fuel line will vaporize, either because it is too hot, or because the pressure drops too low. The vapor does not flow the same way as liquid fuel, causing the fuel to get stuck in the line. This situation is called **vapor lock**. This is a fairly rare condition with today's more efficient vehicles.

Now the fuel enters the cylinder. In order for the fuel to ignite once and push on the piston, the piston has to go through two complete up and down cycles. This type of engine is referred to as a **four-stroke engine**. Here's how it works:

1. The intake valve opens on the top of the cylinder while the piston is brought to the bottom of its stroke by the crankshaft. This motion draws the fuel/air mixture into the cylinder.
2. The intake valve closes tightly. This is called the intake stroke. The crankshaft then pushes up on the piston, compressing all of the air and fuel in the cylinder. The compression ratio is the common way to describe how much this gas is compressed. For example, if the amount of volume that the gas takes up is reduced to a quarter of what it was originally, then the compression ratio will be 4:1. Higher compression ratios are desired. This stroke is called the compression stroke.
3. The sparkplug ignites the fuel/air mixture. The hot, burning mixture wants to expand and pushes out in all directions from inside the cylinder. The only part of the cylinder that can move is the piston. Consequently, the piston is pushed all the way down to the bottom of the cylinder by this explosion. This part of the cycle—the part that actually turns the crankshaft—is called the power cycle. The power cycle provides all the necessary energy to continue the motion of the crankshaft.
4. The exhaust valve opens and the cylinder is pushed back up by the crankshaft, pushing all of the leftover gasses out to the exhaust system. This is called the exhaust stroke.

This cycle continues to run in all of the cylinders. The cylinders are timed in such a way that for each one of these strokes, one of the cylinders is on its power cycle and pushing the crankshaft for the other cylinders. At any moment in a four-cylinder vehicle, one of the cylinders is on the intake stroke, one is on compression, one is on power and one is on exhaust. This keeps the car running smoothly and allows the car to have continuous power. Cars generally run in the range of 600 to 4000 rotations of the crankshaft every minute. The number of revolutions is normally shown to the driver on a gauge on the dash called a **tachometer**. This is not the speed of the car, but only a gauge of how hard the engine is working.

The valves are controlled by a system of components called the **rocker arm** and **camshaft**. The camshaft is driven by the **timing belt**, a special belt with bumps like gear teeth. The camshaft rotates at half the speed of the crankshaft, because the valves need to open and close only one time for each two revolutions of the crankshaft.

The timing belts should be visually inspected every time the oil is changed on the vehicle. If a belt appears to be cracking, or some of the teeth are starting to wear down, it should be replaced. If a timing belt breaks during travel, the engine could be severely damaged. Remember that the timing belt is the link responsible for opening and closing the valves at exactly the right time. If the valves can't open and close, then the fuel can't enter or leave the engine.

A **cam** is a device that attaches to a shaft like a gear, except that, unlike a gear, the cam is not normally connected through the center like a gear and has no teeth. As the **camshaft** turns, the cams push a rod up and down. The rod is connected to a rocker arm that works like a teeter-totter to push the top of the valve down. This allows the valve to open and close when needed. If the valves are not timed to open and close at precisely the right time, then the engine will stop working. The valves are spring-loaded so that they will seal tightly in the closed position.

After the burned fuel leaves the engine through the exhaust valve, it enters the **exhaust system**. The exhaust system consists of everything necessary to take the spent fuel, reduce the pollutants from the gasses, and expel the gas back into the atmosphere. If we lived in a perfect world, all of the exhaust gasses coming from the combustion of the fuel would be carbon dioxide and water vapor. However, three major pollutants—carbon monoxide, nitrogen oxides, and hydrocarbons—are also expelled. Hydrocarbons come from unburned molecules of gasoline. If the fuel/air mixture is rich, then carbon monoxide will be formed instead of carbon dioxide. The nitrogen oxides will form because the source of the oxygen, the atmosphere, is mainly nitrogen and the temperatures at which the hydrocarbons burn is very high. The exhaust gasses leave the cylinders and enter an exhaust manifold, or a chamber, that connects to all of the cylinders. Some of the gasses are then taken back to the air intake and injected back into the fuel air mixture to help to bring down the temperature of the explosion and reduce nitrogen oxides. From the manifold, the gasses travel through a device called the catalytic converter, which contains very small pellets made of a special material that allows the unused hydrocarbons and the carbon monoxide to continue to oxidize at lower temperatures. Upon leaving the catalytic converter, the gasses are almost completely carbon dioxide and water vapor. They then travel through the muffler, which helps deaden the noise of the exhaust, and out of the car.

Another common source of hydrocarbons is from vaporizing fuel in the gas tank or from leftover hydrocarbons in the catalytic converter after the car has been turned off. In order to keep these vapors from escaping into the atmosphere, vent tubes are connected to both devices and to a container filled with charcoal. The charcoal absorbs the hydrocarbon vapors and holds them until the car is started again and they are returned to the engine.

Other materials can also be left behind by the combustion process. It is common to have carbon deposits form in parts of the exhaust system and fuel lines. The carbon deposits can hamper air flow in the exhaust system, but generally, small deposits are not troublesome.

Cooling and Lubrication System

Because of the constant, though controlled, explosions of fuel and air, the temperature inside the engine gets very high—so high that, without a cooling system, the iron or aluminum in the engine would begin to melt! But the heat is reduced by a device that circulates water around the engine. This is similar to putting a cool cloth on the forehead of a fever-stricken child. The water in the cloth absorbs some of the heat, and then the cloth is re-cooled and placed back on the child. The system in the car is a little more complicated, though. Here's how it works:

The turning crankshaft turns a belt called the **fan belt** that connects to the fan and water pump. The **water pump** moves the water from the radiator at the front of the car and into channels, called water jackets, in the engine block. The channels go around the cylinders and the oil reservoir and then out the other side of the engine block. All of the water traveling around the cylinders picks up heat from the hot cylinders and carries it to a special **manifold** on top of the engine. When the coolant in the manifold reaches a certain temperature, a valve called the **thermostat** opens and allows the water to enter the top of the radiator. The **radiator** is simply a network of tubes that have air flowing around them. The fan that is connected to the fan belt helps draw cool air from the environment over the radiator to take heat from the water and carry it back into the atmosphere. When the water in the engine reaches a certain temperature, the thermostat will open again and the now-cooled water will be pushed back into the engine to be heated again.

Sometimes the thermostat will stick and not open, so that the hot water is not permitted to cool in the radiator. The water pump also tends to wear out and will sometimes fail. Both of these situations will result in the car's overheating. The car actually becomes so hot that the coolant trapped in the water jackets and manifold vaporizes and can blow through the tubes it is traveling through. The best thing to do when the car overheats is to pull over and allow it to cool. Consequently, if the fan belt breaks, the cooling system and the electrical generation system will also go down.

The **oil** that you put into the car is also part of the cooling and lubrication system. The oil keeps metal parts from rubbing on each other, creating friction and heat, and damaging components. The oil is pumped through a filter to remove impurities and then throughout the crankcase and camshaft to help lubricate the pistons, rods, cams, and bearings, by forming a thin film on the metal surfaces. The oil is then circulated back to the oil pan on the bottom of the car.

Oil can seep through various parts of the engine and into the combustion chamber. When this occurs, the engine is said to "burn oil." This often results in a blue cloud of smoke from the tailpipe and the need to refill the oil reservoir often. Oil can enter the combustion areas through the head gasket (which seals the engine head with the valves to the engine block) or through the piston rings.

Drive Train

The drive train is the portion of the car that takes the spinning crankshaft and uses it to spin the wheels. The drive train consists of the clutch, transmission, differential gear, axles, wheel bearings, rims, and tires. With the engine running, the flywheel is spinning at a constant rate. If we want to speed up the flywheel, we can depress the gas pedal and open the throttle valve to let more fuel and air into the cylinders. But just connecting the wheels to the crankshaft would allow the vehicle to move at only a small range of speeds. To give the car more speed and power variability, a **transmission** is inserted between the wheels and the engine. There are two main types of transmissions: manual and automatic. We will discuss manual transmissions first.

The **manual transmission** consists of a variety of gears that can be slid back and forth along several shafts and allow several possible arrangements and gear ratios. The gears and shafts convert the revolution rate of the incoming shaft to a new rate at the drive shaft. As we said previously, car engines work best under a limited range of rotation speeds. To keep the car engine working in this range and yet allow the wheels to travel at slower and faster ranges, we need to change the drive-shaft revolution rate.

When two **gears** mesh together, it is important to keep track of the number of teeth on each gear (see chapter 7 for more on this). Let's say that we have a gear with 36 teeth that's spinning in a complete circle one time every second. If we then connect another gear with 18 teeth, how much faster will the second gear be turning? Since the second gear has half as many teeth, it will be turning exactly twice as fast. Using this same idea, we can slide into different gears to allow a different gear ratio and therefore different speeds for the drive shaft.

But, if we were to simply take the car out of one gear and put it in another, we would get a loud noise as the gears traveling at different speeds try to connect and grind into each other. The manual clutch provides a way to connect the two shafts turning at different speeds.

The manual clutch consists of three plates, all aligned with the drive shaft. The plate that is connected to the crankshaft is the **flywheel**. A separate shaft is lined up with the crankshaft and acts as the incoming shaft for the transmission. This shaft has a plate called the **pressure plate** mounted to it. A spring-loaded plate called the **clutch plate** is in between the two. The spring holds the clutch plate tightly between the pressure plate and the flywheel so that all three plates turn together. When the clutch pedal is depressed in the car, the clutch plate is pulled away from the flywheel, disengaging the pressure plate and the drive shaft. This then allows the operator to shift the transmission into a new gear. After the gears have been changed, the operator lifts his or her foot off the clutch pedal, bringing the spinning flywheel and the stationary pressure plate back into contact. By bringing the plates slowly together, the pressure plate can speed up until it is traveling the same speed as the flywheel and the car is in the next gear.

The **automatic transmission** and **torque converter** operate the same way, with slightly different components. The automatic transmission uses a system of planetary gears, which mesh on the inside of the gears as well as the outside. By holding some of the gears or gear housings stationary and allowing others to turn, the car can achieve several different gear ratios. Instead of three plates, as in the manual clutch, the automatic has what looks like three fans. All three of the fans are housed inside a container of hydraulic fluid, which is necessary for the operation of the torque converter. The fan that is connected to the crankshaft is called the pump. The pump is always spinning at the same rate as the crankshaft. When the car is put into gear, the pump starts to spin the fluid inside the transmission in one direction. The second fan, called the stator, helps the fluid to circulate back to the pump, spinning in the same direction that it left and adding to the torque of the pump. A third fan, the turbine, is spun around by the motion of the fluid. A short while after engaging, the pump, turbine, and stator will all be turning at the same rate and therefore the two shafts will be turning at the same rate.

After leaving the transmission, the drive shaft enters another grouping of gears called the **differential gear**. The differential gear sits at the junction between the axle and the drive shaft. As a car turns a corner, the wheels on the outside of the corner will have to travel a slightly longer distance than the wheels on the inside. That means that the outside wheel will need to travel a little faster than the inside wheel to keep up around the corner. The differential gear allows one wheel to turn slower than the other one but still maintain the same average rotation speed for both of the axle halves. It is important to note that the total amount of power going to the wheels does not change, just the distribution. During straight travel, the differential gear allows both of the wheels to turn at the same rate.

The differential gear is attached to the **axles** and the axles to the **wheels**. The wheels consist of wheel bearings, a hub, a rim, and a tire. The wheel bearings allow the wheel to attach to the car chassis and still be able to spin. The **rim** and the **tire** form an airtight seal that allows the tires to be filled and maintain air pressure. Note that this is different from how a bike tire is inflated. A bike tire affixes to the rim in much the same manner, but, unlike a car tire, the bike tire has a separate tube to hold the air.

The tires should always be inflated to the proper air pressure to ensure that the car is getting good traction. When inflated properly, the tire should be bulging slightly at the bottom. If the tire is under inflated, the outsides of the tire will wear quicker than the insides. If the tire is over inflated, the middle part of the tire will wear and the tread will still be good on the outsides. In both cases, the tires will have to be replaced.

Brakes

The car needs to move forward, but it's just as important for the car to stop. There are two types of brakes that help cars to slow down and stop: **disc brakes** and **drum brakes**. Normally, automobiles have disc brakes on the front wheels and drum brakes on the back. Disc brakes have a metal disc, or rotor, connected to the wheel. The rotor spins with the wheel in between two small arms called **calipers**, similar to brakes on a bicycle. On the surface of each side of the calipers are the **brake pads**. Drum brakes have a bowl, or **drum**, attached to the wheel. Two half-circle **brake shoes** fit inside the drum and are attached to two springs to keep them from touching the drum.

When a brake pedal is depressed, it causes brake fluid in a device called the master cylinder to build up pressure. This pressurized brake fluid then travels down hoses, or **brake lines,** to the brakes. On disc brakes, the fluid squeezes the calipers together around the rotor, creating friction and slowing the car. On drum brakes, the fluid causes the shoes to push outward against the drum and create the friction to slow the car. Both types of brakes are spring loaded to disengage the rotor or the drum when the pedal is released. As the brake pedal is pushed harder, more pressure builds up in the brake lines and the wheels stop faster. Over time, the surface of the brake shoes gradually rubs away and the brakes will need to be replaced.

On occasion, the brake lines fail. A few decades ago, the result would be that the car would have no brakes but the parking brake. But cars today have a dual action piston in the master cylinder. If one of the sides fails, the other will be able to provide the friction to stop the vehicle safely. The system will still need to be repaired or replaced afterwards, but that's certainly better than having the car sail uncontrolled down a hill!

Steering

The car's front wheels are connected to a **steering bar** attached to the axle. The steering bar is connected to a **tie rod** that in turn is attached to a flat gear called the **rack**. The teeth of the rack are designed to fit with the teeth on a round gear called the **pinion**. The pinion is attached to the bar that goes through the center of the steering wheel. The pinion is held in place and the rack is allowed to move from side to side. When the steering wheel is turned, the pinion begins to turn and shuttles the rack to one side. This action pulls the back part of the inside wheel toward the center of the car and pushes the back of the outside wheel away from the car.

Vehicles with **power steering** usually have a similar set-up, except that they use hydraulic fluid pumped into an actuator on the steering rod to help to move the bar to the side.

Electrical System

Almost all the systems a car are in one way connected to the electrical system. In order for anything on the vehicle to operate, it needs electrical power. Initially, a battery supplies the electric power. When a key is turned in the ignition switch, a connection is made in the circuit for the starter. The **starter** is an electric motor mounted to the engine block that provides enough torque to the crankshaft so that it starts to turn. At the same time, the other systems in the car start up and supply the engine with fuel and air to allow the engine to run on its own. After the car is started, the starter is not needed.

In the early 20th century, the starter was a hand crank on the front of the car.

The **sparkplugs** in the cylinders need electricity to fire and ignite the gasses to move the pistons. Spark plugs are essentially two metal leads that stick into the cylinders. The metal leads are separated by a small gap. If enough electrical charge builds up across the gap, the electricity will arc across the gap. This arc ignites the fuel air mixture in the cylinder.

While the car is running, the battery does not supply the car with the necessary energy it needs to continue to run. Instead, a device called an **alternator** is used. An alternator is basically a motor that runs in reverse; instead of taking in power and using it to turn a shaft, the alternator takes a spinning shaft (turned by the fan belt on the engine) and produces electricity from it. The electricity travels to a device called a **voltage regulator** and is used to recharge the battery and run other systems in the car. Some of the electricity goes into the **distributor**, which is responsible for sending the right amount of electricity to each sparkplug at the right time, to get the cylinders to fire in the correct sequence. Of course, some of the electricity also goes to the lights, radio, air conditioner, and other systems in the car.

PROBLEM DIAGNOSIS

The auto portion of this section has about 5 to 7 questions asking you to diagnose a vehicle problem by analyzing a few symptoms. Here are some tips to help you answer these questions:

1. Does the question tell you specifically what system is malfunctioning? If so, then you can eliminate all of the answers that have nothing to do with that system.

2. Is the symptom associated with a particular part or system that has not been specified? Once again, you can eliminate the components or answers that are not related to that part or system. Keep in mind that sometimes a malfunction with one part of a system has an impact on another part later in the system or even on another system, so be careful.

3. After you've eliminated answer choices that clearly could not be right, for each answer choice you have left, trace the problem given through the system and try to think what the result might be. Does it match the symptom given in the question? If so, you have found the right answer. You will probably not have time to look at all of the answer choices carefully following this procedure, so be sure to use steps 1 and 2 to eliminate impossible answer choices first.

4. If you feel that you are spending an excessive amount of time and you still can't decide between two or more answer choices, take a guess and move on. Even by eliminating one answer choice, you are improving your chances of answering the question correctly.

7

MECHANICAL
COMPREHENSION

INTRODUCTION TO MECHANICAL COMPREHENSION

This section of the ASVAB contains questions that will test your ability to apply logic to the physical world. The word "mechanical" in the title refers to simple machines such as pulleys and levers, rather than to complex devices such as automobiles. Most of the questions should be familiar to those who have taken high school physics. But if you have never taken a physics course, don't despair; most of the problems in this section are based upon a few general rules that we will cover in this chapter. If you learn these rules and apply them with creativity throughout the section you should be able to survive this portion of the exam.

FORCE

A force is something that changes the motion of an object. In baseball, the pitcher applies a large force to the ball when he throws it towards the plate. After the ball is released, the force of wind resistance will slow the ball down and may cause it to change direction (if the pitcher threw a curveball). Finally, if the batter manages to connect with the ball then the bat will apply a very large force that will change both the direction and the speed of the ball and send it into the field of play.

The forces in the above example originate from very different sources, and yet they have two things in common: direction and size. Both of these features are crucial. The size of a force determines how much effect it will have on the object to which it is applied. The size of a force is usually measured in pounds. (Your weight is actually the amount of force that gravity exerts upon your body.)

The direction of a force determines the direction in which the motion of the object will change. For example, the brakes of an automobile produce a force that points in the opposite direction of the car's motion. This force slows the car down and brings it to a halt. Direction can be measured in degrees (like an angle), but for the purposes of the ASVAB, you will usually only need to pay attention to the relationship that a force has with other forces in the problem. Are they in the same direction, opposite directions, or perpendicular (at right angles) to each other? When two forces act in the same direction then you should add their sizes together. When forces act in opposite directions, you should subtract the size of the smaller force from the size of the larger. When forces act in perpendicular directions, the resulting force will be diagonal to both of them. Imagine two dogs wrestling over a bone. If both dogs pull on the bone with the same amount of force, but in opposite directions, the bone (and the dogs) will remain stationary. If one of the dogs exerts a larger force than the other then both the bone (and the other dog) will move toward the stronger canine. Now imagine that their owner is taking them both for a run on their leashes at the same time. If the dogs are both directly in front of the owner, they will exert a force in the same direction along their leashes and will pull her along with twice the force that a single dog would apply.

Let's take a look at an example force problem to illustrate these ideas:

1. The ropes attached to the girder can each support a maximum of 200 lbs. without snapping. What is the largest weight that the girder can be without breaking a rope?

   A.   100 lbs.
   B.   200 lbs.
   C.   400 lbs.
   D.   800 lbs.

   To solve this problem, let's make a list of the forces that act on the girder. There are two ropes, and they both act in the "up" direction. The only other force that acts on the girder is gravity, and it points "down." The girder is not moving, so the up forces should total to the same size as the down force. Each rope can support 200 lbs., so the total up force is 400 lbs. (remember—"lbs." is the abbreviation for "pounds"). The force of gravity (which is the same thing as the weight of the girder) must also be 400 lbs. The answer is C.

   Let's try another force problem:

180 lbs.

20 lbs.

2. How much weight must the man on the ground support?

   A.   90 lbs.
   B.   100 lbs.
   C.   180 lbs.
   D.   200 lbs.

Again, let's make a list of the forces in the problem. This time there are two forces that push downward, the weight of the plank and the weight of the man. We need to add these two weights together, for a total downward force of 180 lbs. + 20 lbs. = 200 lbs. That means that we need to have a total of 200 lbs. pushing upwards. There are two up forces in this picture. The stepladder pushes up on the left side of the plank and the man pushes up on the right side of the plank. The painter stands in the exact center of the plank, so the man and the stepladder must exert the exact same upward force. That means that we need to divide the total up force by 2 in order to figure out how much weight the man on the ground must support: 200 lbs. ÷ 2 = 100 lbs. The answer is B.

Remember, when you're solving a force problem, follow these steps:

- Make a list of the forces in each direction.

- Add together all the forces that point in the **same** direction.

- Make sure to set the totals of the forces that point in **opposite** directions equal to each other (i.e., be sure to set the total up force equal to the total down force, and the total right force equal to the total left force).

- Use this information to find the missing force.

SIMPLE MACHINES

There are many situations in the modern world where it is difficult or impossible to complete a job with muscle power alone. Imagine a worker who has to lift an 800-pound crate onto a loading dock that's 6 feet above the ground. This crate far exceeds the weight that a normal person can lift. However, the worker can use a simple machine to make the task much easier. He could roll the crate up a ramp or lift it with a system of pulleys. In both cases, the force that the worker must exert in order to complete the job is reduced to a manageable fraction of the total weight of the crate.

It is often possible to solve a problem that involves a simple machine with the techniques that we just learned for force problems. Let's look at a few sample questions:

3. How much force must the person exert on the rope in order to lift the safe?

    A.   50 lbs.

    B.   100 lbs.

    C.   150 lbs.

    D.   200 lbs.

Let's take a look at the forces that act on the safe. Gravity pulls downward on the safe with 200 lbs. of force. The rope pulls upward on the safe. That's it; there are no other forces that act directly upon the safe. That means that the force of the rope must be 200 lbs., exactly equal to the force of gravity. How does this help us to figure out the force with which the person must yank on the rope? The answer is that the force that is transmitted through a rope must be the same everywhere. If the rope pulls up on the safe with 200 lbs. then it must also pull on the person with 200 lbs. of force. That means that the person must exert a force of 200 lbs. in order to lift the safe. The answer is D.

You may have noticed that this pulley did not reduce the force needed to lift the safe. When you use a single pulley that does not move (for instance, a pulley that is attached to the ceiling) then the force needed to lift the load does not change. The only advantage to be gained from this type of pulley arrangement is that you can change the direction of the force that you must apply. In the above example the pulley allows the person to pull downward on the rope. That means that he can use his own weight to help to lift the safe.

Now let's look at a pulley arrangement that really does reduce the force that is needed to lift a load:

200 lbs.

4. How much force must the person exert in order to lift the safe?

    A. 50 lbs.
    B. 100 lbs.
    C. 150 lbs.
    D. 200 lbs.

We use the same technique to answer this question. There is one downward force in this problem: the 200-pound force of gravity. However, now there are two up forces, because the rope pulls upward on both sides of the pulley. Remember, the force transmitted through a rope is the same everywhere, so it must be the same on each side of the pulley. That means that the force in the rope is 200 lbs. ÷ 2 = 100 lbs. The rope transmits this same force back to the person, so he must pull with 100 lbs. of force in order to lift the safe. The answer is B.

MECHANICAL ADVANTAGE

In the last problem we discovered that a system of two pulleys can multiply the force that is applied to a load by a factor of two. This multiplication of force is called "mechanical advantage." The mechanical advantage of a simple machine is equal to the amount that the applied force is multiplied by. For example:

300 lbs.

5. The lever in the above picture provides a mechanical advantage of three. What is the minimum amount that the person must weigh in order to successfully lift the boulder?

   A.   100 lbs.

   B.   300 lbs.

   C.   900 lbs.

   D.   It is impossible to lift the boulder in this fashion.

In this problem, it is stated that the mechanical advantage is 3. That means that the lever applies to the boulder a force equal to three times the person's weight. Since we would need to apply at least 300 lbs. to the boulder in order to lift it, the person must weigh at least 300 lbs. ÷ 3 = 100 lbs. The answer is A.

MECHANICAL DISADVANTAGE

So far we have learned that a simple machine can amplify a person's strength and allow him or her to lift a very heavy load. Alas, nothing in life is free, so along with mechanical advantage there must be a compensating disadvantage. The disadvantage is that the force must be applied over a larger distance. For example, take another look at the pulley arrangement in problem number 4. For every foot that the safe is lifted the rope must also move a foot on *both* sides of the pulley. This means that the person on the other end of the rope must pull two feet of rope for every one foot that the safe is lifted. The disadvantage always multiplies the distance by the same amount that the advantage multiplies the force. Fortunately for test takers, we can turn the mechanical disadvantage into a test taking strategy…

150 lbs.

4' feet

12' feet

6. How much force is needed to push the piano up the ramp?

   A.   30 lbs.
   B.   50 lbs.
   C.   60 lbs.
   D.   100 lbs.

For this problem, we'd have trouble using the force technique that we learned in the last section, because the force that the person applies to the piano is not straight up. Therefore, we can't set it equal to the gravity, the downward force, which is the weight of the piano. It's much easier to look at the mechanical disadvantage instead. The purpose of the ramp is to lift the piano four feet above the ground. In order to travel four feet upward the person must push the piano along twelve feet of ramp. This means that the mechanical disadvantage is three ($12 \div 4 = 3$). The disadvantage and the advantage are always the same number, so the person only needs to push with one third of the weight of the piano in order to move it up the ramp. That means that the force needed is 150 lbs. $\div 3 = 50$ lbs. The answer is B.

LEVERS

A lever is a simple machine that utilizes a length of stiff material that is braced against an object that does not move in order to create mechanical advantage. The immovable object is called the "fulcrum." The mechanical advantage is the ratio of the distance from the fulcrum to the applied force over the distance from the fulcrum to the load (remember, you learned about ratios in chapter 2). If this sounds complicated; don't worry, we will look at several examples to be certain that you understand.

Figure not drawn to scale

7. At what distance from the fulcrum should the adult sit in order to perfectly balance the seesaw?

   A. 3 feet
   B. 4.5 feet
   C. 6 feet
   D. 9 feet

The seesaw in this problem acts like a lever. The fulcrum is the triangle that the seesaw is balanced on. The child is one-third the weight of the adult, so the lever needs to supply the child with a mechanical advantage of 3. The mechanical advantage is the distance from the fulcrum to the child (6 feet) divided by the distance from the fulcrum to the adult (unknown). We can write this as an equation: 6 ÷ ? = 2. We can rearrange this equation so that the question mark is on the other side of the equal sign: 6 ÷ 2 = ?. Six divided by 2 is 3, so the adult must sit three feet from the fulcrum in order to perfectly balance the seesaw. That's answer A!

> **Quick Tip!**
>
> To identify the fulcrum in a lever problem, look for the part of the lever that will never move. That's where the fulcrum is.

Let's look at another problem:

1 ft.   3 ft.

8. 90 pounds of force is required to tip the barrel. How much force must the worker apply to the lever?

    A.   10 pounds

    B.   30 pounds

    C.   45 pounds

    D.   60 pounds

    The mechanical advantage of this lever is the distance from the fulcrum to the worker (3 feet) divided by the distance from the fulcrum to the barrel (1 foot). Three divided by 1 is 3. The worker needs to apply one-third of 90 pounds to his end of the lever in order to tip the barrel. One-third of 90 is 30, so the answer is B.

    Sometimes the load and the force are both on the same side of the fulcrum. Let's look at another problem to see how this works…

1 in.

6 in.

9. If the force required to crack a walnut without using any tool is 30 pounds, how much force must be applied to the nutcracker in the diagram in order the crack the walnut?

    A.   5 pounds

    B.   10 pounds

    C.   30 pounds

    D.   It's too tough a nut to crack

To solve this problem we must first locate the fulcrum. Remember, the fulcrum is the place where the lever does not move. In this case it's at the hinge. The walnut is 1 inch from the hinge and the hand is 6 inches from the hinge. That means that the mechanical advantage is 6 ÷ 1 = 6. We need to apply one-sixth of 30 pounds to the nutcracker in order to crack the walnut. Thirty divided by 6 is 5, so the answer is A.

GEARS

A gear is a wheel with "teeth" along its outside. There's a lot of variety in the shapes and sizes of gear teeth, but in the end they all do the same thing: turn other gears. To calculate the mechanical advantage of a set of gears, count the teeth on each gear. Divide the number of teeth on the gear that is being turned by the number of teeth on the gear that is doing the turning. That's the mechanical advantage. Often, the mechanical advantage for a gear is smaller than one.

10. What is the theoretical mechanical advantage conferred by the gears of this bicycle?

   A. $-\dfrac{1}{2}$

   B. 1

   C. 2

   D. There is no mechanical advantage; the gear system is just a convenient way to transmit muscle power into forward motion.

In this problem, the big gear is turning the small gear. We have to put the number of teeth on the small gear into the numerator (the top number) of our ratio and the number of teeth on the big gear into the denominator (the bottom number). That gives us $\dfrac{10}{20}$, which reduces down to $\dfrac{1}{2}$. The answer is A.

What is the point of using a gear that *increases* the amount of force that we put into it? Remember the compensating disadvantage that goes with mechanical advantage. A simple machine that increases force also reduces distance. In problem 4 we had to pull the rope 2 feet to lift the safe 1 foot. Well, when the mechanical advantage is less than one, the distance is increased. In the bicycle gear above, the small gear turns twice every time the big gear turns once. It's twice as hard to turn, but it goes twice as fast.

Here's another problem where you will need to count teeth...

12 teeth

9 teeth

Gear A

Gear B

11. How many times will gear A turn if gear B turns 20 times?

    A.   9 times

    B.   12 times

    C.   15 times

    D.   20 times

The important concept here is that the teeth of gear A move through the teeth of gear B on a one-for-one basis. We can eliminate answer D immediately, because gear B will only move 9 teeth on gear A per rotation, and that is not enough to turn gear A all the way around. All of the other answer choices are smaller than the number of rotations for gear B, so we can't eliminate any of them yet. Twenty rotations of gear B move $20 \times 9 = 180$ teeth on gear A. Gear A rotates once for every 12 teeth moved, so if we divide 180 by 12 we will find our answer. Twelve goes into 180 15 times, so the answer is C.

There are a few types of gear problems that don't force you to count teeth. For instance, you may need to figure out which direction a gear rotates. Usually, you can solve a problem like this with two simple rules: When 2 gears touch they rotate in opposite directions; when two gears are connected by a chain or a belt, they rotate in the same direction.

12. If gear A rotates clockwise, what direction does gear C rotate?

    A. Clockwise

    B. Counterclockwise

    C. Gear C does not rotate

    D. It is impossible for gear A to rotate clockwise.

Gear A turns gear B, which in turn will then turn gear C, so answers C and D are incorrect. Gear A and B rotate in opposite directions, so B turns counterclockwise. B and C also rotate in opposite directions, so gear C has to rotate clockwise. That means that the answer is A.

There are two more rules that you will need to remember when you tackle a gear problem (actually, these rules apply to *anything* that rotates):

- Two points on the same gear or disk will always rotate at the same rate.
- A point near the outside of a disk will move with a faster linear speed than a point near the center of a disk

Be careful here. If the question asks for *rate of rotation*, you need to use the first rule; if it asks use for the *speed of a point*, you need to use the second. Here are a few examples:

13. Which point on the above bicycle wheel will move at the highest rate of rotation?

    A. point 1

    B. point 2

    C. point 3

    D. They all move at the same rate of rotation.

This is a trick question. All three points are on the same disk, so they all move at the same rate of rotation. The answer is D.

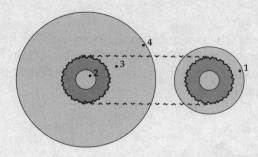

14. The small disk rotates in the clockwise direction at a constant rate. Which of the following is true?

A.   Point 2 rotates in the clockwise direction and has a higher linear speed than point 1.

B.   Point 3 rotates in the counterclockwise direction with the same linear speed as point 1.

C.   Point 4 rotates in the clockwise direction with a higher linear speed than point 1.

D.   Point 4 rotates in the counterclockwise direction with a higher linear speed than point 1.

There are a lot of details to sift through in this problem, so let's look for something simple to start with. The two disks are connected with a chain, so they both have to rotate in the same direction. That means that all of the points move clockwise. We immediately eliminate answers B and D because they give a counterclockwise rotation. At this point, we could guess and have a 50 percent chance of success! However, we can do better than that. The gears that turn these disks are the same size, so the two disks have to move at the same rate of rotation. That means that we can use the second of the two rules above to figure out the relationship between the linear speeds of points 1, 2, and 4. Point 2 is closer to the center of its disk than point 1 is, so it has to move more slowly. Point 4 is further away, so it moves more quickly. Answer choice A is incorrect, because it claims that 2 moves faster than 1. That leaves answer choice D. Point 4 does indeed move more quickly than point 1.

MOMENTUM

Momentum is a subject that most people understand without really knowing why. You already know what will happen if a huge truck collides head on with a compact car: the car will be crushed and the truck will continue to move straight ahead at almost the same speed that it had before the collision. You also know that if two football players of the same size and speed collide head-on they will both stop at the point of collision. And you know that a small bullet can knock down a large man. These examples all illustrate the concept of momentum.

Momentum is a combination of weight and speed. A bullet can knock a man down, even though it is very light, because it has a very high speed. The two football players had the same weight and speed, so they both stopped at the point of collision. The truck kept moving after the collision because it is much more massive than a compact car.

> **Definition of Momentum:**
>
> Technically, momentum is mass times velocity. For the ASVAB, just multiply the weight of the object by its speed and you'll have momentum. (Note: "weight times speed" is not actually the correct way to calculate momentum, but it will allow you to solve any momentum problem that you might encounter on the ASVAB, and that is all that we really care about here.)

Collision problems

There are two types of problems where momentum is important. The first involves collisions. When two objects collide head on and stick together, they will both move in the direction that the object with the larger momentum was moving in before the collision. If they both have the same momentum then they will stop. Here is an example:

Skater A

100 lbs.

5 mph

Skater B

80 lbs.

10 mph

16. Skater A and B will collide and stick together. After the collision which of the following is true?

   A. Both skaters stop at the point of impact.
   B. The skaters will move to the left at a speed greater than 10 mph.
   C. The skaters will move to the right at a speed less than 5 mph.
   D. The skaters will move to the left at a speed less than 10 mph.

The first thing we need to do here is calculate the momentum of each skater. The momentum of skater A is $100 \times 5 = 500$. The momentum of skater B is $80 \times 10 = 800$. That means that skater B has a larger momentum. We can immediately eliminate answer A, because the two skaters will only stop if they have the same momentum. We can also eliminate answer C, because they will only move to the right if the momentum of skater A is larger than the momentum of skater B. Let's take a closer look at answers B and D. We don't know how to calculate the speed of the skaters after the collision, but we *do* know that you need to exert a force on something in order to speed it up. There are no forces acting to the left on skater B, so there is no way that skater B will ever skate faster than 10 mph. That means that answer B is wrong, so the answer must be D.

Let's try another one:

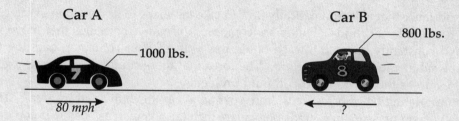

Car A

Car B

1000 lbs.

800 lbs.

80 mph

?

17. How fast must car B travel in order for both cars to come to a complete stop when they collide?

   A.   60 mph
   B.   80 mph
   C.   100 mph
   D.   120 mph

   In this problem we know both the speed and the weight of car A, so let's calculate its momentum: $80 \times 1000 = 80000$. Car B needs to have exactly the same momentum in order to bring the two cars both to a complete stop in the collision. To find car B's speed we must divide 80000 by car B's weight. $80000 \div 800 = 100$, so car B has to go 100 mph. That's answer C.

"Push off" problems

The second type of momentum problem features two objects starting from rest and then pushing off each other. This is the exact opposite of the case where two objects collide and stop, so both objects need to have the same momentum after they push off. Here is an example:

150 lbs.

200 lbs.

18. The person dives out of the boat with a speed of 4 feet per second. What is the speed of the boat after the jump?

   A.   3 feet per second
   B.   4 feet per second
   C.   5 feet per second
   D.   8 feet per second

   Both the boat and the person need to have the same momentum after the jump. The person has a speed of 4 and a weight of 150, so his momentum is 600. We know that the weight of the boat is 200, so the speed of the boat is $600 \div 200 = 3$. That's answer A.

FLUIDS AND PRESSURE

A fluid is a substance that will automatically flow to take the shape of its container. Water and air are two common examples of fluids. Fluids are composed of many molecules that move in random directions and constantly bump into each other, the walls of their container, and any object that happens to be submerged within the fluid. The force that these countless collisions exert is called pressure. Pressure is the key to almost all fluid problems.

The technical definition of pressure is "force per area" or "force divided by area." The ASVAB will usually give you pressure in pounds per square inch (also known as "psi"). If you ever need to translate a pressure into a force, just multiply it by an area. Here is an example:

19. The water pressure surrounding a submarine is 100 psi. Its porthole is 10 square inches. What is the force on the porthole?

    A. 10 pounds
    B. 100 pounds
    C. 1000 pounds
    D. The water exerts no force on the porthole.

A fluid will exert force on any object that is submerged within it, so get rid of answer D. To find the force on the porthole, we need to multiply the pressure of the water by the area of the porthole. That is 100 psi × 10 square inches = 1000 lbs. The answer is C.

LIQUIDS AND PIPES

The **flow rate** of a fluid through a pipe is the volume of liquid that passes through a cross-section of the pipe in a certain amount of time. If you need to calculate the flow rate of a fluid, then you should multiply the velocity of the fluid by the cross-sectional area of the pipe. Often you will just need to compare the flow rate in two different pipes. Here are three rules to keep in mind when you compare flow rates:

- If two pipes have the same area, then the pipe carrying liquid with the greatest velocity (or pressure) will have the highest flow rate.

- If two pipes carry liquids with the same velocity, then the pipe with the greatest area will have the highest flow rate.

- A single pipe has the same flow rate from beginning to end, even if the area of the pipe changes.

Here is an example:

20. Water flows into the pipe from the left at a speed of 8 feet per second. What is the speed of the water as it leaves the pipe from the right?

    A. 1 foot per second
    B. 2 feet per second
    C. 4 feet per second
    D. 8 feet per second

We have a single pipe here, so the flow going into it must be the same as the flow going out of it. The problem gives us enough information to calculate the flow rate through the pipe, but that's a bit complicated, so let's use process of elimination to get rid of a few answers first. The pipe is bigger on the right side than it is on the left side, so that means that for the flow rate to remain the same, the water *must* slow down. Answer D gives the same velocity that the water began with, so eliminate it. The area of a pipe is proportional to the square of its radius. The pipe is twice as big on the right side as it is on the left side, so the area of the right side must be four times the area of the left side. The speed of the water needs to slow down by a factor of four to compensate, so the answer is B.

The pressure of a liquid

Finally, let's talk about how the pressure of a liquid changes as it moves through a pipe. Take another look at the pipe in the last question. How do you think that the water pressure changes as the water moves from the thin part of the pipe to the thick part? Your intuition might tell you that the pressure is higher in the thin part of the pipe, because it is a "tighter squeeze" in there. Actually, that is incorrect; the pressure is lowest in the thin section of the pipe. This is because the speed of the water is high in the thin section of pipe and low in the thick section. Something has to slow the water down as it moves between the sections of pipe, and that something is pressure. Remember, pressure is the force that the molecules inside the fluid exert on everything that they come into contact with, including other parts of the water. As the water flows from the thin part of the pipe to the thick part, it encounters an increase in water pressure that slows it down.

GASES

A gas is a fluid, so it will obey all of the rules for fluids that we've already discussed. However, gases and liquids do have a few differences. A gas will expand to fill any available volume, whereas a liquid will always maintain a constant volume. For instance, a pint of water remains a pint of water regardless of whether it is in a large container or a small container. But a pint of a gas will expand to fill an entire room if you remove the lid of the container that holds it.

The ASVAB may ask you questions about the volume, pressure, or temperature of a gas under many different circumstances. Here is a list of rules that gases follow:

- If the volume of a gas increases, then its pressure will decrease (and vice versa).

- If the temperature of a gas increases, then its pressure will increase (and vice versa).

- If the amount of gas inside a container increases, then the pressure will increase.

- If a gas inside a container has a greater pressure than the air outside the container, the gas will apply a force to the inside of the container, causing it to expand (if the container is too weak to withstand the force). Likewise, if the pressure of the air outside the container is greater, the air will apply a force to the outside of the container, causing it to shrink (again, if the container is too weak to withstand the force). If the pressures inside and outside are the same, then the net force on the container is zero.

- A gas will flow from a region of high pressure into a region of low pressure. If there is no difference in pressure, then there will be no net movement of gas. That also means that if no gas is moving, then there must be no difference in pressure.

Let's take a look at a few problems:

21. A spark ignites the gas within this cylinder. Which of the following is the best explanation of what happens next?

    A.   The explosion increases the temperature of the gas. The increase in temperature causes the pressure to drop; and the piston moves inward.

    B.   The temperature inside the piston is increased dramatically by the ignition of the gas, and this in turn increases the pressure of the gas. The increased pressure forces the piston outward.

    C.   A reduction in the air pressure outside the piston causes the piston to move.

    D.   The force of the explosion causes the piston to move outward.

    Let's go through these options one at a time. Answer A claims that the pressure of the gas will be reduced after its temperature is increased. This violates rule number 2 up above, so let's eliminate answer A. Answer B says that the piston moves because the temperature of the gas increases the pressure inside of the chamber. Rule number 2 above tells us that the pressure of a gas will increase when its temperature increases, so this might be the correct answer. Answer C claims that the pressure outside the piston drops when the gas inside the piston ignites. This option is unlikely, because the spark inside of the piston has no direct impact upon the air outside of the piston. Let's discard answer C. Answer D claims that the "force" of the explosion causes the piston to move outward. It is certainly true that the explosion creates a force that causes the piston to move, but this is not a very informative answer. Answer choice B provides a much more detailed explanation of what this force is. Since we are looking for the best explanation of what happens inside the piston after the ignition, we should choose answer B.

Let's look at another problem:

Chamber A   Chamber B

Moveable partition

Rubber plug

22. Initially, both chambers in the canister contain the same amount of gas at the same temperature and pressure. Then the rubber plug is temporarily removed and half the gas in chamber B is allowed to escape. Which of the following is the best description of what happens after the plug is replaced?

A. The pressure of the gas in chamber B is reduced after the gas escapes. The partition will move to the right until the pressure in the two chambers equalizes.

B. The partition moves a little bit to the right. The pressure in the two chambers will not equalize, because they no longer contain the same amount of gas.

C. The pressure drop in chamber B causes the partition to move to the right. As the gas in chamber A expands, both its pressure and its temperature are reduced. The partition will stop moving when the pressure in both chambers is the same.

D. The pressure drop in chamber B causes the partition to move to the right. As the gas in chamber A expands, both its pressure and temperature are reduced. The partition will stop moving when the temperature in both chambers is the same.

We need to refer back to our list of rules for gases to solve this problem. Rule number 3 tells us that a gas will increase the size of its container as long as the pressure outside of the container is smaller than the pressure inside. This rule also tells us that there will be no expansion if the pressures are equal. Answer B claims that the partition will stop moving before the pressures equalize, so get rid of it. Answer D claims that the partition will stop moving when the temperatures in the two chambers are the same. This may or may not happen when the pressures are equal, so it does not have to be true. Eliminate answer D. Answers A and C both state that the partition will move until the pressures in the two chambers are equal. The only difference between these two answer choices is that answer C claims that the temperature in chamber A will drop as the partition moves. We need to combine rules 1 and 2 to evaluate this extra information. According to rule 1, the pressure will drop as the gas expands. According to rule number 2, the temperature will drop if the pressure drops. This implies that the temperature will drop when the gas expands. That means that answer C is better than answer A, because it provides a more detailed and accurate description of what happens inside the chambers.

8

ELECTRONICS
INFORMATION

INTRODUCTION TO ELECTRONICS INFORMATION

The Electronics Information section of the ASVAB asks questions about the construction and maintenance of simple electronic circuits. There is a fairly large variety in the type of questions you may see in this section, because electricity is used in a wide array of situations throughout the modern world. In this chapter, we will cover the basic ideas on the subject.

A SIMPLE CIRCUIT: THE LIGHT BULB

One of the most common circuits in use today is the circuit that allows you to turn a light bulb on and off. Below is a simplified version of this circuit. In this section we'll talk about how this circuit works.

CURRENT

When the switch is in the on position a countless number of tiny charged particles called electrons flow through the wires of the circuit. This flow of charges is called **current**. Charges flow through a circuit very much like water flows through a river. When people talk about the "size" of a current, they are referring to the amount of charge that flows through a wire during one second. The current is generally measured in **amperes** (this can be abbreviated as "amps" or as "A"). Current also has direction. Current always flows away from the positive terminal of a battery and towards the negative terminal (we'll talk about batteries later in this section). Finally, note that the most common symbol used to represent current in an equation is the letter "I."

AC/DC

Current comes in two different flavors, AC and DC. You need to know the difference between the two. The abbreviation AC means **alternating current**. An alternating current changes direction many times per second. The **frequency** of an AC current refers to the number of times the current changes directions back and forth per second.

DC means **direct current**. A direct current is a steady current that maintains the same direction and the same amperage as long as the circuit is operating. DC current is usually produced by a chemical reaction (such as in a battery) or by a special circuit called a **rectifier** that converts AC current into DC current.

VOLTAGE

Electric current does not flow by itself. Something has to force it to flow—**voltage**. Voltage forces current to flow in a circuit similar to the way gravity forces water to flow in a river. Water flows downhill away from high ground and toward low ground. Electric current flows away from high voltage and towards low voltage. Voltage is measured in units called **volts**, abbreviated simply as V. It is important to remember that volts are always measured as a difference in voltage between two places in a circuit. It makes no sense to say "the voltage at the filament of the bulb is 120V" unless you specify another point in the circuit that has a voltage that is 120V lower than the filament of the bulb. A more likely statement would be "the voltage *across* the filament of the bulb is 120V." This means that the voltage on one side of the filament is 120V higher than the voltage on the other side. This voltage difference is the force that impels the current to flow through the filament of the bulb. If both sides of the filament had a voltage of 120V above some other point in the circuit, there would be no voltage difference across the filament and no current would flow through it. Current and voltage vary in proportion to one another. This means that a large voltage will cause a large current, and a small voltage will cause a small current. We will discuss this further in the next section.

Voltage is sometimes called **electromotive force** (Emf), because it is the force that causes charges to move through a circuit.

Positive and Negative

Technically, electrons are negative particles, so they really flow away from low voltage and towards high voltage. However, circuit designers always pretend that the charged particles in the circuit are positive and that they move away from high voltage and towards low voltage. This practice began in the early days of circuit design when it was believed that the charges in the circuit really were positive. The circuit will work either way, so circuit designers (and ASVAB test writers) have chosen to stick with the accepted practice of pretending that the charges are positive.

RESISTANCE

When the current flows through the light bulb, the electrons bump into the filament of the bulb and lose energy. The electrical energy lost by the electrons becomes the light that is radiated forth from the bulb and the heat that causes the bulb to be hot to the touch. The characteristic of the filament that causes the electrons to lose energy is called "resistance." The current that flows through a circuit varies inversely with the amount of resistance found in the circuit. That means that if you take two circuits with the same voltage, the circuit with the larger resistance will have a smaller current than the circuit with the smaller resistance.

Resistance is measured in **ohms**. The abbreviation for ohms is the capital Greek letter omega (Ω). The letter R is used to represent resistance whenever it appears in an equation. Sometimes the sum of the resistances in all or part of a circuit is called the **load** on the circuit. In a circuit diagram, the symbol for a large resistance is a zigzag line (for instance, the zigzag in the light bulb above).

All parts of a circuit possess some resistance to the flow of current, even the wires that connect the circuit together. However, wires are usually made of material that has a small resistance, so that the current can be delivered to the parts of the circuit that need it (such as the filament of the light bulb) without losing any energy on the way. Materials that have a resistance low enough to be used in wires are called **conductors**. In a circuit diagram, conductors are drawn as straight lines.

Most conductors are metals. In the table below, we list several good electrical conductors. The numbers on this chart are not actually the resistance of the metals, because resistance depends on the shape and size of the metal as well as its composition. The details of how we got the numbers in this chart won't help you on the ASVAB, so for now just use them to compare the metals in the chart. A metal with a small number is a better conductor than a metal with a big number. You should try to memorize the order that the metals appear in the chart, but you won't have to memorize the numbers.

Substance		Specific Resistance (in microhms) at 20 degrees C
Silver	3	1.6
Copper	2	1.7
Gold	4	2.4
Aluminum	8	2.82
Carbon	5	3.9
Tungsten	1	5.5
Brass	0	7.0
Steel	9	15.
Nichrome	9	10

Materials with extremely large resistance are also important in circuits. They are called **insulators**. Insulators are used to prevent currents from entering places where they are not wanted. All of the conductors in a circuit should be insulated from each other so that the currents that they carry do not interfere with each other. It is also important to insulate wires, so that people can safely handle them while a current flows through them. Plastic makes an excellent insulator, because its resistance is high enough to stop all but the largest currents and because it is a flexible and resilient enough to coat a wire. Below is a table of insulators. Try to memorize the order that the insulators appear in the chart.

Good Insulators (starting with the most resistant)
Dry air
Glass
Mica
Ebonite
Gutta percha
Sealing wax
Silk
Dry paper
Porcelain
Oils
Slate

Some materials have a resistance that is too large to be used as a conductor, but too small to be used as an insulator. These materials are called semiconductors. These materials often have other unique characteristics that are very useful in a circuit. For instance, a diode is a device that is constructed from two different types of semiconductors. The properties of the two semiconductors work in such a way that the diode has a very large resistance if current flows in one direction and a very small resistance if current flows in the other direction. We will talk about some important applications of this device later. Many other useful electronic components are also constructed from semiconductors.

CIRCUIT ANALYSIS

Now that we know a bit about the terminology and materials that go into a circuit we need to learn how to analyze a circuit. In this section we will talk about a few of the theories that circuit designers use to build their circuits (and ASVAB designers use to build their questions).

OHM'S LAW

For this section of the ASVAB, you'll need to know the relationship between current, voltage, and resistance. This relationship is called **Ohm's law**. Here it is:

$$V = IR$$

Remember, the V represents voltage, the I represents current, and the R represents resistance. As always, the voltage in this equation is the voltage difference between two places. In this case, it is the voltage difference across something that has a resistance. Ohm's law tells us that the voltage across a resistance is equal to the resistance times the current that flows through it. If the resistance is increased then the voltage must also increase in order to maintain the same current. Alternatively, if the resistance in a circuit is increased, then the current will be decreased (this is the more likely scenario). Here is a sample problem to illustrate this point:

A fuse rated at 1 amp is used to protect a 6-volt DC voltage supply. Which of the following resistances could be placed in series with the fuse in order to guarantee normal operation of the motor?

A.   3 ohms
B.   6 ohms
C.   9 ohms
D.   12 ohms

First: you need to know a new definition: A **fuse** is a device that is designed to break when the current flowing through it exceeds a certain limit. When the fuse breaks, the current can no longer flow in the circuit. Don't worry about the DC voltage supply—we'll talk about that later, but we don't need to know what it is right now in order to solve the problem. Let's use Ohm's law to tell us how much resistance the circuit has when the current is 1 amp. First, let's start with the equation:

$$V = IR$$

The question asks about resistance, so we need to get R alone on one side of the equation. So we divide both sides by I. This gives us:

$$R = V/I$$

If V is 6 volts and I is 1 amp then R must be 6.0 ohms. Does this mean that the answer is B? Not at all! Remember that 1 amp is the point at which the fuse will break. If the resistance of this circuit is exactly 6 ohms, then the current will reach 1 amp and the fuse will blow. That means that we need to choose a larger resistance, to give us a current of less than 1 amp. The next largest resistance is 9 ohms, so the answer is C.

Voltage drop
Ohm's law tells us what the voltage difference is between the two sides of a device, if we know the value of its resistance and the value of the current through the device. This voltage difference is often called the **voltage drop** across the resistance.

POWER

Power is a measure of the amount of work that can be done in a certain amount of time. In an electric circuit, power is measured in **watts** (W). What we mean by "work" really depends upon the type of electric device that we are talking about. A light bulb with a large wattage rating will produce lots of light. A speaker with a large wattage rating can make a loud noise. Basically, more watts mean more light, heat, sound, or more of whatever else it is that the device is supposed to produce. More watts also mean a larger electric bill.

There are three equations that we can use the measure the power in a circuit:

$$P = IV$$
$$P = I^2R$$
$$P = V^2/R$$

All three of these equations will give the exact same answer, so you should pick the equation that has the variables you're given. Here is a sample question to illustrate the point:

How much current will a 60 watt light bulb draw if it is plugged into a 120 volt socket?

A.   0.25 A
B.   0.5 A
C.   0.75 A
D.   1.0 A

This problem involves power, voltage, and current, so the first equation is appropriate. Let's solve it for current:

$$I = P/V$$
$$I = 60/120$$
$$I = 0.5$$

The answer is B.

KIRCHOFF'S LAWS

There are two Kirchoff's laws, one for voltage and one for current. We aren't going to go into detail about what these laws are, but we do want you to know what how they are used for. Kirchoff's laws allow circuit designers to figure out how much current is going to go through each part of a circuit. Basically, if you know the resistance of each part of a circuit and you know the amount of voltage supplied to the circuit, then you can use Kirchoff's laws together with Ohm's law to calculate the current in each and every wire in the circuit.

Note that in a simple circuit all you need is Ohm's law. Kirchoff's laws are needed when you must analyze a circuit that has lots of complicated wiring. You will still use Ohm's law in a complicated circuit, but you must supplement it with Kirchoff's laws in order to fully calculate the current in each part of the circuit. Ohm's law is used in every circuit; Kirchoff's laws are generally just used in complicated circuits. Just knowing that information will help you on the ASVAB.

ELECTRONIC COMPONENTS

In this section we will talk about many of the common devices that are used to build circuits. We are going to tell you a little bit about how each device works and how it's used, and we'll show you the symbol that represents each device in a circuit schematic diagram. You'll need to memorize these symbols.

GROUND

In a circuit, the **ground** is the portion of the circuit that is at the lowest voltage. In a safe circuit, the ground is at the same voltage as the outside world, so that no current will flow through a person who touches the container that houses the circuit. Often, the ground level of a circuit is established by connecting a wire to a metal rod that has been driven into the earth (hence the name "ground").

DC VOLTAGE SOURCE

The source of DC voltage in a circuit is represented as parallel lines, with one line longer than the other. The long line represents the positive terminal of the DC source; the short line represents the negative terminal.

AC VOLTAGE SOURCE

An AC voltage supply is represented as a circle that contains a wavy line. The symbol does not tell you which terminal is positive or negative because the direction of the current (and the voltage) changes several times per second with an AC source.

RESISTORS

The resistor is the most common device in almost any circuit. A resistor is a device built to have a specific resistance to the flow of current. A resistor looks like a small cylinder with a wire protruding from each end. Generally, the manufacturer will paint colored bands around the resistor in a special code that indicates the level of resistance of the resistor. In a circuit diagram, a resistor is depicted as a zigzag line.

A resistor has so many uses that it would be impossible to list them all here. Resistors can be used to regulate the amount of current in a circuit (remember Ohm's law). They can also control the amount of voltage that reaches different parts of a circuit (Ohm's law again). And resistors are commonly used in conjunction with **capacitors** to create timing circuits and bandpass filters (more on these circuits later).

Often, there will be many resistors in a single circuit. The following schematic shows one of the basic ways to connect resistors in a circuit. This is called a **series** circuit. The same current goes through both resistors, so the total resistance that is faced by the current is the sum of the resistances of the two resistors. This relationship works for any number of resistors that are connected in series.

The next drawing shows another very common arrangement, called a **parallel** circuit. The current here has to split into two streams at point 1, so the current through the two resistors is not the same. However, the voltage across both resistors IS the same. The current will take the path of least resistance through the circuit, so most of it will flow through the smaller resistor. Some of it will still flow through the larger resistor, however, so the total resistance of the parallel circuit will actually be less than the resistance of the smaller resistor. Below are the equations for adding series and parallel resistors.

Series and Parallel Resistors

In **series**, add the resistance of each resistor to get the total resistance:

$$R = R_1 + R_2 + \dots R_n$$

In a **parallel** circuit, you take the *inverse* of each figure.

$$\frac{1}{R} = \frac{1}{R_1} + \frac{1}{R_2} + \dots \frac{1}{R_n}$$

You need to memorize both of these equations.

CAPACITORS

A capacitor is a device that stores charged particles. A capacitor is constructed from two pieces of metal that are placed very close to each other but not allowed to touch. When the two pieces of metal are connected to the positive and negative terminals of a battery, the negative charges are drained from the positive sheet and added to the negative sheet. The charge builds up until the voltage across the gap between the two sheets is the same as the voltage across the terminals of the battery. The amount of charge that the capacitor can store per volt is called its **capacitance**. Capacitance is measured in **farads** (f). The letter C is usually used to represent capacitors in equations. Here's the schematic symbol:

One application of the capacitor is in timing circuits, often called RC timing circuits. When a capacitor is placed in series with a resistor, the current that charges the capacitor must flow through the resistor first. The amount of time that it takes to charge or discharge the capacitor depends upon both the size of the capacitor and the size of the resistor. If the capacitance and resistance are chosen carefully, the time to charge can be tuned to any needed value. Some cars use RC timing circuits instead of a distributor to generate the timing for the spark plugs.

Another application of the capacitor is to block DC signals in an AC circuit. In a DC circuit, the capacitor will simply charge up until the voltage across the capacitor is equal to the voltage of the DC supply. The DC current will cease to flow once the capacitor has fully charged. An AC current switches directions repeatedly, so the capacitor will charge and discharge as the current changes directions. Thus, the AC current can pass through the capacitor, but the DC current cannot. Blocking capacitors of this sort are commonly used in stereos. If the blocking capacitor is connected in series to a resistor, then it will block low frequency AC signals as well.

INDUCTORS

An inductor is a wire that is coiled about some material. When a current flows through the inductor, a magnetic field is formed through the center of the coil. The magnetic field resists any change in the current through the coil, so the inductor acts like a resistor in an AC circuit, but does absolutely nothing in a DC circuit. The size of the resistance to current change in an inductor is called **inductance**, and it is measured in *henrys* (h). In an equation, the inductor is represented with an L. The schematic symbol for an inductor looks like a squiggly line.

One important application of the inductor is in the tuner of a radio. Here, an inductor is connected in parallel with a capacitor. The inductor in this circuit blocks high frequency currents, but allows low frequency currents to flow to ground. The capacitor, on the other hand, blocks low frequency currents and allows high frequency currents to flow to ground. There is a very small range of frequencies that cannot pass either the capacitor or the inductor, and these frequencies are passed through to the rest of the radio. The allowed frequency range depends upon the size of the capacitor and inductor. The inductance of the inductor can be changed to tune the radio.

Diodes

A diode is a device that has a very low resistance to current in one direction and a very high resistance to current in the other direction. Basically, a diode acts like a one-way door in a circuit. One application of this unusual property is in a **rectifier**, a device that transforms AC current into DC current. The diode is at the heart of this device, because it does not allow the AC current to pass when it travels in the wrong direction. The symbol for a diode is a triangle with a line through it. The arrow points in the direction that current is allowed to pass through the diode.

Transistors

The transistor is an odd-looking electronic component, because three wires protrude from it instead of two. This makes the transistor look like a tripod. The three legs are called the base, the collector, and the emitter. Very roughly, if the base is at a higher voltage than the collector, any current that flows into the base and out through the emitter is amplified by a fairly large amount. One of the applications of this property is in the amplifier of a radio. The transistor converts the faint radio waves receiving by the antenna into the large currents needed to drive loudspeakers.

PART III

ASVAB Practice Tests

9

Practice Test 1

PART 1

GENERAL SCIENCE

Time: 11 Minutes—25 Questions

1. The nervous system of the body is primarily concerned with

   A. respiration
   B. reproduction
   C. communication
   D. circulation

2. Chromosomes play an important role in

   A. genetics
   B. nutrition
   C. energy transformation
   D. ionization

3. Organisms that sustain their life cycles by producing their own food are

   A. decomposers
   B. producers
   C. scavengers
   D. consumers

4. The mass of an atom is determined by its number of

   A. protons and electrons
   B. electrons and neutrons
   C. isotopes
   D. protons and neutrons

5. Heating food on a stove is an example of

   A. conduction
   B. convection
   C. refraction
   D. reflection

6. The current geologic time period is

   A. Paleozoic
   B. Mesozoic
   C. Cenozoic
   D. Precambrian

7. The smallest planet in the solar system is

   A. Neptune
   B. Pluto
   C. Earth
   D. Mars

8. The chromosomes line up in the middle of the cell during which stage of mitosis?

   A. interphase
   B. anaphase
   C. telophase
   D. metaphase

9. Which is an example of a bryophyte?

   A. mushroom
   B. fern
   C. moss
   D. tree

10. Which biome is being described here: Distinct hot and cold seasons and lots of rain. Trees lose their leaves in the winter and re-grow them in the spring. A large variety of plants and animals are found.

    A. tundra
    B. deciduous forest
    C. taiga
    D. grassland

11. The outermost layer of the earth is called the

    A. crust
    B. mantle
    C. core
    D. photosphere

12. A warm air mass overtaking a cold air mass is called a

    A. cold front
    B. stationary front
    C. warm front
    D. occluded front

GO ON TO THE NEXT PAGE.

13. A solar eclipse occurs when the

    A. earth blocks the sun's light
    B. sun blocks the moon
    C. moon moves behind the sun
    D. moon blocks the sun's light

14. Pepsin is found in the

    A. muscles
    B. stomach
    C. large intestine
    D. spinal cord

15. A person who can donate blood to anybody has

    A. Type O blood
    B. Type AB blood
    C. Sickle cell anemia
    D. Red blood cells

16. A severe deficiency in which of these vitamins can lead to rickets?

    A. Vitamin B$_1$
    B. Vitamin C
    C. Vitamin D
    D. Vitamin K

17. Which organelle is responsible for digesting old organelles and foreign substances?

    A. centrioles
    B. lysosomes
    C. ribosomes
    D. vacuoles

18. Parent A has a genotype of Tt for a particular trait. Parent B has a genotype of tt. Which of the following is a list of the possible genotypes of the offspring of the two parents?

    A. TT, Tt, tt, tt
    B. TT, TT, Tt, Tt
    C. Tt, Tt, Tt, tt
    D. Tt, Tt, tt, tt

19. Plants make their own food through

    A. photosynthesis
    B. meiosis
    C. cell division
    D. respiration

20. The changing sound of a moving fire engine is the result of

    A. electromagnetism
    B. refraction
    C. momentum
    D. the Doppler effect

21. A substance with a pH of 4 is

    A. a base
    B. an acid
    C. a metal
    D. a molecule

22. Water that is 100 degrees Celsius is

    A. at the boiling point
    B. at the freezing point
    C. equal to 32 degrees Fahrenheit
    D. a solid

23. Which is in the correct order from largest to smallest?

    A. kingdom, order, class, genus, phylum
    B. phylum, class, species, order
    C. species, family, order, kingdom
    D. kingdom, class, family, species

24. The cerebrum, cerebellum, hypothalamus, and medulla are parts of the

    A. lymphatic system
    B. endocrine system
    C. brain
    D. heart

25. Plant and animals cells are similar in all of the following ways EXCEPT

    A. both have a nucleus
    B. both have a cell wall
    C. both have vacuoles
    D. both have lysosomes

STOP!
IF YOU FINISH BEFORE THE TIME IS UP, YOU MAY
CHECK OVER YOUR WORK ON THIS PART ONLY.

PART 2

ARITHMETIC REASONING

Time: 36 Minutes—30 Questions

1. Nelly buys a sweater that normally costs $60. It is on sale for 20% off. How much does she end up paying?

   A. $40
   B. $43
   C. $48
   D. $50

2. Mrs. Abbott bought 3 pounds, 8 ounces of hamburger for $3.43. What is the cost of 1 pound of hamburger?

   A. $0.98
   B. $0.99
   C. $1.00
   D. $1.02

3. The town of Orionville loves pets. Every family owns either a dog or a cat. If the ratio of dogs to cats is 4:6 and there are 100 pets total in the town, how many dogs and cats are there?

   A. 30 dogs, 70 cats
   B. 40 dogs, 60 cats
   C. 50 dogs, 50 cats
   D. 60 dogs, 40 cats

4. Tommy is selling chocolate bars for $1.00 and bags of jellybeans for $1.25. If he sold 40 bags of jellybeans and collected $76.00 total, how many chocolate bars did he sell?

   A. 26
   B. 28
   C. 31
   D. 32

5. Gladys opened a savings account 10 years ago with $100. The account earned 4% annually on the original $100 only. She has not deposited or withdrawn any money since opening the account. How much money is in the account now?

   A. $100
   B. $140
   C. $148
   D. $400

6. Alice can knit a scarf in 2 hours and 30 minutes. How many scarves can she knit in 17 hours and 30 minutes?

   A. 4
   B. 5
   C. 6
   D. 7

7. If $x = 7$, then $x^2 + 4x - 6 =$

   A. 64
   B. 67
   C. 71
   D. 89

8. James bought a stereo that was priced at $500. He paid 20% up front, and the remaining balance was paid in 8 equal payments of $60 each. How much more than the original price did he pay?

   A. $60
   B. $70
   C. $80
   D. $480

9. $\sqrt{64} =$

   A. 5
   B. 9
   C. 7
   D. 8

10. Jack bought a coat for $275. Three days later Rob bought the same coat with a 20% discount. How much more did Jack pay for the coat than Rob?

    A. $40
    B. $55
    C. $120
    D. $220

GO ON TO THE NEXT PAGE.

11. When 120 is divided by a certain number, the result has a remainder of 1. What is that number?

    A. 5
    B. 6
    C. 7
    D. 9

12. A man drove 32 miles of a 47 mile trip with his left turn signal on. On what percentage of the trip did he not have his turn signal on?

    A. 32%
    B. 47%
    C. 50%
    D. 68%

13. Jim mowed 33 lawns this week. If his mower uses 0.8 gallons of gas per lawn, how many gallons of gas did he use this week?

    A. 24.4
    B. 26.4
    C. 32.4
    D. 41.2

14. What is the value of x in this equation: $\frac{x}{4} = 24$?

    A. 64
    B. 72
    C. 88
    D. 96

15. Chris is selling hats for $5 and t-shirts for $8. If he sold 35 t-shirts and collected $355 total, how many hats did he sell?

    A. 13
    B. 15
    C. 17
    D. 19

16. Subtract $4x^3 + 2x^2 + 5$ from $12x^3 + 7x^2 - 9$.

    A. $-8x^3 + 5x^2 - 4$
    B. $-8x^3 + 5x^2 - 14$
    C. $8x^3 - 5x^2 - 14$
    D. $8x^3 + 5x^2 - 14$

17. If $-12 \leq x < 5$, then x is

    A. less than 5 but more than –12
    B. less than 5 but more than or equal to –12
    C. more than or equal to 5 or less than –12
    D. more than –12 or more than 5

18. Which of the following lists all the prime numbers between 10 and 20?

    A. 12, 14, 16, and 18
    B. 11, 13, 15, and 17
    C. 11, 13, 17, and 19
    D. 13, 14, 17, and 18

19. The average grade on a final exam for six students was 85%. Five of the students received the following grades: 79%, 83%, 84%, 88%, and 94%. What was the sixth student's grade?

    A. 82%
    B. 78%
    C. 85%
    D. 90%

20. A drawer has 4 blue socks, 5 black socks, 6 white socks, and 3 red socks. If one sock is chosen at random, what is the probability that it will be a black sock?

    A. $\frac{5}{18}$
    B. $\frac{13}{18}$
    C. $\frac{1}{3}$
    D. $\frac{3}{10}$

21. A person's maximum heart rate can be calculated approximately by subtracting the person's age from 220. Using this method, what is the difference between the maximum heart rate of a 15 year old and that of a 60 year old?

    A. 40
    B. 45
    C. 75
    D. 100

GO ON TO THE NEXT PAGE.

22. A movie theater has a total of 180 seats. If the theater sells full-price tickets at a cost of $7 per ticket and sells exactly 70% of its seats on each of three consecutive nights, then what is the theater's total gross income from tickets for those three days?

    A. $3,780
    B. $3,024
    C. $2,646
    D. $1,512

23. A bus has 40 passengers. If $\frac{1}{2}$ of those passengers are traveling to Los Angeles, and $\frac{1}{4}$ of the passengers traveling to Los Angeles departed earlier from Chicago, how many of the total passengers on the bus are traveling from Chicago to Los Angeles?

    A. 20
    B. 15
    C. 10
    D. 5

24. Melanie purchased the following items: 2 dozen eggs at $0.97 a dozen, 2 quarts of milk at $1.39 a quart, and a two-pound melon at $1.10 a pound. Melanie gave the cashier a $20 bill. How much change should she have received?

    A. $1.94
    B. $6.92
    C. $13.08
    D. $14.73

25. $3x^2y^3(2xy^2) =$

    A. $5x^2y^6$
    B. $6x^2y^6$
    C. $6x^3y^5$
    D. $6x^2y^3$

26. Laura can solve 6 math questions in 12 minutes. Working at the same rate, how many minutes would it take Laura to solve 5 math questions?

    A. 6
    B. 8
    C. 9
    D. 10

27. What is the result of dividing 0.675 by 0.6?

    A. 1.125
    B. 11.25
    C. 0.1125
    D. 0.125

28. 500 people attended the annual summer picnic. 70% were adults. How many non-adults were there?

    A. 110
    B. 125
    C. 130
    D. 150

29. On a test with 25 questions, Angela scored 88%. How many questions did she answer correctly?

    A. 20
    B. 22
    C. 23
    D. 24

30. What number multiplied by $\frac{5}{6}$ will give a product of 1?

    A. $-\frac{5}{6}$
    B. $-\frac{6}{5}$
    C. $\frac{6}{5}$
    D. 1

STOP!
IF YOU FINISH BEFORE THE TIME IS UP, YOU MAY CHECK OVER YOUR WORK ON THIS PART ONLY.

PART 3

WORD KNOWLEDGE

Time: 11 Minutes—35 Questions

1. <u>Accuse</u> most nearly means

   A. invite
   B. blame
   C. endure
   D. embitter

2. The <u>unscrupulous</u> politician won the election to the surprise of many in his political party.

   A. popular
   B. wealthy
   C. unpredictable
   D. immoral

3. <u>Prominent</u> most nearly means

   A. productive
   B. popular
   C. noticeable
   D. powerful

4. <u>Conclusive</u> most nearly means

   A. final
   B. inactive
   C. beginning
   D. secure

5. To <u>endure</u> most nearly means

   A. to forgo
   B. to undergo
   C. to include
   D. to hinder

6. He was filled with <u>overwhelming</u> joy.

   A. delusional
   B. continuous
   C. overpowering
   D. fascinating

7. The harvest was <u>abundant</u>.

   A. late
   B. plentiful
   C. destroyed
   D. healthy

8. <u>Chagrin</u> most nearly means

   A. disappointment
   B. deception
   C. impudent
   D. beneficial

9. <u>Anthology</u> most nearly means

   A. ancient
   B. repentant
   C. collection
   D. format

10. To <u>dilute</u> most nearly means

    A. to strengthen
    B. to prevent
    C. to change
    D. to weaken

11. The <u>wretched</u> woman tried to hide her tears.

    A. poor
    B. miserable
    C. exhausted
    D. terrified

12. The child was very <u>precocious</u> for her age.

    A. precious
    B. skilled
    C. advanced
    D. slow

13. To <u>utilize</u> most nearly means

    A. to make use of
    B. to build
    C. to take apart
    D. to create

GO ON TO THE NEXT PAGE.

14. To <u>chastise</u> most nearly means

   A. to donate
   B. to remove
   C. to scorn
   D. to punish

15. The attorney was very <u>cynical</u>.

   A. distrustful
   B. argumentative
   C. expensive
   D. rude

16. The <u>feud</u> between the two families goes back 200 years.

   A. arrangement
   B. dispute
   C. contract
   D. competition

17. To <u>diminish</u> most nearly means

   A. to demand
   B. to enhance
   C. to decrease
   D. to ruin

18. To <u>illuminate</u> most nearly means

   A. to sicken
   B. to brighten
   C. to improve
   D. to support

19. The <u>bizarre</u> story kept the children enthralled for hours.

   A. scary
   B. exciting
   C. strange
   D. long

20. <u>Passive</u> most nearly means

   A. inactive
   B. brief
   C. incapable
   D. sleepy

21. <u>Immense</u> most nearly means

   A. intense
   B. huge
   C. extreme
   D. dangerous

22. His <u>precarious</u> position worried me.

   A. sophisticated
   B. illegal
   C. secretive
   D. risky

23. <u>Nomad</u> most nearly means

   A. outlaw
   B. alien
   C. wanderer
   D. neighbor

24. To <u>rectify</u> most nearly means

   A. to straighten
   B. to correct
   C. to erect
   D. to damage

25. Her <u>candid</u> answer surprised everyone.

   A. honest
   B. eloquent
   C. abrupt
   D. descriptive

26. The <u>pious</u> old man was well respected in the community.

   A. intelligent
   B. quiet
   C. thoughtful
   D. religious

27. <u>Valiant</u> most nearly means

   A. calm
   B. brave
   C. alone
   D. strong

28. <u>Foe</u> most nearly means

   A. stranger
   B. relative
   C. enemy
   D. accomplice

GO ON TO THE NEXT PAGE.

29. Success made him <u>complacent</u>.

    A. worried
    B. self-satisfied
    C. happy
    D. depressed

30. <u>Feeble</u> most nearly means

    A. weak
    B. dizzy
    C. lazy
    D. sleepy

31. The figure was <u>excavated</u> from an ancient burial site.

    A. rescued
    B. divulged
    C. developed
    D. removed

32. He had a <u>zest</u> for life.

    A. regard
    B. enthusiasm
    C. admiration
    D. fear

33. The <u>ingenious</u> plan was the result of serious deliberation.

    A. difficult
    B. detailed
    C. clever
    D. complex

34. <u>Vital</u> most nearly means

    A. necessary
    B. appreciated
    C. incapable
    D. delicate

35. <u>Jubilant</u> most nearly means

    A. opulent
    B. energetic
    C. swift
    D. joyous

STOP!
IF YOU FINISH BEFORE THE TIME IS UP, YOU MAY CHECK OVER YOUR WORK ON THIS PART ONLY.

PART 4

PARAGRAPH COMPREHENSION

Time: 13 Minutes—15 Questions

1. Franklin is widely regarded as the first person to realize that lightning was made of electrically charged air. As a way of testing his theory, he attempted to discover whether lightning would pass through a metal object. To show this, he used a kite to raise a key into the air on a stormy night. From this experiment, Franklin realized that this electricity could be guided to the ground by a metal wire or rod, thereby protecting houses, people, and ships from being hurt.

One of Franklin's discoveries was

A. how to protect houses from lightning
B. the battery
C. the electric generator
D. a hydroelectric dam

2. One way to measure sound is by its frequency, which is the number of complete cycles of a sound wave within one second. One cycle per second is called 1 hertz. Human ears can detect sounds from about 20 hertz (the lowest sound) to 20,000 hertz (the highest sound). Below 20 hertz, humans feel only the vibration of the sound. Above 20,000 hertz, they can't hear the sound at all.

Which of the following can be inferred about a sound wave of 10 hertz?

A. A human could not hear it but a dog could.
B. A human could hear it only with a hearing aid.
C. A human could not hear it, but would feel the vibration.
D. A human could not hear it or feel the vibration.

3. Krakatau, an island located in the Sundra Strait, disappeared on August 27, 1883. It was destroyed by a series of powerful volcanic eruptions. The most violent blew upward with an estimated force of 100–150 megatons of TNT. The sound of the explosion traveled around the world, reaching the opposite end of the earth near Bogota, Colombia, whereupon it bounced back to Krakatau and then back and forth for seven passes over the earth's surface. The sounds, resembling the distant cannonade of a ship in distress, carried southward across Australia to Perth, northward to Singapore, and westward to Rodriques Island in the Indian Ocean. This was the longest recorded distance traveled by any airborne sound in history.

The author mentions "the distant cannonade of a ship in distress" in order to

A. describe a ship damaged by a volcanic eruption
B. show that sound travels very quickly over water
C. help illustrate the sound made by the Krakatau eruption
D. illustrate the distance traveled by the volcano's heat wave

4. The Roman Empire was an autocracy in which power was held by one man—the emperor. Augustus ruled from 27 BC to 14 AD; he brought about fairer taxation and a civil service. This so-called Augustan Age was the start of 200 years of stability, peace, and progress called the Pax Romana.

According to the passage, the Augustan Age

A. lasted 200 years
B. brought about a civil service
C. was a democracy
D. ended the Pax Romana

GO ON TO THE NEXT PAGE.

5. Blood is made up of two main elements: (1) plasma, and (2) the solid components of blood—red blood cells, white cells, and platelets (important for forming blood clots). If a patient has lost a lot of blood, the patient will probably need a transfusion of "whole blood," which induces red blood cells and plasma.However, sometimes the patient only needs an increase in the volume of liquid in the bloodstream, in which case plasma alone can be substituted.A person must be tested for blood type before certain kinds of transfusions because of differences in the way red blood cells react to each other.

When would it be necessary to test a patient for blood type?

A. For whole blood transfusions only
B. For plasma transfusions only
C. For both plasma and whole blood transfusions
D. If the patient requested it

6. Most seeds will germinate when they have moisture, oxygen, and the right temperature, but different seeds need differing proportions of each of these ingredients. Most seeds require a temperature of between 15 degrees and 27 degrees centigrade to germinate, although some seeds, such as the maple, can germinate in far colder climates, and some other seeds, such as corn, require warmer temperatures.

Based on the information above, which of the following is most likely true?

A. Maple seeds can germinate in any temperature.
B. Corn is difficult to grow.
C. Oxygen is not necessary for germination.
D. There are some seeds that do not require a temperature between 15 and 27 degrees for germination.

7. Louis Pasteur, after spending many hours looking through a microscope, discovered that germs could reproduce very rapidly and be very dangerous to humans. This led him to conclude that doctors—who, up until that time, did not always wash their hands or their instruments—were spreading disease and needed to sterilize their equipment and scrub their hands. People began, for the first time, to use antiseptics, and this helped to greatly reduce the number of infections in hospitals.

It can be inferred from the paragraph that an antiseptic is

A. something that kills germs
B. a machine used to heat milk
C. a kind of bacteria
D. a kind of microscope

8. Passive protection is a method by which organisms protect themselves from predators, not by fighting, but by their appearance, smell, or sound. Protective resemblance is one type of passive protection in which an animal's coloring mimics the natural environment, acting as a kind of camouflage. Protective mimicry is another type of passive protection in which a defenseless organism resembles a more powerful organism. Another interesting example of passive protection is the Monarch butterfly, which smells and tastes so bad to other organisms that virtually no other animal or insect will eat it.

The Monarch butterfly is an example of what?

A. An organism that defends itself using protective resemblance
B. An organism that defends itself using protective mimicry
C. An organism that defends itself using passive protection
D. An organism that changes its appearance for protection

GO ON TO THE NEXT PAGE.

9. Coniferous forests grow in colder climates and show little change throughout the year. Rainforests, which tend to grow in tropical climates, get lots of rain and tend to grow year-round.Deciduous forests grow in temperate regions, undergoing seasonal changes each year.

Which of the following statements are true?

I. Rainforests tend to grow year-round.
II. Seasonal changes vary from year to year in deciduous forests.
III. Coniferous forests are found in colder climates.

A. I only
B. II only
C. II and III only
D. I and III only

10. An experiment was undertaken by a scientist to see if men will go bald if exposed to a particular chemical compound.A group of 1000 adult men over the age of 30 were given this compound and it was found that 60 percent of the men eventually did go bald. From this, the scientist concluded that the compound causes baldness in men.

What can be inferred from the paragraph above?

A. The compound does not cause baldness in women.
B. Of the 1000 men in the study, more of them eventually went bald than did not.
C. Men that are not exposed to this chemical compound probably will not go bald.
D. The chemical compound should be studied further to explain why it causes baldness.

11. For years, scientists have debated whether the archaeopteryx, a creature that lived 150 million years ago, was an early species of bird or a dinosaur. Paleontologists argue that the archaeopteryx was a dinosaur that spent most of its time on the ground.Its feathers and wings were of only limited use, they say, and could not sustain life. Ornithologists, on the other hand, believe that the archaeopteryx was first and foremost a bird.As evidence, they point to fossil remains of the creature that show its claws were curved so that it could perch on tree limbs. Curved claws would have prevented the animal from walking or running quickly on the ground.

Scientists' theories about the archaeopteryx are based on

A. studies of the creature in its native habitat
B. examinations of fossilized remains
C. studies of modern descendants of the archaeopteryx
D. old written records

12. The Tower of London is London's most popular tourist attraction. A great deal of fascinating history has taken place within its walls. The tower has served as a fortress, a royal residence, a prison, the royal mint, public records office, observatory, military barracks, place of execution, and city zoo. Today, it houses the crown jewels and a great deal of English history.

The Tower of London was used for all of the following EXCEPT:

A. a place where money was minted
B. a royal residence
C. a place of religious pilgrimage
D. a place where executions were held

GO ON TO THE NEXT PAGE.

13. Mary Shelley was born in 1797. Her parents, Mary Wollstonecraft and William Godwin, were both writers. She was surrounded as a child by some of the greatest literary figures of her day, including Samuel Coleridge and Charles Lamb. Her parents introduced her to these people because they believed that every child had the potential to develop a great intellect. Shelley wrote her best-known work, *Frankenstein*, at the age of 19. She wrote it while staying at Lake Geneva along a group of young poets, which included Lord Byron and Percy Shelley, whom she would later marry.

In approximately what year did Shelley write Frankenstein?

A. 1805
B. 1811
C. 1816
D. 1820

Questions 14 and 15 are based on the following passage.

James Joyce, celebrated Irish author, was born in Dublin on February 2, 1882. The oldest of ten children raised in poverty, he nonetheless graduated from the prestigious University College, Dublin in 1902. After spending a year in Paris studying medicine, he returned to Dublin following his mother's death. In Dublin, he began writing poems. In 1904, he met and married Nora Barnacle. The newlyweds moved to Italy, where they lived until 1915. During his time in Italy, Joyce wrote and published two books: *Chamber Music* and *Dubliners*. His great literary career had begun.

When Italy entered World War I, Joyce moved with his family to Zurich, where he wrote *A Portrait of the Artist as a Young Man* and *Exiles*. *Portrait*, the story of a young boy's childhood in Dublin, is often considered a self-portrait of Joyce. A beautifully written story, it has eventually become viewed one of the great Irish novels.

At the end of the war, Joyce returned to Italy briefly and then moved to Paris. In Paris he published *Ulysses*, a novel that finally brought him the international acclaim he so richly deserved. In 1922 he began work on his next novel *Finnegan's Wake*, which was published in 1939. In December 1940 Joyce returned to Zurich where he died shortly thereafter.

14. Which novel brought Joyce international acclaim?

A. *Dubliners*
B. *A Portrait of the Artist as a Young Man*
C. *Ulysses*
D. *Finnegan's Wake*

15. The tone of the passage can best be described as

A. noncommittal
B. condemnatory
C. uncertain
D. appreciative

STOP!
IF YOU FINISH BEFORE THE TIME IS UP, YOU MAY
CHECK OVER YOUR WORK ON THIS PART ONLY.

PART 5

NUMERICAL OPERATIONS

Time: 3 Minutes—50 Questions

1. $7 \times 0 =$
   A. 0
   B. 7
   C. 10
   D. 12

2. $16 - 5 =$
   A. 8
   B. 9
   C. 10
   D. 11

3. $1 \times 4 =$
   A. 1
   B. 2
   C. 4
   D. 5

4. $8 + 3 =$
   A. 11
   B. 12
   C. 13
   D. 14

5. $21 \div 7 =$
   A. 2
   B. 3
   C. 5
   D. 7

6. $18 \div 2 =$
   A. 9
   B. 13
   C. 16
   D. 18

7. $1 + 9 =$
   A. 5
   B. 8
   C. 10
   D. 13

8. $2 \times 2 =$
   A. 4
   B. 6
   C. 7
   D. 9

9. $28 \div 4 =$
   A. 12
   B. 7
   C. 6
   D. 4

10. $8 \times 2 =$
    A. 16
    B. 10
    C. 20
    D. 19

11. $1 \times 1 =$
    A. 2
    B. 1
    C. 4
    D. 5

12. $13 \div 1 =$
    A. 12
    B. 13
    C. 15
    D. 17

13. $6 - 6 =$
    A. 0
    B. 1
    C. 6
    D. 9

14. $9 + 7 =$
    A. 14
    B. 15
    C. 16
    D. 17

GO ON TO THE NEXT PAGE.

15. 12 − 0 =

   A.   0
   B.   12
   C.   15
   D.   17

16. 10 × 6 =

   A.   45
   B.   50
   C.   60
   D.   16

17. 8 + 7 =

   A.   15
   B.   13
   C.   16
   D.   18

18. 4 + 6 =

   A.   7
   B.   10
   C.   12
   D.   14

19. 15 ÷ 3 =

   A.   18
   B.   3
   C.   12
   D.   5

20. 10 − 7 =

   A.   17
   B.   7
   C.   3
   D.   1

21. 5 × 1 =

   A.   5
   B.   4
   C.   6
   D.   8

22. 0 ÷ 3 =

   A.   3
   B.   0
   C.   2
   D.   5

23. 2 × 10 =

   A.   20
   B.   12
   C.   24
   D.   28

24. 6 − 4 =

   A.   10
   B.   24
   C.   2
   D.   8

25. 3 × 3 =

   A.   0
   B.   1
   C.   9
   D.   11

26. 15 − 1 =

   A.   14
   B.   15
   C.   17
   D.   18

27. 9 ÷ 3 =

   A.   9
   B.   6
   C.   5
   D.   3

28. 10 − 9 =

   A.   19
   B.   0
   C.   1
   D.   6

29. 7 × 2 =

   A.   7
   B.   14
   C.   9
   D.   11

30. 6 × 5 =

   A.   11
   B.   14
   C.   30
   D.   35

GO ON TO THE NEXT PAGE.

31. 17 − 9 =

   A. 8
   B. 26
   C. 11
   D. 10

32. 1 × 7 =

   A. 9
   B. 7
   C. 8
   D. 11

33. 6 − 0 =

   A. 0
   B. 4
   C. 6
   D. 9

34. 3 + 1 =

   A. 4
   B. 6
   C. 7
   D. 10

35. 8 × 6 =

   A. 40
   B. 48
   C. 50
   D. 56

36. 5 × 7 =

   A. 35
   B. 30
   C. 28
   D. 25

37. 9 × 9 =

   A. 18
   B. 2
   C. 78
   D. 81

38. 2 + 7 =

   A. 5
   B. 9
   C. 11
   D. 14

39. 24 ÷ 2 =

   A. 8
   B. 9
   C. 12
   D. 14

40. 8 ÷ 4 =

   A. 12
   B. 9
   C. 2
   D. 1

41. 16 ÷ 4 =

   A. 8
   B. 4
   C. 2
   D. 3

42. 16 − 9 =

   A. 10
   B. 9
   C. 7
   D. 5

43. 5 − 3 =

   A. 2
   B. 3
   C. 7
   D. 9

44. 10 × 9 =

   A. 70
   B. 80
   C. 90
   D. 100

45. 13 − 8 =

   A. 8
   B. 5
   C. 4
   D. 2

46. 6 × 1 =

   A. 6
   B. 7
   C. 9
   D. 10

GO ON TO THE NEXT PAGE.

47. 9 + 9 =

    A. 15
    B. 16
    C. 17
    D. 18

48. 8 + 1 =

    A. 6
    B. 7
    C. 9
    D. 11

49. 11 − 3 =

    A. 12
    B. 8
    C. 7
    D. 4

50. 8 × 4 =

    A. 25
    B. 26
    C. 28
    D. 32

STOP!
IF YOU FINISH BEFORE THE TIME IS UP, YOU MAY
CHECK OVER YOUR WORK ON THIS PART ONLY.

PART 6

CODING SPEED

Time: 7 Minutes — 84 Questions

Key

animal 4619	desert 7214	grade 5248	letter 8741	office 3073
battle 0358	finger 9923	income 1632	nest 2784	root 6977

Questions		Options				
		A	**B**	**C**	**D**	**E**
1.	income	0358	1632	4619	6977	8741
2.	root	1632	2748	3073	5248	6977
3.	desert	2784	5248	6977	7214	9923
4.	battle	0358	1632	2784	3073	4619
5.	office	2784	3073	5248	6977	8741
6.	animal	0358	1632	4619	7214	9923
7.	nest	2784	3073	4619	5248	6977
8.	grade	1632	2784	3073	4619	5248
9.	income	0358	1632	5248	7214	8741
10.	letter	1632	2784	3073	7241	8741
11.	finger	4619	5248	7214	8741	9923
12.	battle	0358	2784	3073	5248	6977

Key

clip 7448	hammer 6827	king 2392	option 4981	sock 8271
ear 3716	joke 5104	market 1063	photo 3362	train 9035

Questions		Options				
		A	**B**	**C**	**D**	**E**
13.	ear	3362	3716	4981	6827	7448
14.	photo	1063	2392	3362	4981	5104
15.	hammer	2392	4981	5104	6827	7448
16.	train	4981	5104	7448	8271	9035
17.	clip	4981	6827	7448	8271	9035
18.	market	1063	3362	5104	6827	8271
19.	sock	2392	3716	6827	7448	8271
20.	joke	1063	2392	4981	5104	6827
21.	king	1063	2392	5104	7448	8271
22.	option	2392	3716	4981	5104	7448
23.	photo	3362	3716	5104	6827	9035
24.	train	4981	5104	7448	8271	9035

Key

bath 4890	diner 9358	globe 5204	laser 0762	rate 6017
cloud 2123	fish 7936	ice 3681	money 1475	waste 8549

Questions	Options				
	A	**B**	**C**	**D**	**E**
25. fish	2123	4890	5204	6017	7936
26. laser	0762	2123	4890	6017	8549
27. bath	1475	2123	4890	5240	6017
28. waste	4890	5204	6017	8549	9358
29. cloud	0762	2123	3681	7936	8549
30. money	1475	3681	4890	5204	7936
31. diner	4890	5204	7936	8549	9358
32. rate	0762	3681	6017	8549	9358
33. ice	0762	1475	2123	3681	5204
34. globe	2123	5204	6017	7936	8549
35. laser	0762	3681	4890	6017	7936
36. diner	1475	2123	5204	8549	9358

Key

anchor 2500	edge 9156	horse 1694	lease 6270	pool 4023
cape 7432	field 3381	job 5749	oath 8917	quail 7835

Questions	Options				
	A	**B**	**C**	**D**	**E**
37. anchor	1694	2500	4023	5749	6270
38. pool	2500	3381	4023	6270	7835
39. horse	1694	3381	5749	7835	9156
40. job	3381	4023	5749	6270	7835
41. quail	2500	5749	6270	7835	8917
42. field	2500	3381	7835	8917	9156
43. oath	3381	4023	6270	7835	8917
44. cape	6270	7432	7835	8917	9156
45. edge	4023	5749	6270	7432	9156
46. lease	3381	5749	6270	7835	8917
47. job	1694	2500	4023	5749	6270
48. pool	4023	5749	6270	7432	8917

Key

bill 5314	chore 9238	giant 7496	knee 4163	nut 2581
camera 2871	dash 1620	idea 3742	manor 6925	phase 8257

Questions   Options

	A	B	C	D	E
49. phase	3742	4163	6925	8257	9238
50. bill	2581	3742	5314	6925	7496
51. manor	1620	2581	3742	5314	6925
52. dash	1620	2581	4163	6925	7496
53. idea	2871	3742	4163	5314	7496
54. knee	4163	5314	7496	8257	9238
55. nut	1620	2581	5314	8257	9238
56. chore	4163	6925	7496	8257	9238
57. giant	3742	4163	5314	7496	8257
58. manor	3742	4163	5314	6925	7496
59. camera	1620	2871	3742	4163	5314
60. idea	2581	2871	3742	5314	7496

Key

contest 4586	exit 5972	health 7308	leaf 0245	note 2796
dial 3451	flaw 1413	ink 8664	meal 6130	order 4827

Questions   Options

	A	B	C	D	E
61. ink	3451	5972	6130	7308	8664
62. note	2796	3451	4586	5972	6130
63. flaw	0245	1413	2796	3451	4586
64. exit	2796	4586	5972	6130	8664
65. meal	0245	1413	3451	6130	7308
66. order	1413	4827	5972	6130	7308
67. contest	0245	1413	2796	4586	5972
68. dial	3451	4586	5972	6130	8664
69. health	2796	3451	4586	6130	7308
70. leaf	0245	1413	3451	5972	8664
71. note	0245	1413	2796	3451	4586
72. contest	2796	4586	5972	6130	7308

Key

agent 9822	debt................ 1975	force................. 8197	latch 3562	prize 7694
base 0046	effect 2434	hawk 9013	peak 4736	umpire........... 6529

Questions

Options

	A	B	C	D	E
73. force	4736	6529	8197	9013	9822
74. prize	2434	3562	4736	7694	8197
75. latch	3562	4736	6529	7694	9013
76. umpire	4736	6529	7694	8197	9822
77. hawk	1975	2434	6529	7694	9013
78. debt	0046	1975	2434	4736	6529
79. agent	2434	3562	4736	8197	9822
80. effect	0046	1975	2434	3562	4736
81. peak	1975	2434	4736	6529	8197
82. base	0046	1975	3562	4736	6529
83. debt	0046	1975	2434	6529	7694
84. force	3562	4736	6529	8197	9822

STOP!
IF YOU FINISH BEFORE THE TIME IS UP, YOU MAY
CHECK OVER YOUR WORK ON THIS PART ONLY.

PART 7

Auto and Shop Information

Time: 11 Minutes—25 Questions

1. All of the following are parts found in a manual transmission EXCEPT

   A. the flywheel
   B. the drive shaft
   C. the rotors
   D. the clutch plate

2. The fuel pump moves fuel from the gas tank to

   A. the intake valve
   B. the intake manifold
   C. the catalytic converter
   D. the float tank

3. Which of the following could result from a faulty voltage regulator?

   A. The electric polarity can switch
   B. The battery can become overcharged
   C. The distributor will malfunction
   D. The battery will completely discharge

4. The temperature gauge on the dash shows the engine is beginning to overheat. The problem could be

   A. too much oil
   B. a lean fuel/air mixture
   C. a broken fan belt
   D. a malfunctioning alternator

5. Most automobiles run on which of the following cycles?

   A. The two-stroke cycle
   B. The four-stroke cycle
   C. The diesel cycle
   D. The gasoline cycle

6. The oil pressure indicator in a car operating under normal conditions suddenly drops and smoke comes out the tail pipe. The cause of this is probably

   A. debris in the oil
   B. not enough oil
   C. too much oil
   D. a blown head gasket

7. The most likely symptom of the water pump failing is

   A. the engine overheating
   B. water entering the combustion chamber
   C. the alternator failing to charge the battery
   D. vapor lock

8. The torque converter contains all the following except the

   A. rotor
   B. stator
   C. turbine
   D. pump

9. Vehicles can stall for all of the following reasons EXCEPT

   A. vapor lock
   B. worn clutch plate
   C. timing belt failure
   D. stuck piston

10. None of the following have gear-like teeth except the

    A. timing belt
    B. fan belt
    C. cams
    D. rocker arm

11. Pistons are always made smaller than the cylinder to

    A. allow enough room for the piston rings
    B. allow vapors from the combustion to slip by the piston
    C. give the car more power
    D. allow the piston to expand when heated and not jam in the cylinder

GO ON TO THE NEXT PAGE.

12. To enlarge the diameter of an existing fastener hole,

    A.   an expansion bolt should be used
    B.   a twist drill should be used
    C.   a hacksaw should be used
    D.   a reamer should be used

13. The kerf of a saw refers to the

    A.   shape of the handle
    B.   total width that the teeth will cut
    C.   angle the teeth are bent to
    D.   number of teeth per inch on the blade

14. The tool shown above is a

    A.   monkey wrench
    B.   pipe wrench
    C.   Allen wrench
    D.   crescent wrench

15. The tool shown above is used to

    A.   cut the tops off of nails
    B.   countersink holes
    C.   smooth and flatten wood
    D.   clamp down on wood while cutting

16. The tool above is a

    A.   hacksaw
    B.   backsaw
    C.   coping saw
    D.   carpenters saw

17. The backsaw is used primarily to cut

    A.   complex curves in wood
    B.   with the grain of wood
    C.   across the grain of wood
    D.   sheetrock

18. What should be put in old nail holes in walls before painting?

    A.   Putty
    B.   Caulk
    C.   Cement
    D.   Drywall dust

19. The tool shown above

    A.   is a pipe cutter
    B.   is a C clamp
    C.   is a vise
    D.   are calipers

20. The tool shown above is a

    A.   twist drill bit
    B.   reamer
    C.   countersink bit
    D.   punch

GO ON TO THE NEXT PAGE.

21. A rubber or wooden mallet is used with a chisel

    A. to keep the chisel from slipping
    B. to transfer more energy to the tip
    C. to protect the worker's hands
    D. to protect the chisel

22. Machine screws are used primarily in

    A. pre-threaded holes in metal
    B. attaching joists to the foundation
    C. attaching saw blades to the handle
    D. power drills

23. Finish sanding should normally be done by

    A. sanding with the grain
    B. sanding across the grain
    C. sanding in small circles
    D. sanding with coarse grit paper

24. Small clearances are best measured with a

    A. rule
    B. caliper
    C. micrometer
    D. feeler gauge

25. Each of the following contains a blade EXCEPT:

    A. dovetail saw
    B. crosscut saw
    C. file
    D. plane

STOP!
IF YOU FINISH BEFORE THE TIME IS UP, YOU MAY
CHECK OVER YOUR WORK ON THIS PART ONLY.

PART 8

MATHEMATICS KNOWLEDGE

Time: 24 Minutes — 25 Questions

1. What is the value of $x^2 + 4x - 3xy + 2y^2$ if $x = 3$ and $y = -4$?

   A. 17
   B. 89
   C. 121
   D. –121

2. If p pieces of candy cost c cents, 10 pieces of candy will cost

   A. $\dfrac{pc}{10}$ cents

   B. $\dfrac{10c}{p}$ cents

   C. $10pc$ cents

   D. $\dfrac{10p}{c}$ cents

3. If the lengths of the sides of a rectangular plot of land with an area of 12 square feet are doubled, what is the new area of the plot in square feet?

   A. 24
   B. 36
   C. 48
   D. 60

4. A drawing of an orchard has a scale of one inch to 25 feet. On the drawing, how far apart are the grape vines from the apple trees if the scale is $2\frac{1}{2}$ inches?

   A. 60 feet

   B. $61\frac{1}{2}$ feet

   C. $62\frac{1}{2}$ feet

   D. 65 feet

5. The formula for converting temperature from Celsius to Fahrenheit is $C = \dfrac{5}{9}(F - 32)$. If the temperature in Celsius is 12 degrees, what is the temperature in Fahrenheit?

   A. 38.7 degrees
   B. 53.6 degrees
   C. 65.4 degrees
   D. 72.1 degrees

6. Vicky, Roger, and Adam want to buy a $90 radio. If Roger agrees to pay twice as much as Adam, and Vicky agrees to pay three times as much as Roger, how much must Roger pay?

   A. $10
   B. $20
   C. $30
   D. $40

7.

   What is the length of x?

   A. 3
   B. 4
   C. 5
   D. 6

GO ON TO THE NEXT PAGE.

8. A statue in the shape of a right triangle has a height of 7 meters, a base of 24 meters, and a hypotenuse of 25 meters. A sculptor is commissioned to make a replica of the statue. If the new hypotenuse is 13 meters long, how long is the new base?

A. 12

B. $12\frac{12}{25}$

C. 13

D. 30

9. Beth is two years older than Debbie and four years younger than Marnie. If Debbie is d years old, how old is Marnie in terms of d?

A. $2d + 4$
B. $d + 2$
C. $d + 4$
D. $d + 6$

10. If rice costs r cents per kilogram, how many kilograms may be bought for $5?

A. $\dfrac{50}{r}$

B. $\dfrac{5}{r}$

C. $\dfrac{r}{500}$

D. $500r$

11. Two less than a certain number is one-third of that number. What is the number?

A. 1
B. 3
C. 6
D. 8

12. A carpenter builds a hexagon-shaped table. If he puts a leg at each corner, how many legs does he need?

A. 3
B. 4
C. 5
D. 6

13. A right triangle has an angle of 25 degrees. How big are the other two angles?

A. 25 degrees and 25 degrees
B. 30 degrees and 60 degrees
C. 45 degrees and 90 degrees
D. 65 degrees and 90 degrees

14. A circle has a diameter of 7 inches. What is its area?

A. 49 π inches
B. 25 π inches
C. 12.25 π inches
D. 3.5 π inches

15. Solve for y: $11y + (2)^3 = -5y + (2)^4$

A. y = 0.5
B. y = −0.5
C. y = 1.2
D. y = 2

16. Jim has built a larger pool than his neighbor Steve. Steve's pool is 9 feet deep, 15 feet long and 10 feet wide. Jim's pool is 12 feet deep, 20 feet long and 12 feet wide. What is the difference in volumes between these two pools?

A. 10 cubic feet
B. 1350 cubic feet
C. 1530 cubic feet
D. 4230 cubic feet

17.

If lines 1 and 2 are parallel, how many degrees does ∠x measure?

A. 45
B. 90
C. 115
D. 135

GO ON TO THE NEXT PAGE.

18. A stop sign has 8 equal sides of length 4. What is its perimeter?

    A. 4
    B. 8
    C. 32
    D. 64

19. One-half the difference between the number of degrees in a square and the number of degrees in a triangle is

    A. 45
    B. 90
    C. 180
    D. 240

20. A sandbox measures 10 feet long, 5 feet wide, and 6 inches deep. How much sand is needed to fill it up?

    A. 21 cubic feet
    B. 25 cubic feet
    C. 50 cubic feet
    D. 250 cubic feet

21. If the area of a square is $9a^2$, what is the length of a side of the square?

    A. $9a^2$
    B. $3a^2$
    C. $3a$
    D. $2a$

22. $x^2 + 3x - 70$ is the product of what?

    A. $(x - 7)$ and $(x + 10)$
    B. $(x + 7)$ and $(x + 10)$
    C. $(x - 3)$ and $(x - 7)$
    D. $(x + 7)$ and $(x + 3)$

23. Points X, Y, and Z lie on a line. Point Y is between points X and Z. If XZ = 10 and YZ = 3, then XY =

    A. 3
    B. 4
    C. 7
    D. 13

24. A right triangle has a hypotenuse that is 7 inches long and a leg that is 4 inches long. How long is the other leg?

    A. 4.00 inches
    B. 5.74 inches
    C. 6.47 inches
    D. 7.40 inches

25. If $10 - x < 14$, which of the following expresses the entire range of possible values for x?

    A. $x < 4$
    B. $x < 2$
    C. $x > -4$
    D. $x > 4$

STOP!
IF YOU FINISH BEFORE THE TIME IS UP, YOU MAY
CHECK OVER YOUR WORK ON THIS PART ONLY.

PART 9

MECHANICAL COMPREHENSION

Time: 19 Minutes—25 Questions

1. A boy kicks a football into the air. The football is moving most slowly

   A. just after it leaves the boy's foot
   B. at the height of its trajectory
   C. just before it hits the ground
   D. Not enough information is available.

2. 32 degrees Fahrenheit is equal to how many degrees Celsius?

   A. 212
   B. 64
   C. 100
   D. 0

3. Gear 1, which has 20 teeth, is turning gear 2, which has 30 teeth. If Gear 1 makes 6 revolutions, how many will Gear 2 make?

   A. 2
   B. 4
   C. 6
   D. 12

4. The ropes attached to the girder can support a maximum of 500 lbs. without snapping. What is the maximum weight that the girder can be before the ropes snap?

   A. 250 lbs.
   B. 500 lbs.
   C. 1000 lbs.
   D. 2000 lbs.

5. Which pulley turns the fastest?

   A. A
   B. B
   C. C
   D. D

6. The lever in the above picture provides a mechanical advantage of 3. What is the minimum amount the person must weigh in order to lift the boulder?

   A. 100 lbs
   B. 200 lbs
   C. 300 lbs
   D. 600 lbs

7. How much force is needed to push the piano up the ramp?

   A. 50
   B. 75
   C. 150
   D. 300

GO ON TO THE NEXT PAGE.

Skater A   Skater B

200 lbs.

150 lbs.

10 mph   5 mph

180 lbs.   90 lbs.

?   6 ft.

Figure not drawn to scale

8. Skater A and B collide and stick together. After the collision, which of the following is true?

   A. Both skaters stop at the point of impact.
   B. The skaters will move to the right at a speed of less than 10 miles per hour.
   C. The skaters will move to the left at a speed of greater than 10 miles per hour.
   D. The skaters will move to the left at a speed of less than 5 miles per hour.

9. If all of the following objects are at the same temperature, which will feel the coldest?

   A. A steel knife
   B. A rubber tire
   C. A wooden chair
   D. A plastic fork

10. The speed of a falling object increases due to gravity at a rate of

   A. 3.2 meters per second squared
   B. 4.5 meters per second squared
   C. 9.8 meters per second squared
   D. 13.1 meters per second squared

11. If water is flowing into a lake at a rate of 120 gallons an hour and flowing out of the lake via another conduit at a rate of 3 gallons a minute, then the amount of water in the lake will

   A. decrease 1 gallon per minute
   B. increase one gallon per minute
   C. decrease 60 gallons per minute
   D. remain the same

12. At what distance from the fulcrum should the person on the left sit in order to perfectly balance the see-saw?

   A. 2 feet
   B. 3 feet
   C. 6 feet
   D. 12 feet

1 in.

6 in.

13. If the force required to crack the walnut is 60 pounds, how much force must be applied to the nutcracker to crack the walnut?

   A. 1 pound
   B. 5 pounds
   C. 10 pounds
   D. 30 pounds

GO ON TO THE NEXT PAGE.

14. If gear A rotates counterclockwise, in which direction does gear C rotate?

    A. Clockwise
    B. Counterclockwise
    C. Gear C does not rotate.
    D. It is impossible for gear A to rotate counterclockwise.

15. Rolling friction is always

    A. less than sliding friction
    B. greater than sliding friction
    C. equal to sliding friction
    D. inversely proportional to sliding friction

16. The best instrument for measuring atmospheric pressure is

    A. a thermometer
    B. a Geiger counter
    C. a Bourdon gauge
    D. a barometer

17. The person jumps off the boat at a speed of 5 feet per second. After he jumps, the boat

    A. will move to the right at a speed of about 2 feet per second
    B. will move to the right at a speed of about 10 feet per second
    C. will move to the left at a speed of about 2 feet per second
    D. will move to the left at a speed of about 10 feet per second

18. The water pressure surrounding a submarine is 200 psi. A porthole on the submarine measures 400 square inches. What is the force on the porthole?

    A. 200 pounds
    B. 800 pounds
    C. 8000 pounds
    D. 80000 pounds

19. If a volume of a gas increases,

    A. its pressure will increase
    B. its pressure will decrease
    C. its mass will increase
    D. its mass will decrease

20. In the pipe above, the water pressure is lowest

    A. at the thickest part of the pipe
    B. at the thinnest part of the pipe
    C. The water pressure is the same throughout the pipe.
    D. There is not enough information available.

21. The tread on a tire is designed to

    A. preserve friction between the car and the road
    B. increase the car's speed when going downhill
    C. increase the car's speed when going uphill
    D. decrease the car's wind resistance

22. If a woman lifts a 10 pound sack 3 feet in the air, how much work is she doing?

    A. 13 ft.-lbs.
    B. 15 ft.-lbs.
    C. 30 ft.-lbs.
    D. 60 ft.-lbs.

23. A device that holds two parts together is called a

    A. coupling
    B. gear
    C. bearing
    D. spring

GO ON TO THE NEXT PAGE.

24. Pi is approximately equal to

    A. 2.54
    B. 3.14
    C. 6.08
    D. 9.2

25. How fast must car B travel in order for both cars
    to come to a complete stop when they collide?

    A. 40 mph
    B. 42 mph
    C. 70 mph
    D. 100 mph

STOP!
IF YOU FINISH BEFORE THE TIME IS UP, YOU MAY
CHECK OVER YOUR WORK ON THIS PART ONLY.

PART 10

ELECTRONICS INFORMATION

Time: 9 Minutes—20 Questions

1. "Hot" wires may be colored

   A. white
   B. green
   C. gray
   D. black

2. Which of the following is the best insulator?

   A. porcelain
   B. sea water
   C. copper
   D. silver

3. How many watts of power are delivered by a 120-V generator that supplies 10 A?

   A. 110 W
   B. 130 W
   C. 500 W
   D. 1200 W

4. The ability of a conductor to induce voltage in itself when the current changes is its

   A. capacitance
   B. resistance
   C. inductance
   D. conductance

5. Certain crystals produce a voltage when they are vibrated. This is known as the

   A. piezoelectric effect
   B. photoelectric effect
   C. generative effect
   D. coaxial effect

6. A good substance for conducting electricity is

   A. copper
   B. rubber
   C. iron
   D. plastic

7. A micrometer would be used to measure a wire's

   A. length
   B. conductivity
   C. voltage
   D. diameter

8. Resistance is measured in

   A. ohms
   B. amps
   C. watts
   D. farads

9. How much current will a 30 watt light bulb draw if it is plugged into a 120 volt socket?

   A. 0.25 A
   B. 0.5 A
   C. 0.75 A
   D. 1.0 A

10. The most commonly used law for solving problems involving voltage, current, and resistance is

    A. Kirchoff's Law
    B. Ohm's Law
    C. Henry's Law
    D. Faraday's Law

11. When an accidental connection is made between two hot wires, the result is

    A. a grounded circuit
    B. a short circuit
    C. a hot circuit
    D. a faulty circuit

12. The frequency of current alternations is measured in

    A. farads
    B. watts
    C. hertz
    D. amperes

13. It's important when soldering to

    A. work in a quiet environment
    B. work in a perfectly level environment
    C. work in a cool environment
    D. work in a well-ventilated environment

GO ON TO THE NEXT PAGE.

14. A diode has low resistance to current in one direction and

   A. negative resistance to current in the other direction
   B. no resistance to current in the other direction
   C. low resistance to current in the other direction
   D. high resistance to current in the other direction

15. Power is equal to voltage times

   A. resistance
   B. capacitance
   C. current
   D. frequency

16. A device that provides a visual representation of variations in voltage or current is

   A. an oscilloscope
   B. a frequency counter
   C. a signal generator
   D. a logic probe

17. The best batteries for supplying a small amount of power for a long period of time are

   A. zinc batteries
   B. alkaline batteries
   C. lead acid batteries
   D. lithium batteries

18. Which of the following metals can be most easily magnetized?

   A. iron
   B. gold
   C. copper
   D. silver

19. The symbol above represents a

   A. resistor
   B. capacitator
   C. transformer
   D. battery

20. The symbol above represents a

   A. resistor
   B. capacitator
   C. transformer
   D. battery

STOP!
IF YOU FINISH BEFORE THE TIME IS UP, YOU MAY
CHECK OVER YOUR WORK ON THIS PART ONLY.

10

ANSWERS AND EXPLANATIONS TO PRACTICE TEST 1

PART 1

GENERAL SCIENCE

1. **C** The nervous system sends and receives information through electrical impulses.

2. **A** Chromosomes determine the genetic traits that offspring inherit from their parents.

3. **B** Producers make their own food. Plants are producers—they make their food through photosynthesis.

4. **D** Protons and neutrons both have a weight of approximately 1 atomic mass unit. By adding them together you get the mass of the atom. Electrons have practically no mass.

5. **A** Conduction occurs when heat travels from something hotter to something cooler.

6. **C** The Cenozoic era started about 65 million years ago and continues today.

7. **B** Pluto is the smallest planet, and the farthest from the sun.

8. **D** The chromosomes line up at the middle of the cell during metaphase.

9. **C** Bryophytes are plants that do not possess stems or leaves.

10. **B** Deciduous forests have distinct seasons, lots of rain, trees that lose their leaves in the winter, and a wide variety of plant and animal life.

11. **A** The crust is a thin layer of rock that covers the earth.

12. **C** A warm front occurs when warm air overtakes cooler air.

13. **D** A solar eclipse occurs when the moon moves between the sun and the earth, blocking the sun's light from the earth.

14. **B** Pepsin is found in the stomach and is used to break down food.

15. **A** Type O is the universal donor.

16. **C** Rickets, a disease of the skeleton, is usually the result of a deficiency of vitamin D.

17. **B** Lysosomes digest old organelles and foreign substances in the cell.

18. **D** Make a Punnett square. From this you will see that the possibilities are: Tt, Tt, tt, and tt.

19. **A** Photosynthesis is the process by which plants convert water, carbon dioxide, and sunlight into food.

20. **D** The Doppler effect occurs when the source of a sound, the receiver of a sound, or both, are moving. The result is a shift in the frequencies detected by the receiver.

21. **B** Anything below 7 on the pH scale is an acid. Anything above 7 on the pH scale is a base.

22. **A** Water boils at 100 degrees Celsius, which is equivalent to 212 degrees Fahrenheit.

23. **D** Remember the mnemonic: King Phillip Came Over From Germany Soaked.

24. **C** They make up the parts of the brain, which is part of the central nervous system.

25. **B** Only plant cells have a cell wall.

PART 2

ARITHMETIC REASONING

1. **C** Plug the information into the formula for percent increases and decreases.

$$\text{Percent increase} = \frac{\text{difference}}{\text{original amount}}$$

$$.20 = \frac{x}{60}$$

$$12 = x$$

2. **A** 16 ounces = 1 pound, so Mrs. Abbott bought 3.5 lbs of hamburger. 3.5 lbs = $3.43, so you divide $3.43 by 3.5 to determine the cost per pound. It is $0.98.

3. **B** Use a ratio box to find the answer.

Dogs	Cats	Total
4	6	10
× 10	× 10	× 10
40	60	100

4. **A** Use Bite Size Pieces to answer this one.

$$1.25(40)+x=76$$

$$50+x=76$$

$$x=26$$

5. **B** Use the formula I = prt

$$I = 100(.04)(10)$$

$$I = 40$$

The interest is 40. So the total in the account is 40 + 100 = 140.

6. **D** This is a proportions question. Match up the categories and solve for x.

$$\frac{1\ \text{scarf}}{2.5\ \text{hours}} = \frac{x\ \text{scarves}}{17.5\ \text{hours}}$$

$$2.5x = 17.5$$

$$x = 7$$

7. **C** $7^2 + 4(7) - 6 = 49 + 28 - 6 = 71$

8. **C** Use Bite Size Pieces to answer this one. First, find out how much he paid up front by multiplying 500 by .20. That gives you $100 for the initial payment. Then, multiply 60 by 8 to find the total for the 8 equal payments, which is 480. $100 + $480 = $580. $580 is $80 more than the original price of $500.

9. **D** $\sqrt{64} = 8$

10. **B** All you need to do for this problem is figure out Rob's discount. To do this, multiply 275 by 0.20. That gives you 55.

11. **C** The easiest way to solve this problem is to use the answer choices. Pick one and divide 120 by it. If it has a remainder of 1, you know it's the correct answer. The first two have no remainders when divided into 120. The fourth answer, 9, leaves you with a remainder of 3 when divided into 120. But $7\overline{)120}$ gives you 17 remainder 1, so that's you're answer.

12. **A** First figure out the percentage of the trip that he had his turn signal on. $\frac{32}{47}$ = .68 Then, subtract that from 100 percent to find how long he had his turn signal off. 100 − 68 = 32

13. **B** $33 \times 0.8 = 26.4$

14. **D** $\frac{x}{4} = 24$

$$x = 96$$

15. **B** Use Bite Size Pieces for this problem. Multiply $35 \times 8 = 280$. That is how much money Chris made from selling t-shirts. 355 − 280 = 75. So he made $75 from the hats. Each hat is $5 so divide 75 by 5. 75 ÷ 5 = 15.

16. **D** Line the equations up and subtract.

$$12x^3 + 7x^2 - 9$$
$$\underline{-(4x^3 + 2x^2 + 5)}$$
$$8x^3 + 5x^2 - 14$$

17. **B** This is a question about inequalities. The $\leq$ sign indicates that x is greater than or equal to -12. The $<$ sign indicates that x is less than 5.

18. **C** Prime numbers are numbers that are only divisible by 1 and themselves. The prime numbers between 10 and 20 are 11, 13, 17, and 19.

19. **A** To solve this averages question, you must first fill in the average pie. The number of items is 6, and the average is 85. Multiply those two numbers and you get the "Total," which is 510.

Subtract the sum of the five grades given from the total: $510 - 428 = 82$. That is the grade of the sixth student.

20. **A** To find the probability that a black sock will be chosen, just add up the total number of socks: $4 + 5 + 6 + 3 = 18$. Out of those 18 socks, 5 are black. The probability that one of the 5 black socks will be chosen is $\dfrac{5}{18}$.

21. **B** Use Bite Size Pieces for this problem. First, find the maximum heart rate for a 15 year old: $220 - 15 = 205$. Then, find the maximum heart rate for a 60 year old: $220 - 60 = 160$. Finally, find the difference between the two:

$$205 - 160 = 45$$

22. **C** Use Bite Size Pieces for this problem. First, find out how many tickets the theater sold each night: $180 \times 0.70 = 126$. Next, find the total number of tickets the theater sold for all three nights: $126 \times 3 = 378$. Finally, find the gross revenue for all the tickets:

$$378 \times 7 = 2{,}646.$$

23. **D** Use Bite Size Pieces for this one. First, find the number of passengers that are traveling to Los Angeles: $40 \times \dfrac{1}{2} = 20$. Next, find the number of passengers traveling to Los Angeles that departed from Chicago: $20 \times \dfrac{1}{4} = 5$.

24. **C** Use Bite Size Pieces to solve this problem. First, find the total cost for each type of item Melanie is buying: $2 \times 0.97 = 1.94$, $2 \times 1.39 = 2.78$, and $2 \times 1.10 = 2.20$. Then add the totals together: $1.94 + 2.78 + 2.20 = 6.92$. Finally, subtract 6.92 from 20.00 to find the amount of change she should receive: $20.00 - 6.92 = 13.08$.

25. **C** Recall that when you are multiplying the same variable with different exponents, you just add the exponents together. Remember that a variable by itself is the same as a variable with an exponent of one. Therefore, $x^2 \times x = x^2 \times x^1 = x^3$, and $y^3 \times y^2 = y^5$. So the answer needs to contain the terms x^3 and y^5. That leaves C.

26. **D** To solve this proportions question, just match the categories.

$$\frac{6 \text{ questions}}{12 \text{ minutes}} = \frac{5 \text{ questions}}{x \text{ minutes}}$$

Then solve for x:
$$6x = 60$$
$$x = 10$$

27. **A** Recall that when you are dividing by a decimal, you have to move the decimal in the divisor out of the way: $0.675 \div 0.6$ becomes $6.75 \div 6$. That equals 1.125.

28. **D** Use Bite Size Pieces to solve this problem. First, find the number of adults at the picnic: $500 \times .70 = 350$. Next, find the number of children by subtracting the number of adults from the total number: $500 - 350 = 150$.

29. **B** $\dfrac{x}{25} = .88$

   $x = 22$

30. **C** When you multiply a fraction by its reciprocal, the product is 1.

   $$\frac{5}{6} \times \frac{6}{5} = \frac{30}{30} = 1$$

PART 3

WORD KNOWLEDGE

1. **B** Accuse: To charge with a fault; to blame

2. **D** Unscrupulous: Without honor or morals

3. **C** Prominent: Noticeable

4. **A** Conclusive: Putting an end to any uncertainty or doubt; final

5. **B** Endure: To undergo (as a hardship)

6. **C** Overwhelm: To affect deeply in mind or emotion

7. **B** Abundant: Marked by great plenty (as of resources)

8. **A** Chagrin: A feeling of embarrassment caused by disappointment

9. **C** Anthology: A collection of literary pieces

10. **D** Dilute: To thin or weaken

11. **B** Wretched: Living in degradation and misery; miserable

12. **C** Precocious: Characterized by early development or maturity

13. **A** Utilize: To put to use

14. **D** Chastise: To punish

15. **A** Cynical: Distrustful of people's motives

16. **B** Feud: A bitter, prolonged quarrel

17. **C** Diminish: To decrease in size, extent, or range; to lessen the authority, dignity, or reputation of

18. **B** Illuminate: To provide or brighten with light

19. **C** Bizarre: Very strange; unusual

20. **A** Passive: Not active

21. **B** Immense: Extremely large; huge

22. **D** Precarious: Dangerously lacking in security or stability; risky

23. **C** Nomad: A person who roams about, wanderer

24. **B** Rectify: To set right; to correct

25. **A** Candid: Free from prejudice; impartial; straightforward

26. **D** Pious: Exhibiting reverent observance of religion

27. **B** Valiant: Possessing or displaying valor; courageous

28. **C** Foe: A personal enemy

29. **B** Complacent: Contented; self-satisfied

30. **A** Feeble: Lacking strength; weak

31. **D** Excavate: To remove by digging

32. **B** Zest: Spirited enjoyment

33. **C** Ingenious: Original and imaginative in design; brilliant

34. **A** Vital: Necessary to the continuation of life

35. **D** Jubilant: Exultingly joyful

PART 4

PARAGRAPH COMPREHENSION

1. **A** The answer to this specific question lies in the last sentence *"Franklin realized that this electricity could be guided to the ground by a metal wire or rod, thereby protecting houses..."*.

2. **C** The passage never mentions dogs or hearing aids so we don't know A or B. The passage states that sound waves below 20 hertz cannot be heard by humans, but they can feel the vibration. So, answer C is correct.

3. **C** The lead words in this specific questions are "the distant cannonade of a ship in distress." Once you find them in the passage, you can see from the context that they are describing the sound made by the explosion, answer C.

4. **B** You have to read carefully to answer this one. The Augustan age was from 27 BC to 14 AD so you can eliminate A. It was an autocracy so you can eliminate C. It brought about the Pax Romana, so you can eliminate D.

5. **A** A person must be tested for blood type if they are going to receive red blood cells. Red blood cells are only found in whole transfusions, so the answer is A.

6. **D** We know D is the answer because the passage states that maple trees and corn do not need temperatures between 15 and 27 degrees centigrade for germination.

7. **A** The lead word is antiseptics and the passage is talking about how the use of them reduced the number of infections in hospitals. The passage never talks about milk so B is out. C really doesn't make sense in the context of the passage, and D is okay but not as good as answer choice A.

8. **C** The lead words in the questions are Monarch butterfly. Find them in the passage and you see that the Monarch butterfly is an example of an organism that uses passive protection. The answer is C.

9. **D** The best way to approach this type of question is step-by-step. First, determine if statement I is true or false. It's true, so eliminate any answer choice that doesn't include it. That gets rid of B and C. We are left with A (I only) and D (I and III only). So we need to know if statement III is true. Since it is, the answer is D.

10. **B** When answering an inference question, look for the answer that has the most support from the argument. Women are never mentioned, so A is out. Men not exposed to the chemical compound were never discussed so C is out. D is never mentioned, so that leaves us with B.

11. **B** The archaeopteryx lived 150 million years ago, so it would be impossible for the scientists to study it in its native habitat because it's dead. So A is out. The passage never mentions any modern descendants or old written records so C and D are out. That leaves us with B.

12. **C** This is an EXCEPT question, so eliminate everything that is mentioned in the passage. The passage mentions A, B, and D, so the answer is C.

13. **C** She was born in 1797 and wrote *Frankenstein* at the age of 19. 1797 + 19 = 1816, answer choice C.

14. **C** The lead words are "international acclaim." By finding them in the passage we see that the answer is C, *Ulysses*.

15. **D** This general question requires that you be familiar with the entire passage. It's asking us for the tone, so we should look for any clues in the passage. The author describes Joyce as a "celebrated Irish author" and says "His great literary career had begun". Later the passage mentions Ulysses, which "finally brought him the international acclaim he so richly deserved." These statements are all very positive, so the answer is D, appreciative.

PART 5

NUMERICAL OPERATIONS

1. A		26. A	
2. D		27. D	
3. C		28. C	
4. A		29. B	
5. B		30. C	
6. A		31. A	
7. C		32. B	
8. A		33. C	
9. B		34. A	
10. A		35. B	
11. B		36. A	
12. B		37. D	
13. A		38. B	
14. C		39. C	
15. B		40. C	
16. C		41. B	
17. A		42. C	
18. B		43. A	
19. D		44. C	
20. C		45. B	
21. A		46. A	
22. B		47. D	
23. A		48. C	
24. C		49. B	
25. C		50. D	

PART 6

CODING SPEED 1

1.	B	29.	B	57.	D
2.	E	30.	A	58.	D
3.	D	31.	E	59.	B
4.	A	32.	C	60.	C
5.	B	33.	D	61.	E
6.	C	34.	B	62.	A
7.	A	35.	A	63.	B
8.	E	36.	E	64.	C
9.	B	37.	B	65.	D
10.	E	38.	C	66.	B
11.	E	39.	A	67.	D
12.	A	40.	C	68.	A
13.	B	41.	D	69.	E
14.	C	42.	B	70.	A
15.	D	43.	E	71.	C
16.	E	44.	B	72.	B
17.	C	45.	E	73.	C
18.	A	46.	C	74.	D
19.	E	47.	D	75.	A
20.	D	48.	A	76.	B
21.	B	49.	D	77.	E
22.	C	50.	C	78.	B
23.	A	51.	E	79.	E
24.	E	52.	A	80.	C
25.	E	53.	B	81.	C
26.	A	54.	A	82.	A
27.	C	55.	B	83.	B
28.	D	56.	E	84.	D

PART 7

AUTO AND SHOP INFORMATION

1. **C** The rotors are not found in the clutch system. The flywheel is connected to the engine and forms part of the connection system. The clutch plate is the friction plate that fits next to the flywheel. The drive shaft is the main shaft leaving the transmission.

2. **D** You can eliminate C right away—the catalytic converter is located in the exhaust system. Before the fuel can be taken into the engine through the intake valves, it has to be mixed with air. The fuel pump moves fuel to the float tank, where it is siphoned out by the carburetor to be mixed with air.

3. **B** The voltage regulator acts as a control to keep the voltage from the alternator from getting too high. With more voltage going into the rest of the car, the distributor will only take what it needs from the system. The increased voltage allowed to pass through the system would overcharge the battery.

4. **C** For this question, it is probably best to look at the answer choices and determine what the effect of each of the answer choices would be on the car. Too much oil in the car might allow some of the oil to enter the combustion chamber and get burned away, but it wouldn't be responsible for overheating the car. A lean fuel/air mix would cool the combustion temperature, but the cooling system would still be able to take the heat off of the engine normally. A malfunctioning alternator would result in a dead battery and stall the car. However, if the fan belt breaks, then the radiator can not pull the heat out of the water fast enough to cool it to normal temperatures before it goes back into the engine, raising the temperature of the coolant and of the engine. The temperature would rise gradually and the car would begin to overheat.

5. **B** C looks like a good answer, but the diesel cycle only runs diesel engines (hence the name diesel engine). The gasoline cycle does not exist. It normally takes two full rotations of the crankshaft, or four strokes (two up and two down), to get just one power stroke.

6. **D** The sudden drop in the pressure is the key. If the oil is too low, then the pressure would drop, but it would most likely be a gradual process and this would not explain the blue smoke. The head gasket is designed to keep the water, oil, and cylinders all separated from each other across the seam between the engine block and the engine head. If it blows, then water and oil can get into the cylinders and start to combust with the fuel, creating the tell-tale blue smoke.

7. **A** Let's trace the problem through the car. If the water pump fails, then the coolant can't be circulated. This would cause the fluid in the engine to get very hot and not be able to cool down, overheating the engine.

8. **A** This question is similar to question 1 above. We already evaluated that the rotor is part of the brakes and not the transmission. The stator, turbine, and pump make-up the three main components in a torque converter that look like fans.

9. **B** Vapor lock is when fuel in the fuel line gets too hot and vaporizes into bubbles, thus preventing the fuel pump from pumping fuel to the carburetor and stalling the car. If the timing belt snaps or is harmed, the valves will not be able to open and close in synch with the piston movements. This will also stall the car. If a piston were to become lodged in one of the cylinders, the crankshaft would not be able to turn, stopping the engine. A worn clutch plate, however, will allow the engine to keep running but not transmit power to the wheels effectively.

10. **A** The timing belt has teeth like a gear so that the belt maintains the proper timing between the crankshaft and the valves and does not slip. Cams are smooth like an egg and push up on the rods leading to the rocker arm. The rocker arm is like a teeter-totter and has no use for teeth. The fan and alternator do not depend on exact timing like the valves. The fan belt has grooves that go along the length of the belt.

11. **D** Answer choice A looks good at first, but the piston rings are designed to expand to fit the cylinder. The vapors slipping past the piston would decrease power and be undesirable. D is the answer. As pistons get heated from the explosions in the engine, the metal starts to expand. Pistons are cut to allow them to expand when they warm up. In fact, cars will not run efficiently until they have had a chance to "warm up" and the pistons expand.

12. **D** A reamer is used to enlarge existing holes, since the cutting parts on the bit are on the sides. Using the standard bit to enlarge a hole is not recommended, as the cutting edges are located at the tip of the bit and not the sides. A hacksaw does not cut corners and circles well. And an expansion bolt is used in masonry to allow a bolt to hold by expanding against the sides of the material.

13. **B** The teeth on a saw are bent slightly outward to allow the saw to move easily in the gap it cuts. The total width of the gap depends on the total width of the saw blades, known as the kerf. The set of the saw is the angle the teeth are bent to.

14. **A** This question requires that you distinguish between different types of wrenches. The pipe wrench has a moveable top jaw. The Allen wrench looks like a hexagonal rod. So we need to decide between the crescent wrench and the monkey wrench. The crescent wrench looks like a crescent and the jaws open at an angle to the handle. The monkey wrench has jaws that open at an angle of about 90 degrees to the handle.

15. **C** The object shown is a plane. Planes are used for smoothing and flattening cut wood.

16. **A** The backsaw and the carpenters saw both consist of a handle and a blade. The hacksaw and coping saw both have blades that are stretched between the handle and an arm. The coping saw has a tall arm to allow the saw to cut into wood or metal farther. The hacksaw is a beefier saw designed for heavier use with a straight arm off of the handle.

17. **C** The stiff back on a backsaw gives it stability when cutting straight across the grain of wood.

18. **A** Answer choices C and D can be eliminated, because drywall dust will not stay in the hole and cement will not adhere to the drywall. Caulk is used to seal various joints to keep out water, such as in a shower or at the corners of walls and windows. Putty is a substance that is easy to spread over the hole and wipe away, leaving the hole filled. Eventually, the putty will harden in place.

19. **B** The device shown consists of a metal arm and a screw attached to one of its feet. There are no points that are used to measure, like on a caliper; no blades to cut into a pipe; and no way to mount the device to a bench, like on a vise.

20. **A** The bit has a twist down the shaft, so it's a twist bit.

21. **D** A metal hammer or mallet would damage the chisel, shortening the life of the tool. Using a rubber or wooden mallet reduces the damage.

22. **A** Machine screws work much like wood screws, except that wood screws can msake their own threads when they are screwed into wood. Metals are too hard for the screw to make the threads, so machine screws can only be fastened into holes with threads already made.

23. **C** Wax on. Wax off. Sanding in small circles will allow the finish to be smooth and even. Sanding in a line or in one direction can put small indentations and ruts into the surface. Although most sanding to remove material is done with the grain, Mr. Miagi's is the best answer.

24. **D** Rules and calipers are not generally small enough to get an accurate measurement in small gaps. A micrometer is good for measuring small distances, but it can't fit inside small gaps. A feeler gauge is set of calibrated pieces of wire that fit into gaps to measure the clearance.

25. **C** Be careful to note the word EXCEPT in the question. The file has teeth and a face, but no part that is called a blade.

PART 8

MATHEMATICS KNOWLEDGE

1. **B** Plug in the values for x and y:
$3^2 + 4(3) - 3(3)(-4) + 2(-4)^2 = 9 + 12 + 36 + 32 = 89$

2. **B** This problem is a little tricky. The easiest way to solve this one is to plug in numbers for the missing variables. For example, make $p = 5$ and $c = 10$ cents. That means that each piece of candy costs 2 cents. 10 pieces of candy will cost 20 cents. Now look at the answers. Plug the values for p and c into the answers and see which one will give you 20 cents. B: $\dfrac{10(10)}{5} = 20$

3. **C** Start by drawing a rectangle with an area of 12. Assign lengths to the sides. It doesn't really matter what lengths you assign as long as the area is 12. For example, you can use 3 and 4. Then, double each of the lengths. Our rectangle becomes 6 and 8. Find the area:

Area = length × width = 6 × 8 = 48

4. **C** One inch equals 25 feet, so 2.5 inches equals 62.5 feet: 2.5 × 25 = 62.5.

5. **B** Plug in 12 for C and solve for F.

$$12 = \frac{5}{9}(F - 32)$$

$$12 = \frac{5}{9}F - 17.77$$

$$29.77 = \frac{5}{9}F$$

$$F = 53.6$$

6. **B** The easiest way to solve this one is to pick one of the answer choices and see if it works. For example, let's look at B. If Roger pays $20 then Adam pays $10 and Vicky pays $60. That adds up to $90, which is the cost of the radio.

7. **C** Use the Pythagorean theorem to find x.

$$3^2 + 4^2 = x^2$$

$$9 + 16 = x^2$$

$$25 = x^2$$

$$x = 5$$

8. **B** This is a similar triangles question. The sides are proportional, so just set up the proportion and solve for the missing side:

$$\frac{25}{24} = \frac{13}{x}$$

$$25x = 312$$

$$x = 12\frac{12}{25}$$

9. **D** The easiest way to solve this problem is to plug in numbers for the missing variables. Since the questions asks us to figure out how old Marnie is in terms of d, let's start with d. Let's make $d = 8$. If $d = 8$, then Beth = 10 and Marnie = 14. Now look at the answer choices for the answer that will equal 14 when $d = 8$. That answer is D, because $d + 6 = 8 + 6 = 14$.

10. **B** The easiest way to solve this problem is to plug in a number for r. Let's make $r = 50$ cents. 50 cents, or 0.50, goes into $5.00 10 times. Now we want to find the answer choice that equals 10 when we plug 0.50 in for r. That answer is B:

$$\frac{5}{.50} = 10$$

11. **B** The easiest way to solve this problem is to use the answer choices. Pick an answer choice, subtract two from it, and see if the result is one-third of the original number. The correct choice is B: $3 - 2 = 1$ and 1 is one-third of 3.

12. **D** A hexagon is a six-sided figure. If you draw one it is easy to see that there would be 6 legs.

13. **D** A right triangle by definition has a 90 degree angle. So the answer must have 90 degrees in it. That eliminates A and B. All triangles have 180 degrees, so the other angle will be 65 degrees: $180 - 90 - 25 = 65$

14. **C** To find the area of a circle use the formula Area = πr^2. The radius here is 3.5 (half the diameter), so Area = $\pi(3.5)^2 = 12.25\pi$

15. **A** First, expand the exponents: $2^3 = 8$ and $2^4 = 16$. The equation is now:

$$11y + 8 = -5y + 16$$
$$16y = 8$$
$$y = 0.5$$

16. **C** Use Bite Size Pieces to solve this problem. First, find the volume of Steve's pool:

Volume = length × width × height

$$9 \times 15 \times 10 = 1350$$

Next, find the volume of Jim's pool

$$12 \times 20 \times 12 = 2880$$

Then subtract the volume of Steve's pool from the volume of Jim's pool:

$$2880 - 1350 = 1530$$

17. **D** Recall Fred's Theorem. If a third line intersects two parallel lines, two types of angles are created: big and little ones. All big angles are equal and all little angles are equal. Any big angle plus any little angle equals 180 degrees. The diagram gives us the size of the little angle. To find the big angle, just subtract the little angle from 180: $180 - 45 = 135$

18. **C** If you know the definition of perimeter this problem should be easy. $8 \times 4 = 32$

19. **B** This problem is a little tricky. A square has 360 degrees. A triangle has 180 degrees. The difference is 180, but the question asks us for one-half the difference, which is 90.

20. **B** This question is asking for the volume of the sandbox. Volume = length × width × height. Be careful: two of the dimensions are in feet and the third is in inches. You need to convert the inches to feet: 6 inches = 0.5 feet. So you end up with:

Volume of the sandbox = $10 \times 5 \times 0.5 = 25$

21. **C** The area of a square is side × side.

$$9a^2 = 3a \times 3a$$

22. **A** Recall that a product is the result of multiplication. By factoring $x^2 + 3x - 70$ you find the answer: $x^2 + 3x - 70 = (x - 7)(x + 10)$

23. **C** Sketch the line being described. If XZ = 10 and YZ = 3, then XY must equal 7.

24. **B** Sketch the right triangle. Use the Pythagorean theorem to find the side:

$$4^2 + b^2 = 7^2$$
$$16 + b^2 = 49$$
$$b^2 = 33$$

Now use Ballparking to find the answer. 33 doesn't have a perfect square, but $5^2 = 25$ and $6^2 = 36$, so you know the answer lies between these two numbers. The only answer that fits this is B.

25. **C** To answer this problem, you need to solve for x:

$$10 - x < 14$$
$$-x < 4$$
$$x > -4$$

Don't forget to flip the inequality sign when dividing by a negative number, -1.

PART 9

MECHANICAL COMPREHENSION

1. B
2. D
3. B
4. B
5. A
6. B
7. B
8. B
9. A
10. D
11. A
12. A
13. C
14. B
15. A
16. D
17. C
18. D
19. B
20. A
21. A
22. C
23. A
24. B
25. D

PART 10

ELECTRONICS INFORMATION

1. D
2. A
3. D
4. C
5. A
6. A
7. D
8. A
9. A
10. B
11. B
12. C
13. D
14. D
15. C
16. A
17. D
18. A
19. A
20. B

11

PRACTICE TEST 2

PART 1

GENERAL SCIENCE

Time: 11 Minutes — 25 Questions

1. Which organism in the food chain is a primary consumer?

   A. cow
   B. tiger
   C. human
   D. shark

2. The mass extinction of many species, including all dinosaurs, occurred during the

   A. Precambrian era
   B. Paleozoic era
   C. Mesozoic era
   D. Cenozoic era

3. The reddish tint of soil in the southern United States is the result of

   A. humidity
   B. temperature
   C. convection
   D. oxidation

4. What do plants require for photosynthesis?

   A. oxygen, water, and sunlight
   B. carbon dioxide, water, and sunlight
   C. water and soil
   D. water, soil, and sunlight

5. Sperm are produced in the

   A. vas deferens
   B. ovaries
   C. seminiferous tubules
   D. urethra

6. A diploid cell possesses

   A. 46 chromosomes
   B. 92 chromosomes
   C. 23 chromosomes
   D. 16 chromosomes

7. When you walk on the beach you are in which marine biome?

   A. aphotic zone
   B. intertidal zone
   C. neritic zone
   D. oceanic zone

8. The atomic number for potassium is 19. Potassium always has

   A. 9 protons
   B. 9 electrons
   C. 19 electrons
   D. 19 protons

9. The three states of matter are

   A. liquid, metal, gas
   B. acid, solid, base
   C. solid, liquid, gas
   D. heat, sound, chemical

10. A blue object is reflecting

    A. blue light waves
    B. all light waves except blue
    C. blue and violet light waves
    D. red, orange, yellow, and green light waves

11. Smooth muscles are found

    A. in the heart
    B. in the stomach
    C. in the arm
    D. attached to bones

12. An organism in the mollusca phylum also belongs to the

    A. Monera kingdom
    B. Protista kingdom
    C. Plantae kingdom
    D. Animalia kingdom

GO ON TO THE NEXT PAGE.

13. The control center of a cell is located in the

    A   mitochondria
    B. nucleus
    C. ribosomes
    D. lysosomes

14. Cytokinesis occurs during

    A. prophase
    B. anaphase
    C. telophase
    D. metaphase

15. Igneous rock forms from

    A. cooling magma
    B. chemical reactions
    C. weathering
    D. oxidation

16. The ionosphere and exosphere are found in the

    A. troposphere
    B. thermosphere
    C. stratosphere
    D. mesosphere

17. Which of the following is a Jovian planet?

    A. Earth
    B. Mercury
    C. Venus
    D. Saturn

18. Energy that is found in a moving object is

    A. kinetic
    B. potential
    C. thermal
    D. nuclear

19. Which of the following is an element?

    A. water
    B. carbon dixide
    C. hydrogen
    D. salt water

20. Which is an example of refraction?

    A. a light bulb shining
    B. a prism bending sunlight
    C. a mirror reflecting sunlight
    D. x-rays

21. Which subatomic particle has a charge of −1?

    A. electron
    B. neutron
    C. proton
    D. isotope

22. The brain is part of the

    A. autonomic nervous system
    B. somatic nervous system
    C. central nervous system
    D. peripheral nervous system

23. Two parents that are homozygous for the dominant trait brown eyes can have which type of offspring?

    A. Brown-eyed and non-brown-eyed
    B. Only brown-eyed
    C. Only non-brown-eyed
    D. Not enough information available

24. Which of the following is a characteristic of fungi?

    A. They are unicellular.
    B. They live off decomposing matter.
    C. They subsist by photosynthesis.
    D. They have stems and leaves.

25. Which biome is characterized by the heaviest rainfall on earth?

    A. tropical rainforest
    B. deciduous forest
    C. taiga
    D. tundra

STOP!
IF YOU FINISH BEFORE THE TIME IS UP, YOU MAY
CHECK OVER YOUR WORK ON THIS PART ONLY.

PART 2

ARITHMETIC REASONING

Time: 36 Minutes — 30 Questions

1. 15 passengers agree to divide evenly the cost of renting a bus for a trip. If all but 7 of the passengers have paid their share, and a total of $177.60 has been collected, what is the total cost of renting the bus?

   A. $246.15
   B. $333.00
   C. $828.00
   D. $1,555.40

2. Lisa and Annette together weigh 222 pounds, and David weighs 168 pounds. What is the average weight of all three?

   A. 130
   B. 140
   C. 175
   D. 180

3. Gina drove for two hours at a rate of 55 miles per hour. She then drove for 3 hours at a rate of 60 miles per hour. How far did she travel?

   A. 180
   B. 240
   C. 290
   D. 300

4. A sack of marbles has 6 red marbles, 9 blue marbles, 2 green marbles, and 4 black marbles. If one marble is chosen from the sack at random, what is the probability that it will be a red marble?

   A. $\dfrac{4}{21}$

   B. $\dfrac{15}{21}$

   C. $\dfrac{6}{13}$

   D. $\dfrac{6}{21}$

5. Leasing a car costs $179 per month plus $0.06 per mile driven. If your monthly car budget is $500, what is the farthest that you can drive in one month (to the nearest mile) and remain within your budget?

   A. 5050
   B. 5240
   C. 5350
   D. 5450

6. Rita received a 90 in History, an 88 in Spanish, and an 85 in Biology. Suppose the classes have the following weights: History 2, Spanish 3, and Biology 4. What is Rita's average, rounded to the nearest tenth?

   A. 86.5
   B. 87.1
   C. 89.3
   D. 90.2

7. Mel bought a TV for $350. Three days later Jack bought the same TV at a 15% discount. How much more did Mel pay for the TV than Jack?

   A. $52.50
   B. $53.50
   C. $252.45
   D. $297.50

8. Kim is building a scale model of an airplane. Each inch represents 7 feet. If the real airplane is 115 feet long, approximately how long, in inches, is the model?

   A. 16.0 inches
   B. 16.5 inches
   C. 17.0 inches
   D. 17.5 inches

9. Dave bought 4 pounds 8 ounces of steak for $16.83. What is the cost of 1 pound of steak?

   A. $3.88
   B. $4.06
   C. $3.74
   D. $4.21

GO ON TO THE NEXT PAGE.

10. Max can build a chair in 2.5 days. Working at the same rate, how many chairs can he build in 55 days?

    A. 21
    B. 22
    C. 23
    D. 24

11. If $x = 9$, then $3x^2 - 7x + 4 =$

    A. 156
    B. 178
    C. 182
    D. 184

12. Farmer Andy expected to harvest 4300 bushels of corn this season. After a season of great weather, Andy harvests 4850 bushels of corn. Approximately what percentage of Andy's original harvest estimate did Andy actually harvest?

    A. 113%
    B. 119%
    C. 89%
    D. 150%

13. The cash register at Pet-A-Rama pet shop always starts with $100 in it every morning. On one day the following purchases were made: 2 dog collars at $8.89 each, 1 litter box at $12.50, 3 goldfish at $.79 each, 2 parakeets at $17.99 each, and 4 hamsters at $7.79 each. What was the total amount of money in the cash register at the end of the day?

    A. $99.70
    B. $100.00
    C. $199.79
    D. $187.43

14. What are the next three terms in the sequence: 1, 3, 7, 13..?

    A. 19, 21, 27
    B. 21, 31, 43
    C. 15, 17, 19
    D. 21, 27, 31

15. In Mr. Kelley's social studies class, $\frac{2}{3}$ of the 36 students are Democrats and the rest are Republicans. In Ms. Richey's social studies class, $\frac{3}{4}$ of the 28 students are Republicans and the rest are Democrats. What are the total numbers of Democrats and Republicans in both classes?

    A. 30 Democrats, 30 Republicans
    B. 31 Democrats, 33 Republicans
    C. 33 Democrats, 31 Republicans
    D. 35 Democrats, 29 Republicans

16. $\sqrt{2} \ \sqrt{8} =$

    A. 2
    B. $2\sqrt{2}$
    C. $4\sqrt{2}$
    D. 4

17. A pet goat eats two pounds of goat food and one pound of grass each day. When the goat has eaten a total of fifteen pounds combined of goat food and grass, how many pounds of grass will it have eaten?

    A. 2
    B. 3
    C. 5
    D. 8

18. If $6x - 4 = 38$, then $x =$

    A. 7
    B. 10
    C. 12
    D. 14

19. A barrel is filled with 50 gallons of lemonade. If every person at a picnic drinks 1 pint of lemonade and the barrel is emptied, how many people are at the picnic?

    A. 50
    B. 200
    C. 400
    D. 500

GO ON TO THE NEXT PAGE.

20. The fraction $\dfrac{9}{72}$ is equal to what percentage?

   A. 9.0%
   B. 10.5%
   C. 12.5%
   D. 17%

21. What is the value of 5^3?

   A. 15
   B. 25
   C. 100
   D. 125

22. During one season, a professional basketball player tried 420 shots and made 294 of them. What percent of his shots did he make?

   A. 65%
   B. 70%
   C. 75%
   D. 80%

23. You are given $20 to buy ice cream for a party. If ice cream costs $3.20 per gallon, how many gallons of ice cream can you buy?

   A. 6.25
   B. 6.50
   C. 7.0
   D. 7.5

24. A backpack usually costs $35.00, but was reduced by 22% for a sale. What was the cost of the backpack on sale?

   A. $24.83
   B. $25.22
   C. $26.35
   D. $27.30

25. A bus travels 420 miles in 8 hours. What was the bus's average speed, in miles per hour?

   A. 50 mph
   B. 52.5 mph
   C. 55.5 mph
   D. 58.5 mph

26. If $3x + 5y = 15$ and $x - 2y = 10$, then $2x + 7y =$

   A. 5
   B. 10
   C. 15
   D. 25

27. If $-9m - 12 > 11 - 3m$, then

   A. $m < -\dfrac{23}{6}$

   B. $m > -\dfrac{23}{6}$

   C. $m > -\dfrac{23}{12}$

   D. $m < -\dfrac{1}{6}$

28. $12.46 \div 100 =$

   A. 1246
   B. 124.6
   C. 0.1246
   D. 1.246

29. $\dfrac{3}{5} + \dfrac{5}{6} =$

   A. $\dfrac{23}{6}$

   B. $1\dfrac{13}{30}$

   C. $2\dfrac{13}{30}$

   D. $\dfrac{25}{30}$

30. Three tankers each carry 10,000 tons of oil, and a fourth tanker carries 12,000 tons of oil. What is the average number of tons of oil carried by each of the four tankers?

   A. 10,000
   B. 10,050
   C. 10,500
   D. 11,500

STOP!
IF YOU FINISH BEFORE THE TIME IS UP, YOU MAY
CHECK OVER YOUR WORK ON THIS PART ONLY.

NO TEST MATERIAL ON THIS PAGE

PART 3

WORD KNOWLEDGE

Time: 11 Minutes — 35 Questions

1. Accidental most nearly means

   A. purposeful
   B. unexpected
   C. taunting
   D. deliverable

2. Refute most nearly means

   A. discuss
   B. clarify
   C. disprove
   D. justify

3. Revolution most nearly means

   A. evolution
   B. overthrow
   C. cure
   D. elect

4. The candidate stressed the importance of having good values.

   A. beliefs
   B. finances
   C. defenses
   D. voters

5. Poll most nearly means

   A. rod
   B. exit
   C. report
   D. survey

6. Conquer most nearly means

   A. create
   B. devise
   C. defeat
   D. watch

7. Disturb most nearly means

   A. bother
   B. classify
   C. invent
   D. listen

8. Larry viewed his co-workers as opponents in the workplace.

   A. friends
   B. compatriots
   C. teammates
   D. enemies

9. Adapt most nearly means

   A. counter
   B. adjust
   C. tear
   D. exercise

10. Awe most nearly means

    A. wonder
    B. sickly
    C. implement
    D. boastful

11. Colleague most nearly means

    A. enemy
    B. predecessor
    C. co-worker
    D. soldier

12. Chris's statement about the movie was misleading.

    A. entertaining
    B. powerful
    C. glorifying
    D. deceptive

13. Pledge most nearly means

    A. commit
    B. clean
    C. taken
    D. coerce

GO ON TO THE NEXT PAGE.

14. Resentment most nearly means

    A. cooling
    B. affirmation
    C. respected
    D. hatred

15. Sufficient most nearly means

    A. choke
    B. limited
    C. enough
    D. excellent

16. The announcer was very animated in his description of the fight.

    A. drawn
    B. lively
    C. pessimistic
    D. terse

17. Transparent most nearly means

    A. opaque
    B. conductive
    C. clear
    D. difficult

18. Graceful most nearly means

    A. beautiful
    B. rude
    C. listless
    D. destructive

19. Indignation most nearly means

    A. independent
    B. aloof
    C. respect
    D. outrage

20. Pam's report on the current state of the economy was insightful.

    A. erroneous
    B. perceptive
    C. classic
    D. plagiarized

21. Skeptical most nearly means

    A. optimistic
    B. doubtful
    C. confident
    D. likely

22. Reaction most nearly means

    A. emotion
    B. explosion
    C. response
    D. therapy

23. Validity most nearly means

    A. truth
    B. candor
    C. search
    D. communicate

24. When Elliot lost his job, his life became full of turmoil.

    A. boredom
    B. commitments
    C. depression
    D. confusion

25. Undermine most nearly means

    A. strengthen
    B. found
    C. weaken
    D. trick

26. Quarrel most nearly means

    A. conflict
    B. fourth
    C. create
    D. declaration

27. Potential most nearly means

    A. possible
    B. knowledge
    C. opportunity
    D. encompass

28. The senator is a very influential person in Congress.

    A. respected
    B. amused
    C. mocked
    D. powerful

GO ON TO THE NEXT PAGE.

29. <u>Infer</u> most nearly means

    A. melt
    B. create
    C. conclude
    D. trap

30. <u>Persuasive</u> most nearly means

    A. beautiful
    B. convincing
    C. destructive
    D. encompassing

31. <u>Precious</u> most nearly means

    A. overpriced
    B. cherished
    C. lively
    D. diminished

32. Lisa thought the fight scene was <u>irrelevant</u> to the plot of the play.

    A. unimportant
    B. ambivalent
    C. crucial
    D. enlightening

33. <u>Nostalgia</u> most nearly means

    A. nasal
    B. royal
    C. longing
    D. tenuous

34. <u>Impulse</u> most nearly means

    A. charge
    B. stance
    C. urge
    D. effective

35. <u>Hazardous</u> most nearly means

    A. forceful
    B. onerous
    C. technical
    D. dangerous

STOP!
IF YOU FINISH BEFORE THE TIME IS UP, YOU MAY
CHECK OVER YOUR WORK ON THIS PART ONLY.

NO TEST MATERIAL ON THIS PAGE

PART 4

PARAGRAPH COMPREHENSION

Time: 13 Minutes—15 Questions

1. In 1896 the United States Supreme Court in the case *Plessy v. Ferguson*, public schools and other institutions were legally segregated under the doctrine of "separate but equal." In 1954 the Supreme Court in the case *Brown v. Board of Education of Topeka*, unanimously reversed this decision and declared this policy unconstitutional. Chief Justice Earl Warren's decision stated that "separate educational facilities are inherently unequal" and ordered that all public schools desegregate.

All of the following statements are true EXCEPT:

A. Since 1954, segregating a public school is illegal.
B. Before 1954, it was legal for schools to be segregated.
C. The doctrine of "separate but equal" applied to segregated schools.
D. Some of the members of the 1954 Supreme Court voted against reversing *Plessy v. Ferguson*.

2. Great artists are not normally confined by the "movements" that others may name for them. Rather, they transcend the conventional structure, working now in one style, then in another, and later in a third. Picasso's work, for example, echoes many of their artistic movements, and other artists too, work their way from one style to another. Indeed, artists are people, and may decide to alter style for no more complex a reason than that which makes most people want to "try something new" once in a while.

The author mentions Picasso in order to

A. describe an artist who didn't reflect numerous movements
B. provide an example of an artist who exhibited many different artistic movements
C. emphasize that not all artists were well regarded until after their deaths
D. show how one artist can have a great influence on many other artists

3. During the Progressive Era in the United States (1900–1920), a group of journalists and writers known as muckrakers went about exposing all the nasty abuses of power and money that went on during the end of the nineteenth century. They stirred up public opinion and helped win public support for various social reforms.

Which of the following is true about muckrakers?

A. They blindly supported politicians.
B. They committed abuses of power and money.
C. They came about in the late twentieth century.
D. They may have had something to do with some social reform.

4. The Boeing 747 is the largest passenger airplane currently in use. It takes about 10 months to build and is built in the largest building in the world. The cost of a 747 is well over $100 million.

What can be inferred from the above passage?

A. The 747 is the fastest commercial airplane built.
B. It takes longer to build a 747 than any other airplane.
C. There is no larger passenger plane than the 747.
D. A 747 costs $140 million.

GO ON TO THE NEXT PAGE.

5. Neanderthals had different facial structures than Homo sapiens. They had virtually no forehead and lacked the jutting chin of Homo sapiens. Neanderthals had a substantial nose, thicker bones, and abnormally large teeth.

Which of the following statements is most likely true?

A. Neanderthals looked very similar facially to Homo sapiens.
B. Neanderthals had a different chin than Homo sapiens.
C. Neanderthals were generally taller than Homo sapiens.
D. Neanderthals had lighter bones than Homo sapiens.

6. Different chemical bonds naturally have different strengths. For instance, the bond between a carbon atom and an oxygen atom is stronger than the bond between two chlorine atoms. When a bond is relatively strong, we say its bond energy is high. Bond energy involves the amount of energy it takes to break a bond.

Which of the following can be inferred about chemical bonds?

A. They all have the same bond energy.
B. The bond between two chlorine atoms and the bond between a carbon and oxygen atom have different bond strengths.
C. The bond between a carbon atom and a chlorine atom has relatively high bond energy.
D. They have low bond energy when the bond is strong.

7. The digestive system of the cow is complex and interesting. Unlike humans, who have a simple stomach, the cow has a large four-chambered stomach. Cows eat plants, primarily grasses, which are only partly digested in one of the four chambers, called the rumen. The cow will then regurgitate, or bring back up, the partially digested plant fibers in a small mass called "cud." The cud is chewed further and swallowed again, this time into the second chamber, called the reticulum. It passes then to the third and fourth chambers, until it is completely digested. It may sound unpleasant, but the cow is able to extract a maximum of nutrients from its food by digesting in this manner. The whole process may take more than three days.

The best title for this passage might be

A. The Cow's Great Gift to Man: Milk
B. Digestive Systems and their Purposes
C. The Diet of the Cow
D. The Digestive System of the Cow

8. Every substance "knows" how to be a solid, liquid, or gas, each of which is called a "state" or a "phase." Whether a substance is in one phase or another depends on temperature and pressure. Water, for instance, turns from solid to liquid or from liquid to solid at zero degrees Celsius and one atmosphere of pressure. It turns from liquid to gas or gas to liquid at one hundred degrees Celsius and one atmosphere of pressure.

Based on the above paragraph, what is true about water?

A. It does not change states.
B. Water freezes at zero degrees Fahrenheit.
C. When pressure equals two atmospheres, water boils at two hundred degrees Celsius.
D. Pressure has an influence on what state a substance is in.

GO ON TO THE NEXT PAGE.

9. This was our last watch fire of the year. Next week the other boys were to file back to their old places in the Sandtown High School, but I was to go up to the divide to teach my first country school in the Norwegian district. I was already homesick at the thought of quitting the boys with whom I had always played; of leaving the river, and going up into a windy plain that was all windmills and cornfields and big pastures; where there was nothing willful or unmanageable in the landscape, no new island, and no chance of unfamiliar birds—such as often followed the watercourses.

Why will the narrator remember this watch fire better than others?

A. It is the narrator's birthday.
B. The narrator is going away soon.
C. The narrator has just been born.
D. The narrator has recently gotten a new job.

10. A piece of rock, named rock number 84001, found in the Arctic, was discovered to be a piece of a meteor from Mars. When studied under a powerful microscope, scientists found what they thought were fossilized remains of microscopic Martian life forms. It turns out that the fossilized remains were mineral deposits and not Martian life.

What can be inferred from the above passage?

A. Remains from Mars can find their way to Earth.
B. There was microscopic life on Mars.
C. All meteors found on earth are from Mars.
D. Most meteors found on earth are found in the Arctic.

11. During the mid-nineteenth century, reformer Dorothea Lynde Dix, a former schoolteacher, carried on a one-person crusade to improve the treatment of the mentally ill. Her efforts were instrumental in the establishment of hospitals and asylums for the mentally ill.

Based on the information above, which of the following is most likely true?

A. Prior to the efforts of Dorothea Lynde Dix, there were relatively few hospitals or asylums for the mentally ill.
B. In the mid-nineteenth century there was a large swell of support to improve the treatment of the mentally ill.
C. There are currently relatively few hospitals and asylums for the treatment of the mentally ill.
D. Treatment of the mentally ill was a social priority at the beginning of the nineteenth century.

12. Making seat belt use mandatory will reduce automobile fatalities. State X has one of the lowest automobile fatality rates in the country, and law there requires seat belt use.

The paragraph means most nearly that

A. state X has low airline fatality rates as well
B. mandatory seat belt use does not work
C. seat belts lower insurance premiums
D. mandatory seat belt use will reduce automobile fatalities

GO ON TO THE NEXT PAGE.

Questions 13–15 are based on the following passage.

Recent studies have confirmed what many people have suspected for years. Emotions can have an effect on your health. Research has shown that people with positive, upbeat attitudes are generally in better health than negative, pessimistic people. Stress, in particular, has been shown to be a factor in immune system functioning. People that are under stress for extended periods of time tend to have weaker immune systems than people that are not under stress. This may put them at risk for developing health problems, or aggravate existing conditions.

Doctors have begun recommending support groups for patients with serious health problems such as cancer. Studies have shown that cancer patients that belong to support groups tend to live longer and feel better than patients that don't. Doctors are not sure why this is, but believe it may have something to do with the emotional support patients receive from each other. For many patients, support groups provide the only opportunity they have to share their feelings with others going through the same experiences.

While these new findings are certainly interesting, there is still a lot of work to be done. Researchers cannot explain why or how emotions affect the immune system. Nor can they explain why different emotions affect the immune system differently. Therefore, further research needs to be done to try and answer these perplexing questions.

13. What is the main point of the paragraph above?

A. Emotions such as unhappiness and loneliness can make you sick.
B. Cancer patients that attend group therapy live longer.
C. More research needs to be done to study the effects of emotions on health.
D. The immune system works independently of the rest of the body.

14. According to the passage, which of the following is NOT true of cancer patients that belong to support groups?

A. They live longer.
B. They learn more about cancer.
C. They feel better.
D. They receive emotional support.

15. Which of the following can be inferred from the passage?

A. If you are under a lot of stress, you will probably get cancer.
B. If you are positive and upbeat you will never get sick.
C. Doctor's with cancer attend their own support groups.
D. There are still a lot of unanswered questions regarding emotions and their effects on health.

STOP!
IF YOU FINISH BEFORE THE TIME IS UP, YOU MAY
CHECK OVER YOUR WORK ON THIS PART ONLY.

PART 5

NUMERICAL OPERATIONS

Time: 3 Minutes — 50 Questions

1. $2 \times 5 =$

   A. 7
   B. 10
   C. 12
   D. 14

2. $36 \div 6 =$

   A. 6
   B. 12
   C. 14
   D. 16

3. $10 \times 8 =$

   A. 50
   B. 60
   C. 80
   D. 90

4. $14 + 7 =$

   A. 16
   B. 18
   C. 20
   D. 21

5. $25 - 12 =$

   A. 11
   B. 12
   C. 13
   D. 15

6. $49 \div 7 =$

   A. 7
   B. 9
   C. 11
   D. 12

7. $9 \times 6 =$

   A. 45
   B. 50
   C. 54
   D. 63

8. $90 \div 10 =$

   A. 8
   B. 9
   C. 19
   D. 11

9. $12 + 12 =$

   A. 20
   B. 22
   C. 24
   D. 27

10. $72 \div 8 =$

    A. 9
    B. 12
    C. 13
    D. 14

11. $8 \times 8 =$

    A. 56
    B. 59
    C. 61
    D. 64

12. $4 \times 7 =$

    A. 20
    B. 28
    C. 32
    D. 34

13. $3 \times 1 =$

    A. 1
    B. 3
    C. 4
    D. 6

14. $10 \div 2 =$

    A. 5
    B. 10
    C. 12
    D. 13

GO ON TO THE NEXT PAGE.

15. 4 + 5 =

    A. 4
    B. 7
    C. 8
    D. 9

16. 7 × 1 =

    A. 6
    B. 7
    C. 9
    D. 10

17. 6 + 3 =

    A. 3
    B. 9
    C. 12
    D. 16

18. 8 ÷ 2 =

    A. 4
    B. 8
    C. 12
    D. 16

19. 2 × 3 =

    A. 5
    B. 6
    C. 12
    D. 14

20. 10 × 0 =

    A. 10
    B. 7
    C. 4
    D. 0

21. 4 × 4 =

    A. 12
    B. 14
    C. 16
    D. 18

22. 5 + 1 =

    A. 6
    B. 7
    C. 8
    D. 9

23. 6 ÷ 3 =

    A. 2
    B. 4
    C. 6
    D. 9

24. 9 ÷ 9 =

    A. 9
    B. 10
    C. 1
    D. 3

25. 1 × 8 =

    A. 8
    B. 9
    C. 12
    D. 16

26. 7 + 4 =

    A. 8
    B. 9
    C. 10
    D. 11

27. 9 − 1 =

    A. 8
    B. 9
    C. 12
    D. 13

28. 3 × 5 =

    A. 12
    B 15
    C. 16
    D. 23

29. 10 − 2 =

    A. 10
    B. 8
    C. 7
    D. 4

30. 18 ÷ 2 =

    A. 9
    B. 12
    C. 18
    D. 21

GO ON TO THE NEXT PAGE.

31. 4 + 0 =

   A. 0
   B. 2
   C. 4
   D. 6

32. 8 + 3 =

   A. 5
   B. 7
   C. 9
   D. 11

33. 9 × 1 =

   A. 9
   B. 10
   C. 12
   D. 13

34. 13 ÷ 1 =

   A. 1
   B. 10
   C. 13
   D. 14

35. 17 − 4 =

   A. 16
   B. 13
   C. 10
   D. 8

36. 56 ÷ 8 =

   A. 6
   B. 7
   C. 8
   D. 9

37. 9 + 6 =

   A. 15
   B. 16
   C. 18
   D. 19

38. 5 − 4 =

   A. 4
   B. 3
   C. 2
   D. 1

39. 25 ÷ 5 =

   A. 2
   B. 5
   C. 6
   D. 7

40. 8 × 3 =

   A. 21
   B. 22
   C. 24
   D. 26

41. 1 × 6 =

   A. 6
   B. 7
   C. 8
   D. 9

42. 2 + 2 =

   A. 3
   B. 4
   C. 5
   D. 7

43. 8 ÷ 4 =

   A. 1
   B. 2
   C. 3
   D. 5

44. 6 + 4 =

   A. 10
   B. 12
   C. 14
   D. 15

45. 10 × 2 =

   A. 12
   B. 16
   C. 18
   D. 20

46. 15 − 7 =

   A. 9
   B. 8
   C. 5
   D. 4

GO ON TO THE NEXT PAGE.

47. $12 \div 3 =$

   A. 10
   B. 7
   C. 6
   D. 4

48. $19 - 6 =$

   A. 14
   B. 13
   C. 10
   D. 9

49. $13 + 3 =$

   A. 12
   B. 14
   C. 16
   D. 17

50. $7 - 6 =$

   A. 1
   B. 3
   C. 6
   D. 7

STOP!
IF YOU FINISH BEFORE THE TIME IS UP, YOU MAY
CHECK OVER YOUR WORK ON THIS PART ONLY.

PART 6
Coding Speed

Time: 7 Minutes — 84 Questions

Key

alley 5784	data 3962	goat 1540	kite 9728	oath 6095
band 8617	face 0439	infant 4873	load 2351	sale 7106

Questions		Options				
		A	**B**	**C**	**D**	**E**
1.	infant	2351	3962	4873	5784	6095
2.	oath	1540	2351	3962	6095	8617
3.	face	0439	1540	3962	5784	7106
4.	sale	1540	2351	4873	6095	7106
5.	data	2351	3962	5784	6095	7106
6.	kite	4873	5784	6095	8617	9728
7.	alley	1540	3962	5784	6095	7106
8.	band	0439	3962	7106	8617	9728
9.	goat	0439	1540	4873	7106	9728
10.	load	2351	4873	6095	7106	8617
11.	data	1540	3962	5784	7106	9728
12.	kite	3962	4873	6095	8617	9728

Key

apple 1119	cake 0204	day 5323	lane 9634	organ 7803
bet...................6095	court 3621	gift 8652	nail 4327	scoop 2629

Questions		Options				
		A	**B**	**C**	**D**	**E**
13.	organ	3621	4327	5323	7803	8652
14.	scoop	0204	2629	3621	4327	6095
15.	lane	5323	6095	7803	8652	9634
16.	apple	1119	3621	4327	6095	7803
17.	court	0204	2629	3621	5323	6095
18.	bet	2629	4327	5323	6095	8652
19.	nail	2629	4327	6095	7803	8652
20.	cake	0204	1119	4327	5323	6095
21.	day	2629	4327	5323	7803	8652
22.	gift	4327	6095	7803	8652	9634
23.	apple	0204	1119	3621	4327	7803
24.	nail	2629	3621	4327	6095	8652

Key

bike 5648	disk 0733	hawk 1157	mop 7796	sale 3509
chore 8276	foot 9329	lunch 4847	plow 2633	vent 6310

Questions			Options		
		A	**B**	**C**	**D**	**E**

Questions		A	B	C	D	E
25.	chore	3059	5648	7796	8276	9329
26.	plow	1157	2633	4847	6310	7796
27.	lunch	0733	3509	4847	6310	8276
28.	vent	2633	4847	5648	6310	8276
29.	disk	0733	2633	3509	5648	7796
30.	foot	4847	6310	4496	8276	9329
31.	sale	1157	2633	3509	7796	8276
32.	mop	3509	5648	7796	8276	9329
33.	hawk	1157	3509	6310	7796	9329
34.	bike	2633	4847	5648	6310	8276
35.	disk	0733	2633	5648	7796	9329
36.	vent	2633	4847	5648	6310	7796

Key

art 3141	cat 7950	floor 9793	meat 6535	pack 8462
bite 5897	dust 2653	key 0649	oat 1592	ranch 4338

Questions			Options		
		A	**B**	**C**	**D**	**E**

Questions		A	B	C	D	E
37.	dust	1592	2653	4338	5897	7950
38.	meat	2653	4338	5897	6535	8462
39.	ranch	1592	3141	4338	7950	9793
40.	key	0649	2653	3141	5897	6535
41.	pack	2653	4338	5897	7950	8462
42.	floor	3141	5897	6535	7950	9793
43.	art	1592	3141	4338	6535	7950
44.	bite	0649	3141	5897	7950	8462
45.	cat	2653	4338	6535	7950	9793
46.	dust	2653	3141	6535	8462	9793
47.	oat	1592	3141	4338	6535	8462
48.	ranch	2653	4338	6535	7950	9793

Key

bear 4118	egg 0854	gate 1982	quote 5674	seed 1730
check 6098	fuel 7717	light 2475	risk 8120	tire 9314

Questions

Options

	A	B	C	D	E
49. egg	0854	2475	4118	6098	7717
50. quote	2475	4118	5674	8120	9314
51. fuel	1982	4118	6098	7717	8120
52. bear	2475	4118	5674	6098	7717
53. risk	0854	2475	5674	7717	8120
54. seed	1730	2475	4118	6098	9314
55. gate	1730	1982	6098	7717	8120
56. check	0854	1982	6098	8120	9314
57. light	0854	1730	1982	2475	4118
58. tire	4118	5674	7717	8120	9314
59. quote	2475	4118	5674	7717	8120
60. gate	1982	4118	6098	7717	9314

Key

area 0492	deck 7529	herd 6121	man.................. 1694	ticket 4875
cable 3687	goal 9453	knob 8428	officer 5524	wave 2001

Questions

Options

	A	B	C	D	E
61. cable	0492	1694	3687	5524	8428
62. goal	2001	4875	5524	6121	9453
63. herd	3687	4875	5524	6121	7529
64. area	0492	2001	4875	7529	9453
65. man	0492	1694	3687	5524	6121
66. ticket	1694	3687	4875	6121	7529
67. deck	3687	4875	6121	7529	8428
68. knob	0492	4875	5524	7529	8428
69. wave	1694	2001	4875	6121	8428
70. officer	0492	4875	5524	7529	9453
71. herd	3687	5524	6121	8428	9453
72. man	1694	3687	7529	8428	9453

Key

belt 9451	end 7622	game 8492	model 0504	shovel 5496
comb 4380	film 1132	iron 6283	navy 3827	village 2772

Questions / Options

	Questions	A	B	C	D	E
73.	navy	1132	3827	5496	7622	9451
74.	village	2772	4380	6283	8492	9451
75.	film	1132	2772	4380	5496	7622
76.	iron	0504	1132	2772	6283	8492
77.	game	0504	2772	4308	7622	8492
78.	belt	4380	5496	6283	7622	9451
79.	end	0504	3827	7622	8492	9451
80.	comb	1132	4380	5496	6283	8492
81.	model	0504	2772	6283	7622	9451
82.	shovel	1132	3827	5496	6283	7622
83.	film	0504	1132	3827	4380	6283
84.	village	2772	4380	5496	6283	7622

STOP!
IF YOU FINISH BEFORE THE TIME IS UP, YOU MAY
CHECK OVER YOUR WORK ON THIS PART ONLY.

PART 7

AUTO AND SHOP INFORMATION

Time: 11 Minutes — 25 Questions

1. If the first stroke on a four stroke engine is the intake stroke, what is the second?

   A. intake
   B. power
   C. exhaust
   D. compression

2. A starter motor does not make any noise when the key is turned in the ignition, but the lights on the car work. The first thing that should be checked is

   A. the fuse box
   B. the battery charge
   C. the distributor
   D. the throttle valve

3. The device used to transfer power from the drive shaft to the rear axle is called the

   A. distributor
   B. differential
   C. master cylinder
   D. torque converter

4. The engine is overheating. One of the possible causes is

   A. not enough fluid in the radiator
   B. malfunctioning distributor
   C. lean air/fuel mixture
   D. vapor lock

5. A thick, black sludge is found in the tailpipe of the car. This is probably due to

   A. oil leaking into a cylinder
   B. rich fuel/air mixture
   C. condensation in the tail pipe
   D. a clogged exhaust manifold

6. The pinion gear is found on the

   A. braking system
   B. steering system
   C. transmission
   D. clutch

7. Condensation inside fuel tanks could lead to

   A. a sludge forming at the bottom of the gas tank
   B. potential for fire in the gas tank
   C. misfiring cylinders
   D. the vehicle stalling

8. An automatic transmission vehicle fails to accelerate as it should and does not shift smoothly. The problem is probably

   A. not enough transmission fluid
   B. jammed differential
   C. damaged wheel bearings
   D. improper timing

9. Spark plugs should be seated in the port with a torque wrench to prevent

   A. the piston from hitting the spark plug on the top of the stroke
   B. changing the timing of the distributor
   C. damaging the spark plug's body
   D. threading the engine block

10. The thermostat controls

    A. oil temperature in the engine
    B. water temperature in the manifold
    C. water temperature in the radiator
    D. the exhaust temperature

11. The engine seems to "run loud" in a car. The problem might be

    A. worn wheel bearings
    B. overextended piston rods
    C. a crack in the exhaust manifold
    D. too much oil.

12. A high-pitched squeak comes from the wheels when stopping. The most likely problem is

    A. the master cylinder over-pressurized the lines
    B. the wheel bearings are damaged
    C. the brake shoes are worn
    D. the rims are rubbing on the wheel bearings

GO ON TO THE NEXT PAGE.

13. To oxidize unburned hydrocarbons, the catalytic converter uses

    A.   special chemical-coated beads
    B.   a burner
    C.   a small oxygen tank
    D.   positive exhaust ventilation

14. Calipers are used to

    A.   clamp objects together
    B.   pick objects up
    C.   measure the outside diameter of a pipe
    D.   remove stuck screws

15. Which of the following can be used when cutting an angle in a piece of wood stock?

    A.   jack plane
    B.   c-clamp
    C.   miter box
    D.   jointer plane

16. The tool pictured above is used to

    A.   cut across the grain of wood
    B.   cut sheet metal
    C.   cut curves
    D.   cut through nails embedded in wood

17. When tapping a hole for a screw, it is important to

    A.   start with a center punch
    B.   keep driving in until the threads are deep enough
    C.   regularly back out the tap
    D.   use a rubber mallet

18. Grinding wheels are used

    A.   in place of a jack plane
    B.   to sand wood
    C.   to cut through sheet metal
    D.   to remove metal burrs

19. The main constituents in concrete are

    A.   cement and sand
    B.   water and cement
    C.   gravel, water, and cement
    D.   sand, gravel, water, and cement

20. The cutting parts of a boring bit are found

    A.   at the tips
    B.   in the screw portion
    C.   between the tips and the center
    D.   in the main shaft

21. The screw length of a flathead screw is the length of the

    A.   threaded portion only
    B.   head, shanks and threaded portion
    C.   the width of the head
    D.   shank and the threaded portion

22. For optimum use, rivets should

    A.   allow $\frac{1}{8}$ of the diameter of motion in the two sheets being joined

    B.   be near a bolted connection
    C.   be of the same material as the sheet metal being joined
    D.   be hot during installation

23. The tool shown above is a

    A.   socket wrench
    B.   box wrench
    C.   open end wrench
    D.   speed wrench

24. A chalk line is often used

    A.   to measure the chalk content in concrete
    B.   when dry lubricant is needed
    C.   to mark a straight line between two points
    D.   to write on wood

25. Which tool is used to determine when two objects are normal to each other?

    A.   miter box
    B.   level
    C.   calipers and rule
    D.   square

STOP!
IF YOU FINISH BEFORE THE TIME IS UP, YOU MAY CHECK OVER YOUR WORK ON THIS PART ONLY.

PART 8

MATHEMATICS KNOWLEDGE

Time: 24 Minutes—25 Questions

1. If $(7x)^2 = 441$, then $x=$

   A. 3
   B. 5
   C. 6
   D. 13

2. An architecture student built a scale model of a building. Each inch in the model represents 15 feet. If the building is 202 feet tall, approximately how high is the model?

   A. 12 inches
   B. $12\frac{1}{2}$ inches
   C. 13 inches
   D. $13\frac{1}{2}$ inches

3. A rectangle has a length of 7 inches and an area of 56 inches. What is its width?

   A. 49
   B. 21
   C. 8
   D. 7

4. There are 7 fruit stands on a road. Each fruit stand has x apples and y oranges. What is the total number of apples and oranges combined in all 7 fruit stands?

   A. $7xy$
   B. $\dfrac{7x}{y}$
   C. $7x + 7y$
   D. $7(x-y)$

5. The perimeter of a swimming pool is 70 feet. The pool's width is 5 feet less than its length. What is the length of the pool?

   A. 20
   B. 40
   C. 50
   D. 70

6. How many more sides does an octagon have than a quadrilateral?

   A. 4
   B. 8
   C. 10
   D. cannot be determined

7. $(x^2 + 6x + 3)(x + 3) =$

   A. $x^2 + 3x + 18x + 6$
   B. $x^3 + 6x^2 + 21x + 9$
   C. $x^3 + 9x^2 + 21x + 9$
   D. $x^2 + 18x + 6x + 18$

8. For what value of m does $2m + 4 = m^3$?

   A. 1
   B. 2
   C. 3
   D. 4

9. A circle has a radius of 4. What is the area? (Use 3.14 for π)

   A. 12.14
   B. 50.24
   C. 25.12
   D. 200.96

10. If the area of a square is $64\pi^2$, what is the length of one side of the square?

    A. $64\pi^2$
    B. $8\pi^2$
    C. 64π
    D. 8π

11. What is the volume of a rectangular box with dimensions 2 by 3 by 4?

    A. 54
    B. 27
    C. 24
    D. 14

12. What is another way to write $2\sqrt{20}$?

    A. $4\sqrt{5}$
    B. $2\sqrt{5}$
    C. $\sqrt{40}$
    D. $4\sqrt{20}$

GO ON TO THE NEXT PAGE.

13. 25 percent of what number is equal to 10?

    A. 30
    B. 40
    C. 45
    D. 50

14. Which of these has 7 in the hundredths place?

    A. 2.0376
    B. 2.3067
    C. 2.7036
    D. 2.3706

15.

If l_1 is parallel to l_2 then $\angle a + \angle b =$

    A. 200
    B. 175
    C. 160
    D. 130

16. If $-9 \leq x < 7$, then x is

    A. less than 7 but more that −9
    B. less than 7 but more than or equal to −9
    C. more than or equal to 7 or less than −9
    D. more than −9 or more than 7

17.

What is the circumference of the above circle?

Diameter = 4

    A. 6π
    B. 8π
    C. 4π
    D. 16π

18. If $6x = 90$ then $x =$

    A. 15
    B. 13
    C. 18
    D. 12

19. Another way to write 3^3 is

    A. 9
    B. 18
    C. 24
    D. 27

20. A hexagon's sides are all 5 inches long. What is the perimeter of the hexagon?

    A. 25
    B. 30
    C. 35
    D. 40

21. Multiply: $2xy(4y - 5x^2)$

    A. $8xy^2 - 10x^3y$
    B. $8x^2y^2 - 10x^2y$
    C. $6xy^2 - 7x^3y$
    D. $8xy - 10xy$

22. If p is an odd integer, which of the following must also be an odd integer?

    A. $p + 1$
    B. $\dfrac{p}{2}$
    C. $p + 2$
    D. $2p$

23.

The surface area of the above rectangular box is
    A. 74
    B. 108
    C. 128
    D. 148

GO ON TO THE NEXT PAGE.

24. Solve: $-5x + 6 < 61$

    A. $x < 11$
    B. $x > 11$
    C. $x > -11$
    D. $x < -11$

25. A car drives south for 3 miles and stops. It then drives east for 4 miles and stops again. How far is the car from its original location?

    A.   7 miles
    B.   5 miles
    C.   4 miles
    D.   3 miles

STOP!
IF YOU FINISH BEFORE THE TIME IS UP, YOU MAY
CHECK OVER YOUR WORK ON THIS PART ONLY.

PART 9

MECHANICAL COMPREHENSION

Time: 19 Minutes — 25 Questions

1. 100 degrees Celsius is equal to how many degrees Fahrenheit?

    A. 100
    B. 32
    C. 0
    D. 212

2. Which pulley turns the slowest?

    A. A
    B. B
    C. C
    D. D

3. How much force is needed to push the piano up the ramp?

    A. 15
    B. 50
    C. 75
    D. 150

4. If the wheel above rotates, which of the dots will rotate at the slowest rate?

    A. 1
    B. 2
    C. 3
    D. All the dots will rotate at the same

5. Skater A and B collide and stick together. After the collision, which of the following is true?

    A. Both skaters stop at the point of impact
    B. The skaters will move to the right at a speed of less than 10 miles per hour
    C. The skaters will move to the left at a speed of greater than 10 miles per hour
    D. The skaters will move to the left at a speed of less than 5 miles per hour

6. A ramp is an example of

    A. a lever
    B. a fulcrum
    C. a block and tackle
    D. an inclined plane

GO ON TO THE NEXT PAGE.

7. If all of the following objects are at the same temperature, which will feel the coldest?

A. A metal teakettle
B. A plastic bucket
C. A wool sweater
D. A blade of grass

8. If rock A weighing 2 lbs and rock B weighing 3 lbs are both dropped at the same time from a height of 100m, which of the two will reach the ground first?

A. Rock A
B. Rock B
C. Both rocks will reach the ground at the same time
D. Not enough information is available.

9. Gear A, which has a diameter of 4 feet, is turning gear B, which has a diameter of 1 foot. If gear A makes one revolution, how many revolutions does gear B make?

A. One revolution
B. Two revolutions
C. Four revolutions
D. Eight revolutions

10. If Mr. Thompson is pouring sand into a sandbox at a rate of 60 lbs per minute and his daughter is removing sand from the sandbox at a rate of 1 lb. per second, then after two minutes the amount of sand in the sandbox will

A. have increased by 60 lbs
B. have increased by 120 lbs
C. have decreased by 60 lbs
D. be exactly the same

Figure not drawn to scale

11. Suppose that the adult is sitting three feet from the fulcrum on the side of the seesaw away from the child. How heavy would the adult need to be in order to balance the seesaw?

A. 30 lbs
B. 60 lbs
C. 120 lbs
D. 180 lbs

12. 160 pounds of force is required to tip the barrel. How much force must the worker apply to the lever?

A. 20
B. 40
C. 60
D. 80

13. What is the theoretical mechanical advantage conferred by the gears of the bicycle

A. $\frac{1}{2}$
B. 1
C. 2
D. 5

14. Which type of belt is least likely to stretch?

A. Leather
B. Rubber
C. Canvas
D. All three are equally likely to stretch.

GO ON TO THE NEXT PAGE.

15. Water condenses on pipes that
    A. contain hot water
    B. contain cold water
    C. contain steam
    D. are empty

16. The water pressure surrounding a submarine is 150 psi. A porthole on the submarine measures 10 square inches. What is the force on the porthole?
    A. 15 pounds
    B. 150 pounds
    C. 1500 pounds
    D. 15000 pounds

17. If the temperature of a gas increases
    A. its charge will increase
    B. its charge will decrease
    C. its pressure will increase
    D. its pressure will decrease

4"   2"

18. Water flows into the pipe from the right at a speed of 12 feet per second. What is the speed of the water as it leaves the pipe?
    A. 2 feet per second
    B. 3 feet per second
    C. 8 feet per second
    D. 24 feet per second

19. If two pipes carry liquids moving at the same velocity, then the pipe with the least area will have the
    A. lowest flow rate
    B. highest flow rate
    C. the same flow rate as the other pipe
    D. highest mass

20. Which of the following is a substance commonly used to reduce friction?
    A. Gravel
    B. Sand
    C. Gasoline
    D. Oil

21. When shafts are not parallel, which type of gears should be used?
    A. Spur gears
    B. Bevel gears
    C. Helical gears
    D. Straight gears

22. Which of the following is a device designed to connect or disconnect driving and a driven member for the purpose of starting or stopping the driven part?
    A. A wheel
    B. An axle
    C. An engine
    D. A clutch

23. The device most commonly used to convey liquids against the force of gravity is the
    A. block and tackle
    B. clutch
    C. generator
    D. pump

24. One mile equals approximately how many meters?
    A. 500
    B. 1000
    C. 1500
    D. 2000

25. Many adhesives are unable to maintain their strength
    A. under high atmospheric pressure
    B. at low temperatures
    C. at high temperatures
    D. at room temperatures

STOP!
IF YOU FINISH BEFORE THE TIME IS UP, YOU MAY
CHECK OVER YOUR WORK ON THIS PART ONLY.

PART 10

ELECTRONICS INFORMATION

Time: 9 Minutes — 20 Questions

1. Which of the following colors signify that a wire is grounded?

   A. Green
   B. Black
   C. Red
   D. Yellow

2. The current through a 100 ohm resistor is 0.5 A. What is the power rating of the resistor?

   A. 5 W
   B. 25 W
   C. 50 W
   D. 100 W

3. Opposition to current flow is known as

   A. capacitance
   B. resistance
   C. inductance
   D. conductance

4. Which of the following is the best conductor of electricity?

   A. Carbon
   B. Brass
   C. Silver
   D. Steel

5. Capacitance is measured in

   A. ohms
   B. amps
   C. watts
   D. farads

6. How much current will a 100 watt light bulb draw if it is plugged into a 120 volt socket?

   A. 0.25 A
   B. 0.5 A
   C. 0.8 A
   D. 1.0 A

7. Three wires protrude from

   A. a resistor
   B. a capacitor
   C. a diode
   D. a battery

8. Common household current is

   A. AC
   B. DC
   C. It varies according to time of year.
   D. It varies according to temperature.

9. A rheostat is a type of

   A. capacitor
   B. resistor
   C. transformer
   D. battery

10. What is the total resistance of a 6 ohm and a 16 ohm resistor in parallel?

    A. 2.67 ohms
    B. 4.5 ohms
    C. 10 ohms
    D. 20 ohms

11. The sum of the voltage drops around a circuit is equal to the source voltage. This is a statement of

    A. Ohm's Law
    B. Kirchhoff's Law
    C. Faraday's Law
    D. Edison's Law

12. Electrical energy, or charge, is measured in

    A. farads
    B. microfarads
    C. watts
    D. coulombs

GO ON TO THE NEXT PAGE.

13. Which household electric appliance uses the most current?

    A. A range
    B. A dishwasher
    C. A television
    D. A freezer

14. A newly soldered joint should be

    A. rough
    B. shiny and smooth
    C. balled up on the joint
    D. gray

15. Five lamps are connected in series. Each lamp requires 16 V and 0.1 amps. The total power used is

    A. 0.1 W
    B. 8 W
    C. 16 W
    D. 80 W

16. Which of the following appliances have the highest wattage?

    A. Clock
    B. Toaster
    C. Broiler
    D. Air conditioner

17. What is the efficiency of a transformer if it draws 600 W and delivers 300 W?

    A. 200%
    B. 100%
    C. 50 %
    D. 25 %

18. It's best to drive grounding rods using a

    A. power drill
    B. claw hammer
    C. ball peen hammer
    D. rotary hammer

19. The symbol above represents a

    A. diode
    B. transistor
    C. inductor
    D. capacitor

20. The symbol above represents a

    A. diode
    B. transistor
    C. inductor
    D. capacitor

STOP!
IF YOU FINISH BEFORE THE TIME IS UP, YOU MAY CHECK OVER YOUR WORK ON THIS PART ONLY.

12

ANSWERS AND EXPLANATIONS TO PRACTICE TEST 2

PART 1

GENERAL SCIENCE

1. **A** A primary consumer is an organism that lives off producers (plants) only.

2. **C** Toward the end of the Mesozoic era, a mass extinction of many species, including dinosaurs, occurred.

3. **D** Oxidation occurs when metallic elements in rock combine with oxygen.

4. **B** Carbon dioxide, water, and sunlight are all required for photosynthesis.

5. **C** Sperm are produced in the seminiferous tubules, which merge into a large duct called the vas deferens.

6. **A** Diploid cells contain 23 pairs of chromosomes. Almost all human cells are diploid, except for sex cells.

7. **B** The intertidal zone is located where the land and water meet.

8. **D** The atomic number of an element is equivalent to the number of protons it has.

9. **C** Matter has three states: solid, liquid, and gas.

10. **A** A blue object reflects blue light waves only.

11. **B** Smooth muscles are found in the stomach, cardiac muscles are found in the heart, and skeletal muscles are attached to bones.

12. **D** Mollusks are technically animals.

13. **B** The nucleus is called the control center of the cell.

14. **C** Cytokinesis is the splitting of the cytoplasm.

15. **A** When magma cools and solidifies it becomes igneous rock.

16. **B** The thermosphere is divided into two regions, the ionosphere and the exosphere.

17. **D** The Jovian planets are Jupiter, Saturn, Uranus, and Neptune.

18. **A** Kinetic energy is energy found in a moving object.

19. **C** An element is a substance that cannot be broken down further by chemical means. Water, carbon dioxide, and salt water all can be broken down further; they are all made up of different elements.

20. **B** Refraction is the bending of light.

21. **A** Electrons have a charge of –1, protons of +1, and neutrons are neutral. Isotopes are not subatomic particles.

22. **C** The central nervous system consists of the brain and spinal cord.

23. **D** The two homozygous parents have a genotype of BB. They can only pass on B genes, never b genes, which they do not have. Therefore, their children will always have the genotype BB and always have brown eyes.

24. **B** Fungi are multicellular, but they do not have stems or leaves and they do not carry on photosynthesis.

25. **A** Tropical rainforests get more rain than anywhere else on earth—hence the name.

PART 2

ARITHMETIC REASONING

1. **B** Use Bite Size Pieces to answer this problem. First, subtract the 7 people who haven't paid from the total number in the group: $15 - 7 = 8$. That means that 8 people have paid. Divide the amount of money collected so far by 8: $177.60 \div 8 = 22.20$. Each person is paying $22.20. Multiply that by the 7 people who still need to pay: $22.20 \times 7 = 155.40$. That is the amount of money that still needs to be collected. Add that to the money already collected and you have the answer: $177.60 + 155.40 = 333.00$.

2. **A** Use the average pie to answer this question. Add David's weight to Lisa and Annette's combined weight to get the total. Put the total and the number of items in the set (3) into the average pie to find the average. $390 \div 3 = 130$

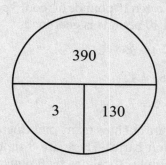

3. **C** Use Bite Size Pieces to answer this problem. First, multiply 55 by 2: $55 \times 2 = 110$. That's how far Gina traveled in the first 2 hours. Then, multiply 60 by 3: $60 \times 3 = 180$. That's how far she traveled in the next 3 hours. Add the sums together: $110 + 180 = 290$.

4. **D** To find the probability that a red marble will be chosen, add all the marbles in the sack together: $6 + 9 + 2 + 4 = 21$. Then put the number of red marbles over the total: $\frac{6}{21}$. That's the probability that a red marble will be selected.

5. **C** Use Bite Size Pieces for this problem. First, subtract the cost to lease the car from the monthly budget: $500 - 179 = 321$. This is the amount of money you have to spend on mileage. Next, divide that by the cost per mile: $321 \div .06 = 5350$.

6. **B** This is a weighted-average problem, so you need to weight the grades accordingly. Multiply each grade by the weight assigned to it: $90 \times 2 = 180$, $88 \times 3 = 264$, and $85 \times 4 = 340$. Add the products together and divide by the total number of weights: $784 \div 9 = 87.111$.

7. **A** To find the answer, all you need to do is figure out what Jack's discount was. To find this, multiply 350 by 15 percent: $350 \times 0.15 = 52.5$.

8. **B** The real plane is 115 feet long and each inch of the model represents 7 feet. Divide 115 by 7 to find the length of the model: $115 \div 7 = 16.43$ inches. The closest answer is B.

9. **C** 1 pound = 16 ounces, so Dave bought 4.5 pounds of steak. Divide the total cost of the steak by 4.5 to find the cost per pound: $16.83 \div 4.5 = 3.74$.

10. **B** To answer a proportions question, match up the categories and solve for the missing item:

$$\frac{1 \text{ chair}}{2.5 \text{ days}} = \frac{x \text{ chairs}}{55 \text{ days}}$$

Then cross-multiply and solve:

$$2.5x = 55$$
$$x = 22$$

11. **D** $3(9)^2 - 7(9) + 4 =$

$3(81) - 63 + 4 =$

$243 - 63 + 4 = 184$

12. **A** Divide the actual harvest by the estimated harvest: $4850 \div 4300 = 1.127$

13. **C** Use Bite Size Pieces for this problem. First, calculate the total cost for each type of item purchased: 2 × 8.89 = 17.78, 1 × 12.50 = 12.50, 3 × 0.79 = 2.37, 2 × 17.99 = 35.98, 4 × 7.79 = 31.16. Then add up the products for the total amount of the day's purchases:

17.78 + 12.50 + 2.37 + 35.98 + 31.16 = 99.79. Add that total to the $100 that is already in the cash register: 100 + 99.79 = 199.79.

14. **B** Subtract the second term from the first term (3 –1 = 2) and the third term from the second term (7 – 3 = 4). The differences are 2 and 4. Subtract the fourth term from the third term (13 – 7 = 6). The difference is 6. The numbers in the sequence are increasing by multiples of two. So the fifth number will be 8 greater than the fourth number, the sixth 10 greater than the fifth, and the seventh 12 greater than the sixth.

15. **B** Use Bite Size Pieces to solve this problem. First, calculate the number of Democrats in Mr. Kelley's class: $36 \times \frac{2}{3} = 24$ Democrats.

Therefore, there are 36 – 24 = 12 Republicans. Next, calculate the number of Republicans in Ms. Richey's class: $28 \times \frac{3}{4} = 21$ Republicans.

That leaves 28 – 21 = 7 Democrats. Add the number of Democrats from each classroom and the number of Republicans from each classroom. Democrats: 24 + 7 = 31. Republicans: 12 + 21 = 33.

16. **D** $\sqrt{2}\ \sqrt{8} = \sqrt{16} = 4$

17. **C** Make a ratio box for this problem and fill in everything you know.

Grass	Food	Total
1	2	3
		15

What multiplied by 3 gives you 15? 5 does, so fill it in.

Gross	Food	Total
1	2	3
× 5	× 5	× 5
5	10	15

From the table you can see that when the goat has eaten 15 pounds of food, 5 pounds is grass and 10 pounds is goat food.

18. **A** 6x – 4 = 38

6x = 42

x = 7

19. **C** Figure out how many pints there are in the 50-gallon barrel. There are 8 pints in a gallon. Multiply 50 gallons by 8 pints: 50 × 8 = 400 pints.

20. **C** Let's start by reducing this fraction into something a little easier to work with: $\frac{9}{72} \div \frac{9}{9} = \frac{1}{8}$.

Recall that a fraction bar implies division. So divide 1 by 8: 1 ÷ 8 = 0.125, or 12.5 percent.

21. **D** $5^3 = 5 \times 5 \times 5 = 125$

22. **B** Divide the number made by the number attempted: $294 \div 420 = 0.7$, or 70 percent.

23. **A** Divide 20.00 by 3.20: $20 \div 3.20 = 6.25$

24. **D** 22 percent of $35.00 is $7.70: $0.22 \times 35 = 7.7$. Subtract that from the regular cost: $35.00 - 7.70 = 27.30$

25. **B** Distance = rate × time

$$420 = 8 \times \text{rate}$$

$$\text{rate} = 52.5$$

26. **A** Subtract $x - 2y = 10$ from $3x + 5y = 15$:

$$
\begin{array}{r}
3x + 5y - 15 \\
-(x - 2y + 10 \\
\hline
2x + 7y = 5
\end{array}
$$

27. **A** $-9m - 12 > 11 - 3m = -6m > 11$ To solve this one you need to isolate the variable. Let's add $3m$ to both sides. This gives us : $-6m - 12 > 11$. Next, add 12 to both side and you get: $-6m > 23$. Finally, divide both sides by -6. Remember, since this is an inequality and not an equal sign, we need to flip the sign around since we're dividing by a negative number. This gives us the answer: $m = -\dfrac{23}{6}$.

28. **C** When dividing by a multiple of ten, move the decimal point to the left one space for each 0. Since we are dividing by 100, which has two 0s, we move the decimal to the left two spaces.

29. **B** Use the Bow tie. Multiply the denominators to find a common factor: $5 \times 6 = 30$. Then cross-multiply to find the new numerators: $3 \times 6 = 18$ and $5 \times 5 = 25$. Then add:

$$\frac{18}{30} + \frac{25}{30} = \frac{43}{30} = 1\frac{13}{20}$$

30. **C** Add the weights of the four tankers to find the total: $10{,}000 + 10{,}000 + 10{,}000 + 12{,}000 = 42{,}000$. The number of items is 4. So divide by 4 to find the average: $42{,}000 \div 4 = 10{,}500$.

PART 3

WORD KNOWLEDGE

1. **B** Accidental: happening by chance or unexpectedly

2. **C** Refute: to disprove

3. **B** Revolution: a political overthrow

4. **A** Values: beliefs of a person or social group

5. **D** Poll: to obtain and analyze information or opinions from people; a survey of people's opinions

6. **C** Conquer: to defeat an opponent

7. **A** Disturb: to interfere with

8. **D** Opponent: one who takes an opposite position

9. **B** Adapt: to adjust or make usable

10. **A** Awe: an emotion combining fear and wonder

11. **C** Colleague: a co-worker

12. **D** Misleading: deceptive

13. **A** Pledge: to make a binding commitment to do or give or refrain from something

14. **D** Resentment: deep hatred

15. **C** Sufficient: enough

16. **B** Animated: filled with life, activity, vigor, or spirit

17. **C** Transparent: clear; see-through

18. **A** Graceful: characterized by beauty of movement, style, form, etc.

19. **D** Indignation: moral outrage

20. **B** Insightful: exhibiting clear and deep perception

21. **B** Skeptical: doubtful; disbelieving

22. **C** Reaction: the act or process or an instance of responding; a response

23. **A** Validity: truth; correctness

24. **D** Turmoil: a state or condition of extreme confusion, agitation, or commotion

25. **C** Undermine: to remove support from; to weaken

26. **A** Quarrel: a verbal conflict between antagonists

27. **A** Potential: possible

28. **D** Influential: having influence or power

29. **C** Infer: to conclude or figure out

30. **B** Persuasive: able to move people to act or believe

31. **B** Precious: highly esteemed or cherished

32. **A** Irrelevant: having no connection to a subject

33. **C** Nostalgia: longing for familiar things or persons, or for a period of time or an occurrence that has past

34. **C** Impulse: force or urge

35. **D** Hazardous: involving risk or danger

PART 4

PARAGRAPH COMPREHENSION

1. **D** This is an EXCEPT question, so you're looking for the answer that is not stated in the passage. D is the answer because the court voted unanimously.

2. **B** Choices A and B are saying the opposite of each other, so one of them is probably the correct answer. By referring back to the passage, we see that Picasso was an example of an artist who demonstrated many artistic styles in his work. Hence, the answer is B.

3. **D** Politicians are never mentioned in the passage, so get rid of A. They exposed abuses of power and money, so get rid of B. They came about in the beginning of the 20th century, so get rid of C. That leaves you with D.

4. **C** Look for a paraphrase of the passage. C paraphrases the first sentence, so it's the answer.

5. **B** The passage says that Neanderthals had different facial structures than Homo sapiens so eliminate A. C is never mentioned, and D is the opposite of what the passage says, so the answer is B.

6. **B** Since it's an inference question, look for a paraphrase of the passage, which B is.

7. **D** This is a main idea question in disguise. The main idea of the passage is not milk or the diet of the cow, so eliminate A and C. B is too general, so the answer is D.

8. **D** Choice A isn't true, so cross it off. Water freezes at zero degrees Celsius, not Fahrenheit, so cross off B, and the passage never mentions C, so the answer is D.

9. **B** The passage states that the author is leaving home next week.

10. **A** Choice A can be inferred from the passage because remains from Mars must be able to find their way to Earth if a meteor from Mars was found in the Arctic. The passage doesn't say B or D, and C is extreme.

11. **A** The passage states "Her efforts were instrumental in the establishment of hospitals and asylums for the mentally ill." This supports answer choice A.

12. **D** Choices A and C are never mentioned, and B is the opposite. So, the answer is D.

13. **C** Choices A and B are mentioned in the passage, but are not the main point. D is never stated. C is a nice paraphrase of the last sentence, which is the main point.

14. **B** Use the lead words "cancer patients" to guide you to the answer. Cross off answers that are mentioned in the passage and that leaves you with B.

15. **D** Look for the sentence that paraphrases the question. A and C are never stated, and B is extreme. D is a paraphrase of the main point.

PART 5

NUMERICAL OPERATIONS

1. B
2. A
3. C
4. D
5. C
6. A
7. C
8. B
9. C
10. A
11. D
12. B
13. B
14. A
15. D
16. B
17. B
18. A
19. B
20. D
21. C
22. A
23. A
24. C
25. A
26. D
27. A
28. B

29. B
30. A
31. C
32. D
33. A
34. C
35. B
36. B
37. A
38. D
39. B
40. C
41. A
42. B
43. B
44. A
45. D
46. B
47. D
48. B
49. C
50. A

PART 6

Coding Speed 2

1. C		29. A		58. E	
2. D		30. E		59. C	
3. A		31. C		60. A	
4. E		32. C		61. C	
5. B		33. A		62. E	
6. E		34. C		63. D	
7. C		35. A		64. A	
8. D		36. D		65. B	
9. B		37. B		66. C	
10. A		38. D		67. D	
11. B		39. C		68. E	
12. E		40. A		69. B	
13. D		41. E		70. C	
14. B		42. E		71. C	
15. E		43. B		72. A	
16. A		44. C		73. B	
17. C		45. D		74. A	
18. D		46. A		75. A	
19. B		47. A		76. D	
20. A		48. B		77. E	
21. C		49. A		78. E	
22. D		50. C		79. C	
23. B		51. D		80. B	
24. C		52. B		81. A	
25. D		53. E		82. C	
26. B		54. A		83. B	
27. C		55. B		84. A	
28. D		56. C			
		57. D			

PART 7

AUTO AND SHOP INFORMATION

1. **D** After the air and fuel is taken into the cylinders, the valves close and the piston returns to the top of the cylinder. This is the compression stroke. Next is the power stroke, during which the sparkplug ignites the fuel/air mixture. Then the exhaust valve opens and the piston returns back to the top of the cylinder to expel the exhaust gasses.

2. **A** When looking for problems in the vehicle, it is important to start from the source and work back toward the malfunctioning component. This allows you to identify big-picture problems that could be cheaper to fix. The lights on the car work but not the starter. That means that the battery works. Following the power from the working battery, the next problem could be a blown fuse in the fuse box. After that, the connection of the electrical cables leading to the starter should be checked. If you still can't find the problem at this point, then the starter itself is probably at fault.

3. **B** The distributor controls the timing and distribution of electricity to the sparkplugs. The master cylinder is in the braking system. The torque converter works like a clutch in an automatic transmission. The differential gear is a grouping of gears that connects the driveshaft to the rear axles.

4. **A** Answer choice D would cause the engine to stall. Answer choice B would cause the engine to stall out or to sputter and misfire. A lean fuel/air mix would actually cool the engine a bit, as it reduces the combustion temperature. But if there is not enough coolant in the cooling system, then the coolant will not be able to cool significantly before it re-enters the engine block to take up more heat.

5. **A** A thick black sludge normally forms in the tail pipe due to something burning and depositing in the exhaust system. A is incorrect because unburned fuel usually evaporates and leaves the vehicle. D is wrong because a clogged exhaust system would not allow anything to pass out of the system. C is wrong because, though water can mix with built-up carbon deposits and accumulate in the exhaust system, its sludge is normally thin and runny. Oil, however, is heavy and, when burned, does not always exit the exhaust system, leaving a thick black sludge.

6. **B** The pinion is used in conjunction with the rack gear to turn the wheels.

7. **A** If you have ever seen an oil slick on water, you have seen that the water tends to sink and the oil moves to the surface of the water. This is true in a gas tank as well. The water moves to the bottom of the tank, where it mixes with the impurities that settle out of the gas. This typically causes sludge to form at the bottom of the tank. As for B, the only way to start a fire in the gas tank is to put it near a heat source or spark. And water in the cylinders still allows the fuel to burn and the cylinder to go through its power stroke, though the combustion will not be as complete.

8. **A** Choices B and C both deal with problems that would occur farther down the drive train. Improper timing prevents the cylinders from firing in the right sequence and would affect the smoothness of the engine. But, because automatic transmissions use a torque converter, if there is not enough fluid, the pump will not be able to turn the turbine properly.

9. **D** The torque wrench allows the user to know how much force is being applied to the bolt. This prevents the tool from over-tightening and potentially from stripping the threads.

10. **B** The thermostat opens when the water in the manifold reaches a certain temperature and then closes again to allow the water into the radiator to cool. The water in the radiator can't get back into the engine without the thermostat opening, but its opening is based only on coolant temperatures in the manifold.

11. **C** Answer choice A can be discarded because the wheels are not part of the engine. One of the purposes of the exhaust system is to help to quiet the car. If there is a crack in the manifold before the gases can go through the exhaust system, then the car will "run loud." Too much oil will generally quiet the vehicle.

12. **C** Since the sound only comes when stopping, the sounds are probably coming from the brakes. Damaged wheel bearings would make noise whether the vehicle is stopping or just cruising down the road.

13. **A** The oxidation process in the catalytic converter is entirely chemical. The chemical coating on the beads works to push ahead the oxidation process without burning the gasses.

14. **C** Calipers are strictly a measuring device and should not be used for anything else.

15. **C** A miter box is used to hold the saw's blade in line while cutting angles. Planes are used to shape wood surfaces. A C clamp just holds objects together.

16. **C** The first step is to identify the picture as a coping saw. The coping saw has a thin blade to allow it to flex and cut curves and corners in wood.

17. **C** If a tap is not taken completely out of the hole while the threads are being made, the shavings will clog in the end of the tap and jam the tap in the hole. The tap should be taken out of the hole every 5 turns to clean off the shavings.

18. **D** Grinding wheels are not used to remove large pieces of material; they are designed to remove small pieces of metals or to smooth or polish a surface. The jack plane is used on wood, not metal.

19. **D** To make concrete, you need all of these components mixed wet and allowed to dry.

20. **C** A boring bit uses a different method from that of standard bits. The boring bit uses a threaded part to draw it into a piece of stock. Two points then scribe a circle that is to be drilled. The material is then removed from within this circle by the cutting blades located between the center and the tips.

21. **D** The length of a screw is the distance that it will sink into a piece of wood. So if the head is a standard round head, the length is the shank and threaded portion only, since the head will stick up above the surface of the wood. If the head is a countersink head, then the length of the screw is the full length of the fastener including the head. The question does not tell us that the screw is a countersink head, so assume it's a standard.

22. **C** Rivets should fit snuggly into the rivet holes, but the materials *must* be the same. If they are not the same, then chemical reactions can take place at the interface between the two metals and the joint will be very weak.

23. **B** Since the end of the wrench is closed, this must be a box wrench.

24. **C** Chalk lines are ropes covered in chalk that are stretched between two points and laid on the ground. The line is then snapped upward and some of the chalk falls off, leaving a temporary line of chalk between the two points. As for A, there is no chalk in concrete. And a pencil, not a chalk line, is the best thing for writing on wood.

25. **D** "Normal" means at a right angle. The tool to use in this case is a square. A level only allows the user to see if something is horizontal or vertical and is therefore not the best tool for the job.

PART 8

MATHEMATICS KNOWLEDGE

1. **A** The easiest way to solve this problem is to plug in the answers. If we plug in 3 (answer choice A) for x we get: $[7(3)]^2 = [21]^2 = 441$.

2. **D** The scale is 1 inch = 15 feet. Divide 202 by 15 to find the height of the scale model: 202 ÷ 15 = 13 remainder 7, or 13.4.

    That's approximately $13\frac{1}{2}$ feet.

3. **C** If the area is 56 inches and the length is 7 inches then you can use the area formula to find the width.

    $$\text{Area} = \text{length} \times \text{width}$$

    $$56 = 7w$$

    $$w = 8$$

4. **C** Use Plugging In to solve this problem. Let's say each fruit stand has 5 apples and 4 oranges. That's 9 pieces of fruit at each stand. Then we multiply that number by 7, since there are seven stands, for a total of 63 pieces of fruit. So 63 is our target number. Now we need to plug in 4 and 5 into the answer choices to find our target number. When we plug in our numbers, only answer choice C works: 7(5) + 7(4) = 35 + 28 = 63.

5. **A** Perimeter is found by adding the lengths of all sides. The best way to find the length of the pool is to plug in numbers from the answer choices. If you plug in answer choice A, 20 then you get: length = 20 and width = 15.

    $$20 + 20 + 15 + 15 = 70$$

6. **A** An octagon has 8 sides and a quadrilateral has 4. The difference is 4.

7. **B** Multiply each term in $x^2 + 6x + 3$ by x, then multiply each term by 3:

    $x(x^2 + 6x + 3) = x^3 + 6x2 + 3x$, and $3(x^2 + 6x + 3)$ $= 3x^2 + 18x + 9$.

    Then add the results together:

    $x^3 + 6x2 + 3x + 3x^2 + 18x + 9 = x^3 + 6x^2 + 21x + 9$

8. **B** Plug in the answer choices to find the one that works. If you plug in answer B, which is 2, then you get:

    $$2(2) + 4 = 2^3$$

    $$4 + 4 = 8$$

9. **B** Area = πr^2, so here, area = 16π. The problem tells us that $\pi = 3.14$, so we have $16 \times 3.14 = 50.24$

10. **D** The area of a square is side², or side × side, so we have $\sqrt{64\pi^2} = 8\pi$.

11. **C** Volume = length × width × height. So here, volume = 2 × 3 × 4 = 24.

12. **A** Two factors of 20 are 4 and 5. 4 has a square root, 2, which can be pulled out. So we have:

    $$2\sqrt{20} = 2\sqrt{4 \times 5} = 2\sqrt{2 \times 2 \times 5} = 2 \times 2\sqrt{5} = 4\sqrt{5}$$

13. **B** 25 percent = $\frac{1}{4}$. So ask yourself: $\frac{1}{4}$ of what number equals 10? Try the answer choices. When you get to B, you have $\frac{1}{4}$. That's the answer.

14. **D** Recall that the order after the decimal point is: tenths, hundredths, thousandths.

15. **C** Remember Fred's Theorem. $\angle a = 65$ and $\angle b = 95$, so a + b = 160.

16. **B** $x < 7$ means that x is less than 7, and $-9 \leq x$ means that x is greater than or equal to –9.

17. **C** Circumference = $2\pi r$, or π diameter. Since the diameter is 4, the answer is 4π.

18. **A** Solve for x by dividing both sides of the equation by 6. $x = 15$.

19. **D** $3^3 = 3 \times 3 \times 3 = 27$

20. **B** A hexagon has six sides, and the perimeter is the sum of the lengths of all the sides, so: 6 × 5 = 30.

21. **A** Multiply $2xy$ by both of the terms inside the parentheses. Remember that when multiplying exponents, you add them together, and that any variable by itself without an exponent is the same as that variable with an exponent of 1: $y = y^1$. So $2xy \times 4y = 8xy^2$ and $2xy \times 5x^2 = 10x^3y$. The answer is A.

22. **C** Use Plugging In on this one. Choose any odd integer and plug it into the answer choices. Let's use 3. If we plug 3 into the answer choices, the only answer that is also an odd integer is C: $3 + 2 = 5$.

23. **D** Find the area of each side of the box and add the areas together: front = 30, back = 30, top = 24, bottom = 24, side = 20, side = 20. $30 + 30 + 24 + 24 + 20 + 20 = 148$.

24. **C** Remember, you must always flip the inequality when multiplying or dividing by a negative number:

$$-5x + 6 < 61$$

$$-5x < 55$$

$$x > -11$$

25. **B** Draw a picture of the car's route. Then sketch a line from the end point to the starting point. That is the distance you are trying to find. Your sketch should look something like this:

Does this look familiar? It should—it's a right triangle. Use the Pythagorean theorem to find the distance:

$$3^2 + 4^2 = x^2$$

$$9 + 16 = x^2$$

$$25 = x^2$$

$$x = 5$$

PART 9

MECHANICAL COMPREHENSION

1. D
2. B
3. A
4. D
5. D
6. D
7. A
8. C
9. C
10. D
11. C
12. B
13. C
14. B
15. B
16. C
17. C
18. B
19. A
20. D
21. B
22. D
23. D
24. C
25. C

PART 10

ELECTRONICS INFORMATION

1. A
2. B
3. B
4. C
5. D
6. C
7. C
8. A
9. B
10. B
11. B
12. D
13. A
14. B
15. B
16. D
17. C
18. D
19. A
20. B

13

PRACTICE TEST 3

PART 1

GENERAL SCIENCE

Time: 11 Minutes — 25 Questions

1. Milk, eggs, dairy and fish are good sources of which type of vitamin?

   A. vitamin A
   B. vitamin C
   C. vitamin D
   D. vitamin K

2. Kinetic energy can be found in

   A. a motionless object
   B. a moving object
   C. a battery
   D. a chemical reaction

3. The main source of energy for bodily metabolism is

   A. carbohydrates
   B. proteins
   C. minerals
   D. vitamins

4. Water freezes at what temperature?

   A. 100° C
   B. 32° C
   C. 212° F
   D. 273° K

5. Which subatomic particle carries a charge of –1?

   A. proton
   B. electron
   C. neutron
   D. atom

6. Which of the following is a terrestrial planet?

   A. Jupiter
   B. Saturn
   C. Earth
   D. Uranus

7. A hot air balloon rises because of

   A. convection
   B. conduction
   C. radiation
   D. magnetism

8. Oxygen enters the bloodstream from the lungs through the

   A. aorta
   B. arterioles
   C. alveoli
   D. capillaries

9. Food is broken down and absorbed into the body primarily in the

   A. stomach
   B. small intestine
   C. large intestine
   D. appendix

10. Which of the following is NOT part of the electromagnetic spectrum?

    A. microwaves
    B. visible light
    C. heat
    D. x-rays

11. A lack of vitamin A can cause

    A. night blindness
    B. scurvy
    C. anemia
    D. beriberi

12. A lunar eclipse occurs when

    A. the moon blocks the sun's light
    B. the sun blocks the moon's light
    C. the earth blocks the moon's light
    D. the earth blocks the sun's light

13. The third stage of mitosis is

    A. telophase
    B. anaphase
    C. metaphase
    D. prophase

GO ON TO THE NEXT PAGE.

14. Nitrogen has an atomic number of 7. From this we know that

   A. nitrogen has 7 electrons in one atom.
   B. one atom of nitrogen has a mass of 7.
   C. nitrogen has 7 neutrons in one atom.
   D. nitrogen has 7 protons in one atom.

15. A substance with a pH of 4 is a(n)

   A. acid
   B. base
   C. solvent
   D. compound

16. An animal that breathes through gills and has scales belongs to which class?

   A. mammalia
   B. reptilia
   C. amphibia
   D. pisces

17. What is an effect of epinephrine?

   A. It stimulates adrenal cortex.
   B. It regulates metabolic rate.
   C. It decreases blood sugar.
   D. It increases blood calcium concentration.

18. Which biome is characterized by its arid environment?

   A. taiga
   B. grasslands
   C. desert
   D. deciduous forests

19. Which of the following is an autotroph?

   A. a mushroom
   B. a spider
   C. yeast
   D. a tomato plant

20. The earliest geologic time period is the

   A. Paleozoic era
   B. Precambrian era
   C. Mesozoic era
   D. Cenozoic era

21. What will you never find in the aphotic zone?

   A. living organisms
   B. fossils
   C. light
   D. fish

22. Cellular protein synthesis occurs in the

   A. vacuole
   B. mitochondria
   C. centriole
   D. ribosome

23. Water is a

   A. mixture
   B. compound
   C. solution
   D. element

24. A car with mass of 200 kg is traveling at 5 meters per second. What is the momentum of the car?

   A. 1,000 N
   B. 2,000 N
   C. 400 N
   D. 40 N

25. Parent A has the genotype CC. Parent B has the genotype Cc. What are the possible genotypes of their offspring?

   A. CC, CC, CC, Cc
   B. CC, CC, Cc, Cc
   C. CC, Cc, Cc, Cc
   D. CC, Cc, Cc, cc

STOP!
IF YOU FINISH BEFORE THE TIME IS UP, YOU MAY
CHECK OVER YOUR WORK ON THIS PART ONLY.

PART 2

ARITHMETIC REASONING

Time: 36 Minutes — 30 Questions

1. A mechanic is paid $5 for every tire he changes, $3 for every spark plug he changes, and $2 for every oil change. If the mechanic replaces 6 tires and 8 spark plugs and does 3 oil changes, how much will he be paid?

   A. $10
   B. $15
   C. $40
   D. $60

2. How many 28-passenger ferries will it take to carry 196 people?

   A. 5
   B. 7
   C. 9
   D. 10

3. One yard is equal to approximately 3 feet. A bicyclist can ride 15 feet in 10 seconds. How long will it take her to ride 45 yards?

   A. 1 minute
   B. 1 minute and 15 seconds
   C. 1 minute and 30 seconds
   D. 1 minute and 45 seconds

4. A baker bakes 500 muffins in 8 hours. How many muffins does he bake on average every hour?

   A. 50.5
   B. 62.5
   C. 70.5
   D. 72.5

5. What is the next term in the sequence:

   2, 8, 14, 20, _____?

   A. 26
   B. 28
   C. 29
   D. 30

6. A lightbulb inspector inspects 200 lightbulbs an hour. 7% of the lightbulbs she inspects are defective. How many good lightbulbs does she inspect in 4 hours?

   A. 744
   B. 775
   C. 804
   D. 832

7. A teacher divides 22.5 pounds of candy into 15 separate packages. How much candy is in each package?

   A. 1.25 pounds
   B. 1.40 pounds
   C. 1.50 pounds
   D. 1.75 pounds

8. A movie theater charges $6.75 for adults and $4.25 for children. If three adults and two children go to the movies, how much do the tickets cost?

   A. $25.25
   B. $28.75
   C. $30.50
   D. $32.25

9. A sweater originally priced at $45 is reduced 17%. What is the sale price?

   A. $17.65
   B. $25.35
   C. $32.00
   D. $37.35

10. A small pizza feeds 2 people and costs $10. A large pizza feeds 5 people and costs $18. How much more would it cost to feed 50 people with small pizzas than with large pizzas?

   A. $70.00
   B. $60.00
   C. $55.00
   D. $50.00

GO ON TO THE NEXT PAGE.

11. Tickets for a charity fundraiser cost $75 each. If 30% of the money per ticket goes to administrative costs for the fundraiser, how much money from each ticket goes to the charity?

    A. $45
    B. $50
    C. $52
    D. $55

12. An architect designs a square room with 10-foot long walls. Another architect decides to increase the length of the walls by 20%. What is the area of the new room?

    A. 100 square feet
    B. 144 square feet
    C. 150 square feet
    D. 166 square feet

13. A store owner increases the price of a $100 stereo by 40%. Then he decreases the price by 15%. What is the final price of the stereo?

    A. $119
    B. $125
    C. $131
    D. $140

14. A truck driver drives from 6:30 a.m. to 4:45 p.m., stopping once for 15 minutes and once for 45 minutes. How much time did he spend driving?

    A. 7 hours
    B. 8 hours
    C. 8 hours 45 minutes
    D. 9 hours 15 minutes

15. Five percent of the students at Greenville High study Chinese. If 10 students study Chinese, how many students attend Greenville High?

    A. 50
    B. 150
    C. 200
    D. 250

16. A widges company has 8 employees. Each employee can build 12 widges an hour. If all employees work 8-hour shifts, five days a week, how many widges can the company manufacture in a week?

    A. 3,240
    B. 3,840
    C. 4,020
    D. 4,840

17. Dan works a total of $17\frac{1}{4}$ hours in a week. If he is paid $8.25 an hour, how much will his paycheck be, rounded to the nearest penny, before taxes?

    A. $142.31
    B. $142.32
    C. $143.00
    D. $143.31

18. An auto factory has 1,450 sheets of metal. If each car built uses $6\frac{3}{4}$ sheets, how many cars can the factory build?

    A. 160
    B. 200
    C. 214
    D. 241

19. Sue charges $0.05 per square foot of lawn that she mows. If she mows a lawn measuring 15' x 30', how much money will she make?

    A. $22.50
    B. $25.00
    C. $30.50
    D. $32.50

20. A student purchases 3 notebooks at $3.25 each, 2 boxes of pencils at $1.99 per box, a package of pens at $2.59 per package, and a bookbag at $23.00. If the bookbag was 15% off, how much did the student pay for everything?

    A. $39.32
    B. $39.00
    C. $37.75
    D. $35.87

GO ON TO THE NEXT PAGE.

21. The ratio of boys to girls in a class is 3 to 5. If there are 32 students in the class, how many of them are girls?

    A. 12
    B. 16
    C. 20
    D. 24

22. The price of a jacket is reduced 30%, and the jacket then sells for $143.50. What was the price of the jacket before the reduction?

    A. $173.50
    B. $205.00
    C. $209.00
    D. $230.00

23. A group of students received the following grades on a test: 75, 83, 87, 88, 92, and 96. What was the students' average grade, rounded to the nearest whole number?

    A. 84
    B. 85
    C. 86
    D. 87

24. If pencils cost 12 cents each for the first 100, 10 cents each for the next 50, and 8 cents each for every pencil after, how many pencils can be purchased with $25.00?

    A. 250
    B. 225
    C. 200
    D. 175

25. A car leaves Detroit at 12:00p.m. EST on July 12th and arrives in San Diego at 4:00p.m. PST on July 17th. How long did it take the car to get to San Diego?

    A. 107 hours
    B. 115 hours
    C. 123 hours
    D. 127 hours

26. Admission to a park costs $3 for every car, plus 60 cents for every passenger. How many people were in a car for which the admission cost was $6?

    A. 3
    B. 4
    C. 5
    D. 6

27. A savings account with $500 earns 4% interest annually. How long will it take for the account to reach $600?

    A. 1 year
    B. 2 years
    C. 4 years
    D. 5 years

28. A man buys a pair of boots for $45. If sales tax is 6%, and he pays with a $100 bill, how much change does he receive?

    A. $45.00
    B. $50.70
    C. $52.30
    D. $55.00

29. A man plans to make a 3,500-mile journey by bike. If he travels 70 miles a day for five days straight and then rests for two days before continuing the trip, how many days, including those in which he does not travel, will it take him to complete the journey?

    A. 100
    B. 90
    C. 80
    D. 70

30. A seamstress can sew 26 dresses a day. Approximately how long will it take the seamstress to sew 500 dresses?

    A. 15 days
    B. 19 days
    C. 23 days
    D. 25 days

STOP!
IF YOU FINISH BEFORE THE TIME IS UP, YOU MAY
CHECK OVER YOUR WORK ON THIS PART ONLY.

PART 3

WORD KNOWLEDGE

Time: 11 Minutes — 35 Questions

1. <u>Anxious</u> most nearly means

   A. angry
   B. terrible
   C. worried
   D. atrocious

2. <u>Inhibit</u> most nearly means

   A. undress
   B. live
   C. distress
   D. hinder

3. Joan felt great <u>sympathy</u> for Jim's troubles.

   A. compassion
   B. contempt
   C. apathy
   D. feelings

4. <u>Modify</u> most nearly means

   A. shy
   B. alter
   C. tempt
   D. ease

5. <u>Labor</u> most nearly means

   A. admire
   B. open
   C. refute
   D. work

6. <u>Vivid</u> most nearly means

   A. timely
   B. artistic
   C. bright
   D. dark

7. <u>Loyalty</u> is an attribute Bill desires in a friend.

   A. devotion
   B. strength
   C. happiness
   D. jealousy

8. <u>Hesitate</u> most nearly means

   A. plan
   B. pause
   C. defend
   D. contain

9. <u>Abolish</u> most nearly means

   A. abstain
   B. outlaw
   C. decipher
   D. furnish

10. <u>Implement</u> most nearly means

    A. river
    B. program
    C. furniture
    D. tool

11. The child <u>revered</u> his hero.

    A. punished
    B. cajoled
    C. honored
    D. melted

12. <u>Harsh</u> most nearly means

    A. simple
    B. cruel
    C. enlightened
    D. immoral

13. The flavor of the dish was <u>enhanced</u> by his use of a rare spice.

    A. improved
    B. destroyed
    C. flavorless
    D. burned

14. <u>Quest</u> most nearly means

    A. legend
    B. game
    C. search
    D. distance

GO ON TO THE NEXT PAGE.

15. Characterize most nearly means

   A. describe
   B. scrutinize
   C. employ
   D. diminish

16. Paul has the <u>authority</u> to make the decision.

   A. gall
   B. audacity
   C. power
   D. responsibility

17. <u>Benefactor</u> most nearly means

   A. supporter
   B. entertainer
   C. farmer
   D. scientist

18. <u>Obedience</u> most nearly means

   A. aggression
   B. compliance
   C. disgust
   D. fix

19. <u>Morose</u> most nearly means

   A. emotional
   B. energetic dreary
   C. lively
   D. dreary

20. As Tom got older the <u>prosperity</u> in his life increased.

   A. stress
   B. debt
   C. affluence
   D. anxiety

21. <u>Prohibit</u> most nearly means

   A. forbid
   B. allow
   C. scold
   D. entice

22. <u>Persist</u> most nearly means

   A. diminish
   B. glorify
   C. liquefy
   D. continue

23. <u>Abandon</u> most nearly means

   A. destroy
   B. desert
   C. anger
   D. sweeten

24. The principal thought it was necessary to <u>penalize</u> the student for his behavior.

   A. applaud
   B. clarify
   C. punish
   D. cajole

25. <u>Standard</u> most nearly means

   A. common
   B. height
   C. plan
   D. obligation

26. By the end of the day, it was apparent that he was <u>ignorant</u>.

   A. talented
   B. selfish
   C. intelligent
   D. uneducated

27. <u>Devious</u> most nearly means

   A. delicious
   B. illegal
   C. deceitful
   D. cleanly

28. <u>Devise</u> most nearly means

   A. destroy
   B. create
   C. serenade
   D. scramble

29. <u>Hilarious</u> most nearly means

   A. funny
   B. relaxed
   C. tall
   D. medical

GO ON TO THE NEXT PAGE.

30. Little Bobby wanted his dinner <u>immediately</u>.

   A. spicy
   B. served
   C. delicious
   D. directly

31. <u>Diligent</u> most nearly means

   A. careful
   B. sloppy
   C. talented
   D. ill

32. <u>Lack</u> most nearly means

   A. contain
   B. deficiency
   C. slide
   D. ease

33. The king showed <u>mercy</u> for the man who stole a loaf of bread.

   A. disdain
   B. disgust
   C. admiration
   D. forgiveness

34. <u>Mere</u> most nearly means

   A. expensive
   B. majority
   C. weak
   D. only

35. <u>Phenomenon</u> most nearly means

   A. event
   B. weather
   C. ancient
   D. elicit

STOP!
IF YOU FINISH BEFORE THE TIME IS UP, YOU MAY
CHECK OVER YOUR WORK ON THIS PART ONLY.

PART 4

PARAGRAPH COMPREHENSION

Time: 13 Minutes — 15 Questions

1. A family of amateur archeologists discovered the fossilized skeleton of what is believed to be a baby velociraptor, a prehistoric predatory dinosaur. The family identified the fossilized bones as a velociraptor by analyzing the jaw-bone. Expert archeologists have confirmed that the discovery is in fact a velociraptor and that it is the most complete skeleton found of a baby velociraptor. This is significant because much can be learned about the life cycle of velociraptors by looking at the remains of a baby.

Based on the information above, which of the following is most likely true?

A. Velociraptors eat plants and vegetables to survive.
B. Amateur archeologists never make significant discoveries.
C. The remains of a baby dinosaur can be a significant discovery.
D. A dinosaur fossil can only be identified by looking at the entire skeleton.

2. Doctors conducted an experiment to find a cure for the flu. Two thousand patients were used in the experiment. A thousand were given a new drug and 1000 were given a placebo, a harmless sugar pill that makes the patients in that group believe they are being given the drug, when in fact they are not. Placebos are important because they make sure that the results seen in the study are because of the drug itself and not because of the psychological effects of a patient believing he is taking a drug that will cure his flu.

Which of the following is true about a placebo?

A. Placebos contain the drug that is being tested.
B. Placebos can be important to an experiment that involves a new drug.
C. A cure for the flu has been found.
D. Psychological effects have no effect on drug experiments.

3. Bison and buffalo are not the same animal. For years, the American bison were mistakenly referred to as buffalo. Buffalo are actually found in Asia, Africa, and South America. Bison roamed the Northern American western plains by the millions just a couple of centuries ago. Because they were so widely hunted, however, their numbers fell greatly. In fact, as of a century ago, there were only about 500 left. They were deemed near extinction, but due to conservation efforts, their numbers have increased. Today, there are approximately 50,000 bison living in protected parks. Though they may never be as abundant as they once were, they are not in danger of extinction as long as they remain protected.

The paragraph implies that the primary difference between the buffalo and the bison is

A. their geographic location
B. their size
C. their number
D. when they lived

4. In the field of economics, the more demand there is for a product, the greater the price of that product will be. Also, the more available or the greater supply of a products the cheaper it will be. The price of a product is generally set when the amount people are willing to spend on a given amount of product comes into equilibrium with the amount a producer is willing to accept for that given amount of product produced.

What can you infer from this passage?

A. Price has nothing to do with supply.
B. The higher priced an item is, the greater its quality is.
C. If demand for a product increases, its price may increase.
D. A product comes into equilibrium when price and demand are equal.

GO ON TO THE NEXT PAGE.

5. War broke out in Europe in 1914, and because of a lot of secret alliances among the European nations, most were drawn into the fight within a few months. Britain, France, and Russia led the Allies; Germany and Austria-Hungary led the Central Powers. U.S. President Woodrow Wilson and many Americans desperately wanted to stay out of the war and maintain U.S. neutrality. Circumstances, however, made this difficult to do. Which of the following statements are true?

    I.   Americans were eager to enter the war.

    II.   There were secret alliances among the European nations.

    III.   Russia and Britain were allies.

A. I
B. III
C. II and III
D. I, II and III

6. The cocoa plant, from which chocolate is made, is native to Central and South America. Many of the native cultures—most notably, the Aztecs—cultivated and ate the fruit of the cocoa plant. In certain cultures, the cocoa beans were even used as a form of money. The Aztecs made the cocoa beans into a hot drink with no sugar at all. In fact, the Aztecs used chili peppers to make it spicy. It was bitter and strong, and they called it xocoatl. When Spanish explorers arrived in South America, they discovered the cocoa bean and brought them back to Europe in huge quantities. This was how chocolate was introduced to Europeans. At the beginning, the Europeans drank it in the Aztec fashion—hot, spicy, and unsweetened.

The people who brought chocolate to Europe were the

A. Mayans
B. Aztec
C. Spanish
D. Dutch

7. Howard Hughes built an airplane called the Spruce Goose. It had a wingspan of 300 feet and weighed 300,000 pounds. Its wings were so thick a person could stand in one. It could hold 700 passengers. It was the largest airplane ever built. The controls used hydraulics to move the flaps.

Which of the following is true about the Spruce Goose?

A. Howard Hughes built many Spruce Goose–like airplanes.
B. The Spruce Goose was made of lightweight metals.
C. The Spruce Goose was torn apart and used for scrap.
D. The wings of the Spruce Goose were at least as thick as a person is tall.

8. All elements can be classified as a metal, non-metal, or semi-metal. Metals share certain physical characteristics. They are usually shiny. Metals are generally good conductors of heat and electricity. Many metals are said to be malleable. This means they can be hammered into thin sheets like aluminum foil.

Which of the following statements is true about metals?

A. Metals have no common characteristics with other metals.
B. Metals have the ability to conduct electricity.
C. All metals are very heavy.
D. Nonmetals are usually shiny.

GO ON TO THE NEXT PAGE.

9. Mandatory minimum sentences require that people who are convicted of certain crimes are sentenced to a minimum number of years as mandated by legislation. Normally a judge uses his discretion to sentence a convicted criminal. Mandatory minimums take any discretion out of a judge's hands, and provide the sentence for the criminal, regardless of the circumstances of the crime.

Based on the above passages all of the following are true EXCEPT:

A. All crimes have mandatory minimum sentences.
B. Traditionally a judge has discretion in determining sentence length.
C. Legislation determines the length of mandatory minimum sentences.
D. The circumstances of a crime are irrelevant to sentencing for crimes that have mandatory minimum sentences.

10. Napoleon Bonaparte sold the Louisiana territory to the United States in the Louisiana Purchase. He needed cash to establish an empire. Originally President Jefferson sent emissaries to France to gain control of the Mississippi River and the Port of New Orleans, invaluable trade routes for the Ohio Valley and western settlers. U.S. representatives were shocked to be offered the entire Louisiana territory. President Jefferson quickly approved the purchase.

The primary purpose of this paragraph is

A. to describe why Napoleon wanted an empire
B. to describe the events that surrounded the Louisiana Purchase
C. explain how important control of the Mississippi River was
D. to describe the greatness of President Jefferson

GO ON TO THE NEXT PAGE.

Questions 11-15 are based on the following passage.

Ancient Greece is often considered the birthplace of European heritage. The Greeks helped develop science, philosophy, democracy, art, and literature. Three of the greatest philosophers of all time lived in Athens: Socrates, Plato, and Aristotle. These men are often considered the founders of Western philosophy.

Everything that is known about Socrates comes from the writings of others, for he wrote nothing down. He never lectured, and never claimed to have any knowledge. Instead, he taught by asking questions of his students. He asked his students a series of questions, leading them to reveal the inconsistencies in their beliefs. This method, now known as the "Socratic method," is often used in law schools today. Unfortunately, his methods caused Socrates to make as many enemies as he had followers, and he was sentenced to death in 399 BC.

Plato, a student of Socrates, is well known for his theories on everyday life, which he expressed through written dialogues, often between he and Socrates. One of his best-known dialogues is titled *The Symposium* and discusses his views on love. Plato is also well known for his political views, which are explained in his book *The Republic*. He founded a school in Athens called the Academy.

Aristotle, a student of Plato's at the Academy, was the son of a doctor. He taught with Plato for 20 years before moving to Macedonia to tutor Alexander the Great. In addition to his influence on Western philosophy, Aristotle also had a large influence on science in the Middle Ages and Renaissance. Eventually he founded his own school in Athens called the Lyceum.

11. Which of the following CANNOT be attributed to ancient Greece?

    A. art
    B. democracy
    C. music
    D. philosophy

12. Who wrote about everyday life through dialogues?

    A. Plato
    B. Aristotle
    C. Alexander the Great
    D. Socrates

13. Which of the following can be inferred from the passage?

    A. Plato, while a student of Socrates, did not like him very much.
    B. Aristotle is not mentioned in any of Socrates' writings.
    C. Socrates inspired Plato to write as much as he did.
    D. The work of Aristotle was used during the Middle Ages.

14. The purpose of the passage is to

    A. describe in detail the beginnings of Western philosophy
    B. briefly discuss the three founders of Western philosophy
    C. demonstrate the influence Socrates had on history
    D. describe education in ancient Greece

15. Which of the following is true?

    A. Plato was a student of Socrates.
    B. Plato was a student of Aristotle.
    C. Aristotle was a student of Socrates.
    D. Alexander the Great was a student of Plato.

STOP!
IF YOU FINISH BEFORE THE TIME IS UP, YOU MAY
CHECK OVER YOUR WORK ON THIS PART ONLY.

PART 5

NUMERICAL OPERATIONS

Time: 3 Minutes — 50 Questions

1. $\dfrac{2}{2}$ =

   A. 0
   B. 1
   C. 2
   D. 4

2. 12 − 4 =

   A. 6
   B. 7
   C. 8
   D. 9

3. 8 + 9 =

   A. 13
   B. 14
   C. 16
   D. 17

4. 2 × 4 =

   A. 8
   B. 9
   C. 10
   D. 12

5. 6 − 5 =

   A. 4
   B. 3
   C. 1
   D. 2

6. 8 × 3 =

   A. 21
   B. 24
   C. 26
   D. 27

7. 2 + 5 =

   A. 4
   B. 5
   C. 6
   D. 7

8. 5 × 5 =

   A. 25
   B. 30
   C. 20
   D. 15

9. 15 − 5 =

   A. 5
   B. 7
   C. 10
   D. 12

10. $\dfrac{12}{3}$ =

    A. 3
    B. 4
    C. 5
    D. 6

11. 1 + 0 =

    A. 0
    B. 1
    C. 2
    D. 3

12. $\dfrac{8}{2}$ =

    A. 4
    B. 5
    C. 6
    D. 8

13. 4 × 1 =

    A. 1
    B. 2
    C. 3
    D. 4

GO ON TO THE NEXT PAGE.

14. $8 \times 2 =$
   A.   14
   B.   15
   C.   16
   D.   18

15. $15 - 9 =$
   A.   5
   B.   6
   C.   7
   D.   8

16. $14 + 8 =$
   A.   22
   B.   23
   C.   24
   D.   26

17. $\frac{27}{3} =$
   A.   8
   B.   9
   C.   10
   D.   11

18. $7 \times 3 =$
   A.   18
   B.   20
   C.   21
   D.   22

19. $6 + 7 =$
   A.   16
   B.   15
   C.   14
   D.   13

20. $\frac{30}{5} =$
   A.   6
   B.   7
   C.   8
   D.   9

21. $\frac{75}{25} =$
   A.   1
   B.   2
   C.   3
   D.   4

22. $19 - 7 =$
   A.   9
   B.   12
   C.   13
   D.   14

23. $6 \times 6 =$
   A.   30
   B.   32
   C.   34
   D.   36

24. $\frac{18}{9} =$
   A.   2
   B.   3
   C.   4
   D.   5

25. $7 + 5 =$
   A.   10
   B.   12
   C.   14
   D.   16

26. $3 + 4 =$
   A.   5
   B.   6
   C.   7
   D.   8

27. $9 - 4 =$
   A.   4
   B.   5
   C.   6
   D.   7

GO ON TO THE NEXT PAGE.

28. $\frac{10}{5} =$

   A. 1
   B. 2
   C. 3
   D. 4

29. $\frac{16}{4} =$

   A. 4
   B. 5
   C. 6
   D. 7

30. $9 \times 4 =$

   A. 32
   B. 33
   C. 34
   D. 36

31. $\frac{11}{1} =$

   A. 10
   B. 11
   C. 12
   D. 13

32. $20 - 12 =$

   A. 8
   B. 10
   C. 12
   D. 14

33. $2 \times 12 =$

   A. 14
   B. 18
   C. 24
   D. 28

34. $8 - 3 =$

   A. 3
   B. 4
   C. 5
   D. 6

35. $3 \times 2 =$

   A. 6
   B. 5
   C. 4
   D. 3

36. $7 - 7 =$

   A. 1
   B. 0
   C. 3
   D. 4

37. $9 \times 9 =$

   A. 71
   B. 77
   C. 81
   D. 88

38. $12 + 1 =$

   A. 10
   B. 11
   C. 12
   D. 13

39. $7 - 2 =$

   A. 4
   B. 5
   C. 7
   D. 9

40. $\frac{15}{5} =$

   A. 3
   B. 5
   C. 6
   D. 7

41. $10 - 7 =$

   A. 1
   B. 2
   C. 3
   D. 4

GO ON TO THE NEXT PAGE.

42. 6 + 8 =

    A.   10
    B.   12
    C.   13
    D.   14

43. 8 × 1 =

    A.   9
    B.   8
    C.   7
    4D.   6

44. 2 + 4 =

    A.   2
    B.   4
    C.   6
    D.   8

45. $\dfrac{30}{3}$ =

    A.   10
    B.   9
    C.   7
    D.   6

46. 21 − 7 =

    A.   18
    B.   16
    C.   15
    D.   14

47. 5/1 =

    A.   4
    B.   5
    C.   6
    D.   7

48. 4 − 0 =

    A.   0
    B.   2
    C.   4
    D.   5

49. 7 × 0 =

    A.   0
    B.   6
    C.   7
    D.   10

50. 11 × 8 =

    A.   80
    B.   88
    C.   90
    D.   96

STOP!
IF YOU FINISH BEFORE THE TIME IS UP, YOU MAY
CHECK OVER YOUR WORK ON THIS PART ONLY.

PART 6

CODING SPEED

Time: 7 Minutes — 84 Questions

Key

accent 5515	desk 4201	guard 3003	knight 2511	number 8463
blank 7288	engine 1691	igloo 9926	ledge 6789	phone 4597

Questions		Options				
		A	**B**	**C**	**D**	**E**
1.	number	3003	4201	6789	7288	8463
2.	desk	1691	3003	4201	5515	6789
3.	blank	2511	4201	5515	7288	9926
4.	igloo	4597	5515	6789	8463	9926
5.	guard	2511	3003	4201	4597	5515
6.	engine	1691	2511	3003	5515	6789
7.	ledge	2511	3003	4597	6789	7288
8.	knight	1691	2511	3003	4201	6789
9.	accent	1691	2511	5515	6789	8463
10.	phone	2511	4597	6789	7288	9926
11.	blank	1691	4201	5515	7288	8463
12.	igloo	3003	4597	6789	8463	9926

Key

album 0298	doctor 3070	hat 1400	rock 6341	unbrella 2651
card 7866	family 5445	paint 8797	track 9921	violin 4097

Questions		Options				
		A	**B**	**C**	**D**	**E**
13.	umbrella	0298	2651	3070	4097	5445
14.	card	1400	3070	6341	7866	8797
15.	doctor	1400	2651	3070	6341	9921
16.	album	0298	2651	4097	5445	6341
17.	hat	0298	1400	2651	4097	5445
18.	track	3070	4097	5445	8797	9921
19.	paint	0298	2651	4097	8797	9921
20.	family	1400	3070	5445	6341	7866
21.	violin	4097	5445	6341	7866	8797
22.	rock	1400	3070	4097	5445	6341
23.	card	3070	4097	6341	7866	8797
24.	doctor	0298	3070	4097	5445	6341

Key

alarm .... 434 6 | drill .... 2705 | garden .... 8882 | lesson .... 5083 | saw 1121

bell .... 9328 | fortune .... 6391 | income .... 2789 | native .... 3271 | theater 7427

Questions	Options				
	A	**B**	**C**	**D**	**E**
25. native	2705	3271	5083	6391	8882
26. alarm	1121	2705	3271	4346	7427
27. lesson	1121	2705	2789	5083	6391
28. fortune	2789	4346	6391	7427	8882
29. bell	3271	4346	5083	8882	9328
30. saw	1121	2705	3271	5083	7427
31. garden	2705	3271	6391	7427	8882
32. income	1121	2789	4346	6391	7427
33. theater	3271	4346	6391	7427	9328
34. alarm	1121	3271	4346	5083	8882
35. drill	2705	2789	3271	5083	6391
36. lesson	2705	5083	6391	7427	9328

Key

bread .... 5461 | empire .... 9949 | health .... 7594 | manager .... 3457 | reptile 1979

carton .... 6695 | future .... 2802 | journey .... 0842 | ocean .... 4281 | vault 8943

Questions	Options				
	A	**B**	**C**	**D**	**E**
37. future	1979	2802	4281	7594	8943
38. vault	0842	3457	5461	8943	9949
39. bread	1979	3457	5461	7594	8943
40. ocean	1979	2802	3457	4281	6695
41. health	2802	3457	5461	6695	7594
42. future	2802	3457	4281	6695	8943
43. carton	1979	2802	5461	6695	7594
44. manager	2802	3457	4281	7594	8943
45. journey	0842	2802	3457	4281	5461
46. empire	3457	4281	6695	8943	9949
47. reptile	0842	1979	3457	5461	7594
48. ocean	1979	2802	4281	5461	6695

Key

book 6219	glove 2405	judge 8225	orbit 5278	rent 3579
deal 1418	home 4491	master 7062	park 9878	watch 0698

Questions

Options

		A	B	C	D	E
49.	master	1418	5278	6219	7062	8225
50.	glove	2405	3579	5278	6219	7062
51.	book	0698	4491	6219	7062	9878
52.	orbit	3579	5278	7062	8225	9878
53.	judge	0698	2405	4491	7062	8225
54.	watch	0698	2405	5278	6219	7062
55.	rent	1418	3579	4491	5278	6219
56.	deal	1418	2405	3579	7062	9878
57.	park	3579	4491	6219	7062	9878
58.	home	0698	1418	3579	4491	6219
59.	book	1418	3579	6219	7062	8225
60.	glove	0698	2405	5278	6219	7062

Key

crate 2230	feast 4533	labor 8725	path 1614	scale 7775
eraser 6543	helmet 3144	needle 9106	quilt 5095	tent 9963

Questions

Options

		A	B	C	D	E
61.	scale	2230	4533	7775	8725	9963
62.	helmet	1614	3144	5095	6543	7775
63.	crate	2230	3144	5095	7775	8725
64.	labor	1614	2230	4533	8725	9963
65.	feast	3144	4533	5095	6543	8725
66.	quilt	1614	4533	5095	7775	9963
67.	tent	3144	5095	7775	8725	9963
68.	needle	2203	7775	8725	9106	9963
69.	path	1614	3144	5095	7775	9106
70.	eraser	4533	5095	6543	8725	9106
71.	crate	1614	2230	4533	5095	6543
72.	labor	3144	4533	6543	7775	8725

Key

bench 4900	dish 1288	issue 8143	party 7204	scout 3790
circuit 9195	flag 6423	motor 2845	reward 5916	truck 0300

Questions   Options

		A	B	C	D	E
73.	flag	2845	4900	5916	6423	7204
74.	circuit	0300	3790	4900	5916	9195
75.	scout	1288	3790	4900	7204	8143
76.	reward	0300	2745	5916	6423	7204
77.	dish	1288	2845	6423	8143	9195
78.	circuit	2845	4900	7204	8143	9195
79.	bench	0300	4900	5916	7204	8143
80.	party	3790	5916	6423	7204	8143
81.	truck	0300	2845	4900	5916	6423
82.	issue	1288	2845	5916	7204	8143
83.	motor	0300	1288	2845	5916	6423
84.	flag	2845	6423	7204	8143	9195

STOP!
IF YOU FINISH BEFORE THE TIME IS UP, YOU MAY
CHECK OVER YOUR WORK ON THIS PART ONLY.

PART 7

AUTO AND SHOP INFORMATION

Time: 11 Minutes — 25 Questions

1. Piston rings can get stuck in the groves around a piston because

   A. the oil is dirty
   B. the piston is too big for the cylinder
   C. the oil is too hot
   D. the fuel combustion welds them in place

2. The power train contains the following parts EXCEPT the

   A. transmission
   B. torque converter
   C. differential
   D. pinion gear

3. The engine block contains the

   A. cylinders
   B. oil pan
   C. radiator
   D. carburetor

4. The indicator on the dash of a car shows that the battery charge is low. What should be checked first?

   A. The fuse box
   B. The water level in the battery
   C. The alternator
   D. Spark plug clearance

5. Water is found to be coming out of the tailpipe of a car. This situation

   A. is normal
   B. is caused by oil in the crankcase
   C. indicates that the exhaust valve is leaking
   D. indicates a malfunctioning catalytic converter

6. The gas pedal controls

   A. the throttle valve
   B. the distributor timing
   C. the amount of fuel moved by the fuel pump
   D. the water pump

7. A tire is found to be worn only on one outside edge. This is probably caused by

   A. incorrect balancing
   B. improper alignment
   C. under-inflation
   D. over-inflation

8. All of the following are part of the electrical system EXCEPT the

   A. distributor
   B. alternator
   C. current booster
   D. voltage regulator

9. A car is overheating but the radiator is cold. The first diagnostic to check is for a

   A. stuck thermostat
   B. leaking radiator
   C. failed waterpump
   D. plugged waterjackets

10. Engines without enough oil will generally

    A. run a little hot
    B. run the same as with the right amount of oil
    C. "burn" more oil
    D. idle a little smoother

11. An automobile is idling fast. This could be caused by

    A. improper distributor timing
    B. air leaking into the intake manifold
    C. broken water pump
    D. overcharged battery

12. The master cylinder is

    A. in the braking system
    B. the main source of engine power
    C. the biggest cylinder in the car
    D. used to pump air

GO ON TO THE NEXT PAGE.

13. The tool that should be used with a punch is

    A. ball peen hammer
    B. mallet
    C. carpenters hammer
    D. sledge hammer

14. Which of the following should be used to allow faster assembly with a screwdriver?

    A. Flathead screw
    B. Philips head screw
    C. Wing nut
    D. Standard screws

15. The tool above is a

    A. file
    B. flathead screwdriver
    C. chisel
    D. reamer

16. Arc welding uses which of the following to melt the metal?

    A. Nitrogen
    B. Acetylene gas
    C. Hydrogen and oxygen
    D. Electricity

17. The cut of a file refers to

    A. the shape
    B. the size of the tang
    C. the smoothness of the surface when finished
    D. its teeth

18. A torque wrench allows the user to measure

    A. how tight the bolt is
    B. how big the bolt is
    C. how many times the bolt has been turned
    D. when the bolt will break

19. The tool shown above is used to

    A. cut circles and arcs
    B. cut through metal
    C. cut with the grain of wood
    D. cut across the grain of wood

20. Sheet metal should be cut with

    A. kitchen shears
    B. tin snips
    C. a hack saw
    D. heavy-duty bolt cutters

21. What is the consequence if the tang on a file is bent?

    A. The file will be able to work in corners.
    B. The handle may not be able to attach.
    C. The face will be bent upwards.
    D. The teeth will not be able to function properly.

22. The tool shown above is a

    A. pipe wrench
    B. monkey wrench
    C. caliper
    D. ratchet wrench

23. Oil and grease are used to

    A. remove rust and corrosion
    B. lubricate joints and bearings
    C. allow drill bits to work properly
    D. coat sheet metal before shaping

GO ON TO THE NEXT PAGE.

24. What is the tool pictured above?

   A. Pliers
   B. Vise grips
   C. Box wrench
   D. Crescent wrench

25. If a pipe cutter is not available, which of the
    following could be used to cut through an
    aluminum pipe?

   A. Grinding wheel
   B. Compass saw
   C. Hacksaw
   D. Circular saw

STOP!
IF YOU FINISH BEFORE THE TIME IS UP, YOU MAY
CHECK OVER YOUR WORK ON THIS PART ONLY.

PART 8

MATHEMATICS KNOWLEDGE

Time: 24 Minutes — 25 Questions

1. If you subtract $5x - 2y - 8z$ from a polynomial, you get $7x + 6y + z$. What is the polynomial?

   A. $12x - 4y + 7z$
   B. $12x + 4y - 7z$
   C. $2x + 8y - 9z$
   D. $-2x + 8y + 9z$

2. $(x + 5)(x - 4) =$

   A. $x^2 + 9x - 20$
   B. $x^2 + x - 20$
   C. $x^2 - x + 9$
   D. $x^2 - 9x + 20$

3. If $4x = -12$, then x equals

   A. 3
   B. -3
   C. 4
   D. -4

4. The square root of 144 is

   A. 10
   B. 11
   C. 12
   D. 13

5. A square has an area of 25. What is the perimeter of the square?

   A. 5
   B. 10
   C. 15
   D. 20

6. A right triangle has sides measuring 3 inches and 4 inches. What is the length of its hypotenuse?

   A. 5 inches
   B. 6 inches
   C. 6.5 inches
   D. 7 inches

7. The perimeter of an equilateral triangle is 16.5. What is the length of one of its sides?

   A. 4
   B. 4.5
   C. 5
   D. 5.5

8. A line crosses two parallel lines, creating angle c, which measures 50 degrees. How many degrees would an angle vertical to c measure?

   A. 50 degrees
   B. 90 degrees
   C. 130 degrees
   D. 180 degrees

9. If one plant costs x dollars, how much do y plants cost?

   A. $x + y$
   B. xy
   C. $x - y$
   D. $\dfrac{x}{y}$

10. The area of a rectangular room 10 yards by 12 yards is equal to

    A. 120 yards
    B. 240 yards
    C. 360 yards
    D. 480 yards

11. Given the formulas $y = wx$ and $z = \dfrac{y}{x} + w$, which formula below expresses the value of z without using y?

    A. $z = wx$
    B. $z = w + 2x$
    C. $z = 2w + x$
    D. $z = 2w$

GO ON TO THE NEXT PAGE.

12. Which of the following will result in a prime number?

    A. $13 + 3$
    B. $11 + 2$
    C. $17 - 5$
    D. 10×2

13. What is the approximate circumference of a circle with a radius of 4 (use 3.14 for pi)?

    A. 12
    B. 20
    C. 25
    D. 50

14. If $x = 2y$ and $6y = 9z$, then $x =$

    A. $3z$
    B. $\dfrac{4}{3}z$
    C. $\dfrac{8}{3}z$
    D. $\dfrac{8}{6}z$

15. 4 factorial equals

    A. 120
    B. 100
    C. 75
    D. 24

16. Factor: $x^2 - x - 6$

    A. $(x + 3)(x + 2)$
    B. $(x - 3)(x - 2)$
    C. $(x - 3)(x + 2)$
    D. $(x + 6)(x - 1)$

17. If $P(S) = R + T$, then $S =$

    A. $\dfrac{P}{R + T}$
    B. $P(R + T)$
    C. $(R + T) - P$
    D. $\dfrac{R + T}{P}$

18. The perimeter of a rectangle is 60. Two sides of the rectangle are twice the length of the other two sides. What is the length of the longer sides?

    A. 20
    B. 10
    C. 5
    D. 2

19. Which of the following is correct?

    A. Similar triangles have equal sides and proportional angles
    B. Isosceles triangles have 3 equal sides and 3 equal angles
    C. A trapezoid has 4 right angles
    D. A quadrilateral has 360 degrees.

20. Approximately what is the radius of a circle with an area of 201? (use 3.14 for pi)

    A. 6
    B. 7
    C. 8
    D. 9

21. Evaluate the expression $4x - 3y + 7z$ if $x = -3$, $y = 6$, and $z = -5$.

    A. 65
    B. −65
    C. −5
    D. 5

22. If 4 less than the product of b and 6 is 44, what is the value of b?

    A. 2
    B. 4
    C. 6
    D. 8

GO ON TO THE NEXT PAGE.

23.

In the figure above, if l_1 is parallel to l_2, then
$x + y =$

A. 80
B. 100
C. 160
D. 180

24. Solve for x: $16x - 4x = 36$

A. 3
B. 4
C. 5
D. 6

25. If the sides of a square are increased by 2, how much does the perimeter increase?

A. 2
B. 4
C. 6
D. 8

STOP!
IF YOU FINISH BEFORE THE TIME IS UP, YOU MAY
CHECK OVER YOUR WORK ON THIS PART ONLY.

PART 9

MECHANICAL COMPREHENSION

Time: 19 Minutes — 25 Questions

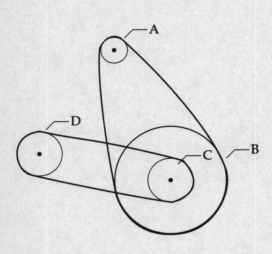

1. Which pulley turns the fastest?

A. A
B. B
C. C
D. D

150 lbs.

1' foot

5' feet

2. How much force is needed to push the piano up the ramp?

A. 15
B. 30
C. 60
D. 150

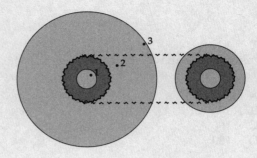

3. If the wheel above rotates, which of the dots will move at the fastest linear speed

A. 1
B. 2
C. 3
D. All the dots will move at the same linear speed.

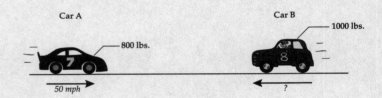

Car A   Car B
800 lbs.   1000 lbs.
50 mph   ?

4. How fast must car B travel in order for both cars to come to a complete stop when they collide?

A. 40 mph
B. 50 mph
C. 80 mph
D. 100 mph

5. A ball thrown straight up in the air will reach its maximum height when its speed is

A. at zero
B. at half its maximum
C. at the square root of its maximum
D. at its maximum

GO ON TO THE NEXT PAGE.

6. Gear A, which has a diameter of 1 foot, is turning gear B, which has a diameter of 2 feet. If gear A makes one revolution, how many revolutions does gear B make?

   A. Half a revolution
   B. One revolution
   C. Two revolutions
   D. Four revolutions

7. If a man lifts a 20 pound box 5 feet in the air, how much work is he doing?

   A. 15 ft.-lbs
   B. 25 ft.-lbs
   C. 50 ft.-lbs
   D. 100ft.-lbs

1 ft.   3 ft.

8. 120 pounds of force is required to tip the barrel. How much force must the worker apply to the lever?

   A. 20
   B. 30
   C. 40
   D. 60

1 in.
4 in.

9. If the force required to crack the walnut is 20 pounds, how much force must be applied to the nutcracker to crack the walnut?

   A. 1 pound
   B. 4 pounds
   C. 5 pounds
   D. 10 pounds

15 teeth

5 teeth

10. What is the theoretical mechanical advantage conferred by the gears of the bicycle

   A. $\dfrac{1}{3}$

   B. $\dfrac{1}{2}$

   C. 1

   D. 3

11. A good device for measuring hydraulic pressure is

   A. a thermometer
   B. a barometer
   C. a Schrader gauge
   D. an altimeter

GO ON TO THE NEXT PAGE.

Figure not drawn to scale

12. The person jumps off the boat at a speed of 6 feet per second. What is the speed is the boat after the jump?

    A. 2 feet per second
    B. 3 feet per second
    C. 6 feet per second
    D. 10 feet per second

13. If the amount of gas inside a container increases,

    A. its volume will increase
    B. its volume will decrease
    C. its pressure will increase
    D. its pressure will decrease

14. Which of the following is a type of fastener?

    A. A screwdriver
    B. A cotter pin
    C. A gear
    D. A drill

15. Water flows into the pipe from the right at a speed of 5 feet per second.

    What is the speed of the water as it leaves the pipe?

    A. 5 feet per second
    B. 10 feet per second
    C. 20 feet per second
    D. 40 feet per second

16. Suppose that a weight is placed eight feet from the fulcrum on the side of the seesaw away from the child. How heavy should the weight be in order to balance the seesaw?

    A. 20 lbs
    B. 40 lbs
    C. 80 lbs
    D. 100 lbs

17. When coupling two shafts that aren't in the same plane, you should use

    A. a sleeve coupling
    B. a universal joint
    C. a clutch
    D. a tube coupling

18. The distance between the ridges of screw threads is the

    A. pitch
    B. torque
    C. kerf
    D. kearning

19. Each of the following is an example of a lever EXCEPT

    A. a crowbar
    B. a seesaw
    C. a pair of pliers
    D. a pulley

GO ON TO THE NEXT PAGE.

20. Bearings are used to reduce

    A. gravity
    B. friction
    C. acceleration
    D. wind resistance

21. A lever in which the fulcrum is placed between the force and the resistance is an example of

    A. a first-class lever
    B. a second-class lever
    C. a third-class lever
    D. a fourth-class lever

22. The tread on a tire is designed to

    A. preserve friction between the car and the road
    B. increase the car's speed when going downhill
    C. increase the car's speed when going uphill
    D. decrease the car's wind resistance

23. Plastic is sometimes used when manufacturing pipes because plastic is

    A. stronger than metal
    B. less corrosive than metal
    C. heavier than metal
    D. more expensive than metal

24. A major disadvantage of glass as a material is its

    A. toughness
    B. opacity
    C. strength
    D. brittleness

25. When drilling into glass or masonry, you should use a

    A. normal drill bit
    B. plastic drill bit
    C. gold-tipped drill bit
    D. carbide-tipped drill bit

STOP!
IF YOU FINISH BEFORE THE TIME IS UP, YOU MAY CHECK OVER YOUR WORK ON THIS PART ONLY.

PART 10

ELECTRONICS INFORMATION

Time: 9 Minutes—20 Questions

1. The ability to store an electric charge is known as

   A. capacitance
   B. resistance
   C. inductance
   D. conductance

2. Overheating of a circuit could be caused by

   A. too many fuses
   B. too little current
   C. too little fuse amperage
   D. too much fuse amperage

3. When working with electricity, you should only use a ladder made of

   A. steel
   B. nichrome
   C. fiberglass
   D. aluminum

4. Power is measured in

   A. volts
   B. amps
   C. watts
   D. farads

5. How much current will a 120 watt light bulb draw if it is plugged into a 120 volt socket?

   A. 0.25 A
   B. 0.5 A
   C. 0.75 A
   D. 1.0 A

6. Which of the following devices are usually flat or tube-shaped?

   A. Capacitors
   B. Resistors
   C. Transistors
   D. Batteries

7. Which of the following are most commonly used as automobile batteries?

   A. Zinc batteries
   B. Alkaline batteries
   C. Lead acid batteries
   D. Lithium batteries

8. If a magnetized needle is broken into two parts, the parts

   A. will each become complete magnets
   B. will not be magnetized
   C. will have four times the previous magnetism
   D. will begin to move apart

9. A unit of inductance is known as

   A. an ohm
   B. a farad
   C. a watt
   D. a henry

10. Resistors that are larger in size can handle more _____ than smaller resistors.

    A. power
    B. voltage
    C. charge
    D. frequency

11. Higher gauge wire will be

    A. heavier than lower gauge wire
    B. stronger than lower gauge wire
    C. more expensive than lower gauge wire
    D. thinner than lower gauge wire

12. As temperature rises, wire resistance generally

    A. rises
    B. falls
    C. remains the same
    D. rises at first, and then falls

GO ON TO THE NEXT PAGE.

13. Three lamps are connected in series. Each lamp requires 8 V and 0.2 amps. The total power used is

A. 2 W
B. 4.8 W
C. 16 W
D. 32 W

14. The electrical pressure that causes electrons to move through a wire is called

A. voltage
B. current
C. flow
D. power

15. Green wire connectors should only be used for connecting

A. grounding wires
B. hot wires
C. live wires
D. low gauge wires

16. A transformer draws 240 W from a 120 V line and delivers 24 V at 5 A. What is its efficiency?

A. 200%
B. 100%
C. 50 %
D. 25 %

17. A conductor consists of generators doing what in a magnetic field?

A. Vibrating
B. Undulating
C. Cooling
D. Rotating

18. Which of the following have largely replaced fuses as the preferred method of preventing electrical overload in houses?

A. Capacitors
B. Resistors
C. Circuit breakers
D. Inductors

19. The symbol above represents

A. ground
B. switch
C. AC voltage source
D. DC voltage source

20. The symbol above represents

A. ground
B. switch
C. AC voltage source
D. DC voltage source

STOP!
IF YOU FINISH BEFORE THE TIME IS UP, YOU MAY
CHECK OVER YOUR WORK ON THIS PART ONLY.

14

ANSWERS AND
EXPLANATIONS TO
PRACTICE TEST 3

PART 1

GENERAL SCIENCE

1. **C** Make sure you are familiar with the section on nutrition. The ASVAB loves to ask questions about vitamins!

2. **B** A moving object has kinetic energy. Potential energy exists due to an object's position in space.

3. **A** Review the section on nutrition. The ASVAB always asks questions about it.

4. **D** Remember the following chart:

	Water Freezes	Water Boils
Celsius	0	100
Fahrenheit	32	212
Kelvin	273.15	373.15

5. **B** Protons have a charge of +1, neutrons are neutral, and atoms are not subatomic particles.

6. **C** Jupiter, Saturn, and Uranus are all outer planets. The terrestrial planets are the four planets closest to the sun: Mercury, Venus, Earth, and Mars.

7. **A** A hot air balloon uses heat to raise the temperature of the air inside the balloon. The hot air inside the balloon rises as it becomes less dense and takes the balloon with it.

8. **C** Oxygen leaves the lungs through small sacs called alveoli.

9. **B** Food is completely broken down in the small intestine, and most nutrients are absorbed into the body here as well. What little remains is absorbed in the large intestine.

10. **C** Heat is not a part of the electromagnetic spectrum.

11. **A** Be sure to review the nutrition section.

12. **C** During a lunar eclipse, the earth moves between the sun and the moon, blocking the sunlight from the moon. What you actually see during the eclipse is the earth's shadow on the moon!

13. **B** The four stages of mitosis are prophase, metaphase, anaphase, and telophase.

14. **D** The atomic number indicates the number of protons in one atom of the element.

15. **A** Substances with a pH of less than 7 are acidic, greater than 7 are a base, and exactly 7 are neutral.

16. **D** An animal that breathes through gills and has scales is a fish, and therefore belongs in the pisces class.

17. **B** Make sure you know the chart on hormones and their effects.

18. **C** Deserts are very arid and have little plant or animal life.

19. **D** An autotroph, also known as a producer, is an organism that makes its own food. Plants make their own food through photosynthesis.

20. **B** The first geologic era is the Precambrian era, followed by the Paleozoic, Mesozoic, and Cenozoic eras.

21. **C** The aphotic zone is the part of the ocean where light does not reach. While there are very few organisms living in this area, a few highly adapted species do exist.

22. **D** You need to be familiar with all the parts of the cell and their functions.

23. **B** Water, or H_2O, is a compound of two atoms of hydrogen and one atom of oxygen.

24. **A** Use the equation for momentum: mass $\times$ speed = momentum.

25. **B** Draw a Punnett Square!

	C	C
C	CC	CC
c	Cc	Cc

PART 2

ARITHMETIC REASONING

1. **D** Use Bite Size Pieces to solve this one. The mechanic is paid $5 for 6 tires: $5 \times 6 = 30$. He is paid $3 for 8 spark plugs: $8 \times 3 = 24$. He is paid $2 for 3 oil changes: $2 \times 3 = 6$. Now add them all up: $30 + 24 + 6 = 60$.

2. **B** This is a division problem in disguise: $196 \div 28 = 7$.

3. **C** Use Bite Size Pieces to solve this one. First, note that we are asked how long it will take the bicyclist to ride 45 yards but are only given her speed in relation to feet. Let's convert the 45 yards to feet using 1 yard = 3 feet: $45 \times 3 = 135$ feet. Now we need to figure out how long it takes her to travel 135 feet. We know that it takes her 10 seconds to travel 15 feet, so let's see how many times 15 divides into 135: $135 \div 15 = 9$. This tells us that 135 feet is the same as 9 units of 15 feet. We know that it takes the bicyclist 10 seconds to travel 15 feet, so just multiply 9 by 10: $9 \times 10 = 90$. That is the total number of seconds it takes her to ride 135 feet. But the answer choices are in minutes, not seconds, so we need to convert. There are 60 seconds in a minute, and we have 90 seconds, which gives us 1 minute and 30 seconds.

4. **B** This is a division problem: $500 \div 8 = 62.5$.

5. **A** This is an arithmetic sequence. The difference between any two consecutive numbers is 6. So the next number in the sequence is $20 + 6 = 26$.

6. **A** You can solve this problem a few different ways. Here's how we did it. The problem tells us that 7 percent of the light bulbs inspected are defective. That means 93 percent are good. 200 light bulbs are inspected every hour, so a total of 800 light bulbs were inspected over 4 hours. We can find 93 percent of 800 through multiplication: $800 \times 0.93 = 744$.

7. **C** This is a division problem: $22.5 \div 15 = 1.5$.

8. **B** Use Bite Size Pieces for this problem. First, multiply the price of an adult ticket by the number of adults: $6.75 \times 3 = 20.25$. Next, multiple the price of a child's ticket by the number of children: $4.25 \times 2 = 8.50$. Then add the two results to find the answer: $20.25 + 8.50 = 28.75$.

9. **D** Use the formula we gave you to solve this problem:

$$\text{percent decrease} = \frac{\text{difference}}{\text{original amount}}$$

Now plug in the discount and the price of the sweater, and solve.

$$0.17 = \frac{\text{difference}}{45.00}$$

Difference $= 0.17 \times 45.00 = 7.65$. That's the difference, or the change in the price. Now subtract the change from the original to find the sale price: $45.00 - 7.65 = 37.35$.

10. **A** Use Bite Size Pieces to answer this question. First, figure out how many small pizzas you would need to feed 50 people. Each small pizza feeds 2 people, so you would need 25 pizzas. Next, calculate the cost of 25 small pizzas: $25 \times \$10 = \$250$.

Then, calculate the number of large pizzas needed to feed 50 people. Each large pizza feeds 5, so you would need 10 pizzas. Calculate the cost of 10 large pizzas: $10 \times \$18 = \$180$. The difference between $250 and $180 is $70.

11. **C** To solve this percent question, first multiply the cost of the ticket by the percent given: $\$75.00 \times 0.30 = \$22.50$. That is the amount that goes towards administrative costs. Now subtract that amount from the total ticket price to find the amount that goes to the charity: $\$75.00 - \$22.50 = \$52.50$.

12. **B** The original room with 10-foot walls has an area of 100, because the area of a square is side^2: 10^2 or $10 \times 10 = 100$. 20 percent of 10 is 2, so the length of the walls of the new room is $10 + 2 = 12$. So the new area of the room is 12^2, or 12×12, which equals 144.

13. **A** Use Bite Size Pieces to solve this problem. First, figure out the price of the stereo after the 40 percent increase: $100 \times 0.40 = 40$, and $100 + 40 = 140$. That's the new price. Next, decrease the new price by 15 percent: $140 \times 0.15 = 21$, and $140 - 21 = 119$.

14. **C** The amount of time between 6:30 am and 4:45 pm is 9 hours and 45 minutes. The truck driver stopped for 15 minutes and 45 minutes, or a total of 1 hour. Subtract that time from the total time and you end up with 8 hours and 45 minutes.

15. **C** This problem is asking us for a specific amount, so the best way to solve it is to plug in the answers and see which one works. What is 5 percent of 50? It's 2.5, but the answer we want is 10 (because the question tells us that 10 students study Chinese), so A must be wrong. What is 5 percent of 150? It's 7.5, so eliminate B. What is 5 percent of 200? It's 10 and that's out target answer! But just to make sure, let's try D. What is 5 percent of 250? It's 12.5, so we can also eliminate D.

16. **B** There are a couple of ways to solve this one. Here how we did it. First, figure out how many widges are built by all employees each hour. There are 8 employees and each builds 12 widges per hour, so that gives us $8 \times 12 = 96$. Next, figure out how many widges are built each day. The work day is 8 hours long, and 96 widges are built each hour: $8 \times 96 = 768$. Finally, multiply the number of widges built each day by the number of work days in a week: $768 \times 5 = 3,840$.

17. **A** To answer this question, you need to convert $17\frac{1}{4}$ to 17.25 and then multiply with decimals: $17.25 \times 8.25 = 142.3125$.

The question asks you to round the answer to the nearest penny, so that leaves us with 142.31.

18. **C** This question is testing your ability to divide with decimals. Recall that the best way to handle this types of problem is to get rid of the decimal point all together: $1450 \div 6.75$ becomes $145000 \div 675$. Now do the division. 675 divides into 1450 2 times, giving us a remainder of 100. Drop down a 0 and now we have:

$$
\begin{array}{r}
2.6 \\
675\overline{)\,145000} \\
-1350 \\
\hline
1000
\end{array}
$$

675 divides into 1000 once and another 0 drops down, giving us:

$$
\begin{array}{r}
21 \\
675\overline{)\,145000} \\
-1350 \\
\hline
1000 \\
-675 \\
\hline
3250
\end{array}
$$

We can stop here because we have enough information to answer the question. Only one answer has the first two numbers "21," and that's C. If we couldn't eliminate all of the other answers we would have to complete the division to solve this one. But this we could eliminate the others, we might as well save ourselves the time and hassle of unnecessary math.

19. **A** First, find the area of the lawn: $15 \times 30 = 450$ square feet. Then, multiply $0.05 by 450: $0.05 \times 450 = \$22.50$.

20. **D** Use Bite Size Pieces to solve this one. Multiply the price of notebooks by the number purchased: $3.25 \times 3 = \$9.75$. Multiply the cost of pencils by the number purchased: $1.99 \times 2 = \$3.98$. One bag of pens was purchased at $2.59. Now figure out the sale price of the backpack: $23.00 \times 0.15 = \$3.45$ and $23.00 - \$3.45 = \$19.55$. Now add up all the prices of the purchased items: $9.75 + \$3.98 + \$2.59 + \$19.55 = \$35.87$.

21. **C** Use a ratio box to solve this problem:

Boys	Girls	Total
3	5	8
		32

Once you've filled everything in, figure out which number multiplied by 8 gives you 32. Four does, so fill in the rest of the ratio box and solve.

Boys	Girls	Total
3	5	8
× 4	× 4	× 4
12	20	32

22. **B** Plug in the answers to solve this one. What is 30 percent of $173.50? It's $52.50. $173.50 - 52.50 = \$121.00$, not $143.50, which is the number we're looking for, so cross off A. What is 30 percent of $205.00? It's $61.50. $205.00 - \$61.50 = \$143.50$, so B is the answer. Let's check the last two just to make sure. What is 30 percent of $209.00? It's $62.70. $209.00 - \$62.70$ is $146.30, so cross off C. What is 30 percent of $230.00? It's $69.00. $230.00 - \$69.00 = \$161.00$, so cross off D.

23. **D** To find the average of the students' grades, add up all the grades and divide by the number of grades: 75 + 83 + 87 + 88 + 92 + 96 = 521, and 521 ÷ 6 = 86.8333. Then round to the nearest whole number, which is 87.

24. **A** The cost of the first 100 pencils is 12 cents each, or $12.00. The cost of the next 50 pencils is 10 cents each, or $5.00. $12.00 + $5.00 is $17.00, so that leaves us with $8.00 for the remaining pencils, which cost 8 cents each. $8.00 divided by $0.08 is 100, so the total number of pencils that can be purchased is 100 + 50 + 100 = 250.

25. **D** Eastern standard time (EST) is 3 hours ahead of Pacific standard time (PST), so let's adjust our departure time to 9:00a.m. PST on July 12th. This will make it easier for us to calculate the traveling time. The car arrives in San Diego on July 17th at 4:00p.m. That's 5 whole days and 7 hours later. Each day has 24 hours in it, so 5 days = 120 hours. 120 + 7 = 127.

26. **C** First, subtract the $3 for the car from the total bill: $6–$3 = $3. That is the total cost for the passengers. Divide that amount by 60 cents and you get 5.

27. **D** Use I = prt to solve this one. The interest (I) is 100 because 600 − 500 = 100. Plug everything in and solve:

    $100 = 500(.04)t$

    $100 = 20t$

    $t = 5$

    It will take 5 years for account to reach $600.

28. **C** First figure out the total cost of the boots with tax: 45.00 × 0.06 = 2.70. That's the tax. Add it to the price of the boots, and we get 45.00 + 2.70 = 47.70. Now deduct the total cost from 100 to find the change from a $100 bill: 100 − 47.70 = 52.30.

29. **D** If the man travels 70 miles a day for five days straight, he has traveled 350 miles. After every 5 days of travel he rests for 2 days before continuing on. In other words, he travels 350 miles every 7 days. The total length of the trip is 3,500 miles, which, when divided by 350, equals 10. Multiply 10 by 7 and you get 70 days.

30. **B** Divide 500 by 26 and you get approximately 19.

PART 3

WORD KNOWLEDGE

1. **C** Anxious: mentally upset over possible misfortune or danger, etc.; worried

2. **D** Inhibit: to check; to hold back; to restrain; to hinder; to discourage from free or spontaneous activity

3. **A** Sympathy: compassion

4. **B** Modify: to make partial changes in; to make different

5. **D** Labor: work; effort

6. **C** Vivid: bright or lively

7. **A** Loyalty: the quality of being unswerving in allegiance

8. **B** Hesitate: to pause or hold back in uncertainty or unwillingness

9. **B** Abolish: to do away with

10. **D** Implement: tool

11. **C** Honor: to regard or treat with esteem or respect; to revere

12. **B** Harsh: very strict; unkind or cruel

13. **A** Enhanced: to make better or stronger

14. **C** Quest: a long search

15. **A** Characterize: to describe the qualities of

16. **C** Authority: power to influence or command thought, opinion, or behavior

17. **A** Benefactor: someone who takes care of or gives money to another person

18. **B** Obedience: compliance with that which is required by authority

19. **D** Morose: sad and dreary

20. **C** Prosperity: the state of being successful; economic well-being

21. **A** Prohibit: to forbid by authority

22. **D** Persist: to continue

23. **B** Abandon: to forsake or desert

24. **C** Penalize: to inflict a penalty or punishment on

25. **A** Standard: common or ordinary

26. **D** Ignorant: lacking knowledge or comprehension

27. **C** Devious: characterized by insincerity or deceit; evasive; deviating from a straight course

28. **B** Devise: to imagine or create

29. **A** Hilarious: marked by or causing boisterous merriment or convulsive laughter

30. **D** Immediate: direct; without anything in between

31. **A** Diligent: careful and steady in application to one's work or duties

32. **B** Lack: deficiency or absence of something

33. **D** Mercy: a disposition to be kind and forgiving

34. **D** Mere: only; nothing more than

35. **A** Phenomenon: an observable fact or event

PART 4

PARAGRAPH COMPREHENSION

1. **C** Choice C paraphrases the passage. A is never mentioned, B is extreme, and D is the opposite of what the passage says.

2. **B** Choice B is a paraphrase of the last sentence. A is false, C is never stated, and D contradicts the passage.

3. **A** Buffalo are found in Asia, Africa, and South America, whereas Bison are found in North America.

4. **C** Choice C is a paraphrase of the first sentence. A contradicts the passage, B is never stated, and D is incorrect.

5. **C** Use POE to answer this question. First, determine if statement I is true or false. It's false, so eliminate A and D. Next, determine if statement II is true or false. It's true, so eliminate B. That leaves you with C.

6. **C** Use the lead word "Europe" to find the answer in the passage. It leads you to C, Spanish.

7. **D** The passage never states the quantity of Spruce Goose airplanes built, so cross off A. It weighed 300,000 pounds, so cross of B. C is never mentioned, so the answer is D.

8. **B** Choice A contradicts the passage, C is never stated, and D doesn't answer the question. That leaves us with B.

9. **A** Use POE to get rid of the answers that are mentioned in the passage. That eliminates B, C, and D.

10. **B** The passage never discusses A, C, or D, so B is the answer.

11. **C** Use POE to cross off the answers that are mentioned in the passage. That gets rid of A, B, and D.

12. **A** The word "dialogues" will lead you to the correct answer choice: Plato.

13. **D** There is no evidence that A is true, nor is there any evidence that B or C is true. D paraphrases the passage.

14. **B** Could a short passage describe the beginnings of Western philosophy in detail? Probably not, so cross off A. While the passage discusses the influence Socrates had on history, that is not the purpose of the passage, so cross off C. D is mentioned only briefly, so cross it off.

15. **A** The passage says "Plato, a student of Socrates…". Hence, the answer is A.

PART 5

NUMERICAL OPERATIONS

1. B	28. B
2. C	29. A
3. D	30. D
4. A	31. B
5. C	32. A
6. B	33. C
7. D	34. C
8. A	35. A
9. C	36. B
10. B	37. C
11. B	38. D
12. A	39. B
13. D	40. A
14. C	41. C
15. B	42. D
16. A	43. B
17. B	44. C
18. C	45. A
19. D	46. D
20. A	47. B
21. C	48. C
22. B	49. A
23. D	50. B
24. A	
25. B	
26. C	
27. B	

PART 6

CODING SPEED 3

1.	E	29.	E	57.	E
2.	C	30.	A	58.	D
3.	D	31.	E	59.	C
4.	E	32.	B	60.	B
5.	B	33.	D	61.	C
6.	A	34.	C	62.	B
7.	D	35.	A	63.	A
8.	B	36.	B	64.	D
9.	C	37.	B	65.	B
10.	B	38.	D	66.	C
11.	D	39.	C	67.	E
12.	E	40.	D	68.	D
13.	B	41.	E	69.	A
14.	D	42.	A	70.	C
15.	C	43.	D	71.	B
16.	A	44.	B	72.	E
17.	B	45.	A	73.	D
18.	E	46.	E	74.	E
19.	D	47.	B	75.	B
20.	C	48.	C	76.	C
21.	A	49.	D	77.	A
22.	E	50.	A	78.	E
23.	D	51.	C	79.	B
24.	B	52.	B	80.	D
25.	B	53.	E	81.	A
26.	D	54.	A	82.	E
27.	D	55.	B	83.	C
28.	C	56.	A	84.	B

PART 7

AUTO AND SHOP INFORMATION

1. **A** If the oil in the car is dirty, then it can form a sludge that accumulates around the piston rings, locking them in place. If the piston is too big for the cylinder, it will lock in the cylinder and the engine will stop.

2. **D** The pinion gear is in the steering system.

3. **A** The engine block, the main part of the engine, contains the cylinders. The oil pan is underneath the engine block and the carburetor on top of the block.

4. **B** Before replacing the battery, you should check it for low fluid levels inside. If the water level is low in the battery, it will not be able to charge completely. If a fuse were out, the battery would not be working and the car would not start. The alternator is a good device to check, but there are easier things to check first that are closer to the real problem.

5. **A** Water is one of the byproducts of combustion, and should be removed from the car via the exhaust system. Sometimes water vapor condenses in the cooler tailpipe.

6. **A** The gas pedal controls the throttle valve. The throttle valve allows more or less fuel and air to enter the cylinders, increasing the power for each power stroke. The fuel pump only transports fuel to the float tank that the carburetor draws from to mix the fuel with the air.

7. **B** If the tire were under-inflated, the tire would be worn on both the outsides of the tread. If it were over-inflated, the tire would be worn down the center of the tread. If the tire is out of alignment, the tire may be worn on one side of the tire.

8. **C** There is no such thing as a current booster in a car.

9. **A** The fact that the radiator is cold means that there is cold fluid in the radiator that's not getting into the engine. The easiest and cheapest thing to check for is a stuck thermostat. The water jackets might be plugged, but that is very uncommon and difficult to fix. The water pump is also difficult and expensive to change. Always look first at the easiest thing to fix.

10. **A** The oil in the engine helps to remove a little of the heat by reducing friction. If the engine does not have enough oil, then the car will typically run a little hot. If the car is running with no oil, the frictional heat is so high that the engine parts can actually start to weld together.

11. **B** We can find the right answer here through Process of Elimination. A broken water pump would cause the engine to overheat, not idle fast. Improper distributor timing means that the spark plugs would not fire at the right time, leading to engine knock or misfires. An overcharged battery does not have an impact on the mechanical timing of the engine, only on the electrical system. That leaves answer choice B. If air is leaking into the intake manifold, the fuel air mix will run lean and the engine will tend to idle faster.

12. **A** With a name like the master cylinder, it can be easy to confuse this part with other parts of the car. The master cylinder is used to pressurize the brake lines and squeeze the brake shoes against the drums or rotors.

13. **B** Anytime a tool must be struck with a hammer, a mallet should be used, in order to prevent damage to the tool.

14. **B** The flathead and the standard are the same type of screw head. The Philips was developed to allow the screwdriver to move to the center of the screw faster and easier, so that it does not slip out of the grove.

15. **C** The chisel has a flat blade for gouging out wood. The file would have teeth along the face.

16. **D** Arc welding uses an electrical arc between the welding tool and the material to generate heat to melt the metal.

17. **D** The cut of a file refers to the configuration of the teeth on its face.

18. **A** A torque wrench has some way to measure the torque being used to tighten the bolt. It does not count the number of times the bolt has been turned or measure the stress in the bolt.

19. **B** We first identify the tool as a hacksaw. Hacksaws are used for cutting through metal and other objects. The arm on the hacksaw does not allow it to cut curves and circles.

20. **B** Thin metal with tin snips. A saw would not be able to cut the metal because it is too thin. Kitchen shears are too weak and bolt cutters would not cut the surface correctly. Remember, bolt cutters have jaws that are close to parallel all the time. This is not ideal for cutting sheet metal.

21. **B** The tang is the part of the file that is inserted into a handle. If the tang is bent, the handle might not be able to slide on the file.

22. **B** The pipe wrench and monkey wrench look similar, except that on the pipe wrench, the bottom jaw is fixed, while on the monkey wrench, the top jaw is fixed. The picture shows the top jaw fixed, so this is a monkey wrench.

23. **B** Oil and grease are the two main types of lubricants. They can be effective in preventing rust and corrosion, but they can not remove it.

24. **A** Since the handles move on the device pictured, we can rule out answer choices C and D. The device does not have a mechanism to lock it in place when grabbing something, so it is not vise grips.

25. **C** The only tool listed that is used to cut through metal is the hacksaw.

PART 8

MATHEMATICS KNOWLEDGE

1. **B** This problem gives you the answer and asks you how you would get that result. The easiest way to answer this question is to just add the two polynomials in the question together. Think about it like this: some polynomial, minus $5x - 2y - 8z$, gives you $7x + 6y + z$. By adding the two polynomials together, you will end up with the missing polynomial.

2. **B** Remember FOIL:

   First: $x \times x = x^2$

   Outer: $x \times 4 = 4$

   Inner: $5 \times x = 5x$

   Last: $45 \times -4 = -20$.

   That gives you $x^2 - 4x + 5x - 20$, or $x^2 + x - 20$.

3. **B** $4x = -12$, so isolate the variable by dividing both sides by 4. That gives you $x = -3$.

4. **C** $12 \times 12 = 144$, so the square root of 144 is 12.

5. **D** A square has four equal sides. The area of a square is side $\times$ side, or side^2. The area of the square in the problem is 25, so each side has a length of 5. $\sqrt{25} = 5$. To find the perimeter of an object, add up the lengths of all of the sides. For this square that will be: $5 + 5 + 5 + 5 = 20$.

6. **A** This is one of the special right triangles you should know, the 3-4-5 triangle. Whenever a right triangle has a side with length 3 and a side with length 4, the hypotenuse will have a length of 5. The ASVAB loves to test this, so make sure you remember it!

7. **D** An equilateral triangle has three equal sides. The perimeter is the sum of all the sides, so we can find the length of one side (the base) by dividing the perimeter by 3: $16.5 \div 3 = 5.5$.

8. **A** First, draw it. You should have something like this:

Recall that vertical angels are across from each other, and that vertical angles, by definition, are always equal. So the answer is 50°.

9. **B** This is a great problem for Plugging In. Plug in numbers for each of the variables, for example: $x = \$5$ and $y = 2$ plants. If you bought 2 plants for \$5 each, you would pay \$10. Now plug your numbers into the answer choices. The answer that gives you 10 is the correct one. A $5 + 2 = 7$, nope. Choice B: $5 \times 2 = 10$, that's correct. Choice C: $5 - 2 = 3$, nope. D: $5 \div 2 = 2.5$, nope.

10. **A** First, draw it. You should have a rectangle that looks like this:

Recall that the area of a rectangle is length $\times$ width, or 12×10, which is 120.

11. **D** This question looks a little tricky at first glance, but really isn't that bad. We need to get rid of the y. We know that $y = wx$, so plug in wx for y in the formula $z = \dfrac{y}{x} + w$. This gives you $z = \dfrac{wx}{x} + w$, which reduces to $z = 2w$.

12. **B** Recall that a prime number is a number divisible only by 1 and itself. Perform the functions for each answer choice and see if the result is prime. Choice A: $13 + 3 = 16$ is divisible by 1, 2, 4, 8, and 16. Choice B: $11 + 2 = 13$ is divisible by 1 and 13, so it's prime. Choice C: $17 - 5 = 12$ is divisible by 1, 2, 3, 4, 6, and 12. Choice D: $10 \times 2 = 20$ is divisible by 1, 2, 4, 5, 10, and 20.

13. **C** The formula for circumference is $2\pi r$. The question tells us that r = 4 and that $\pi = 3.14$. Plug in those values and solve: $C = 2(3.14)(4) = 25.2$.

14. **A** In order to solve for x, we must figure out what y is. Isolate y in $6y = 9z$ and you get $y = \dfrac{9z}{6}$, which reduces to $y = \dfrac{3z}{2}$. Plug that value into $x = 2y$ and you get $x = 2\dfrac{3}{2}z$. Multiply and you get $x = \dfrac{6}{2}z$, or $x = 3z$.

15. **D** 4 factorial means $1 \times 2 \times 3 \times 4 = 24$.

16. **C** Factor out and you get: $(x - 3)(x + 2)$. You can check this through FOIL.

   First: $x \times x = x^2$

   Outer: $x \times 2 = 2x$

   Inner: $-3 \times x = -3x$

   Last: $-3 \times 2 = -6$.

17. **D** To solve for S, you must isolate it. Divide both sides by P and you end up with

$$S = \frac{R+T}{P}$$

18. **A** Draw the building and label the sides. It should look something like this:

We use x and $2x$ to denote the lengths of each side. Recall that the perimeter of an object is the sum of the sides. We know that the perimeter is 60, so your equation looks like this: $2x + x + 2x + x = 60$, or $6x = 60$. Solve for x: $x = 10$, so the length of the longer side is $2 \times 10 = 20$.

19. **D** Similar triangles have equal angles, but their sides are not necessarily of equal lengths, so A is out. Isosceles triangles have two equal sides and angles, not three, so B is out. Trapezoids do not have 4 right angles, so C is out. That leaves us with D, which is correct.

20. **C** Recall that the formula for the area of a circle is area = πr^2. First, fill in what you know: $201 = 3.14\, r^2$. Then solve for r.

$$r^2 = \frac{201}{3.14} = 64$$

$$r = \sqrt{64} = 8$$

21. **B** Plug the values into the expression and solve:

$$4(-3) - 3(6) + 7(-5) = -12 - 18 + -35 = -65$$

22. **D** Convert the math jargon into an equation you can solve. Recall that a product is the result of multiplication, so we have $b \times 6$. That product is 4 more than 44, or 48. Our equation is therefore $b \times 6 = 48$. Now solve for b by dividing both sides by 6. You end up with $b = 8$.

23. **C** Use Fred's Theorem to solve this one. Recall that when a line crosses two parallel lines, any big angle plus any small angle is 180°. We know the big angle is 100, so the small angle is 80. All big angles are the same size and all small angles are the same size. Knowing this we can figure out that $x = 80$ and $y = 80$. $80 + 80 = 160$.

24. **A** To solve for a variable, you need to isolate it. $16x - 4x = 12x$, so $12x = 36$. Divide both sides by 12 and you have $x = 3$.

25. **D** Squares have four sides, and their perimeter is the sum of the sides. If you add 2 to each side, you will increase the perimeter by 8, because $4 \times 2 = 8$.

PART 9

MECHANICAL COMPREHENSION

1. A
2. B
3. C
4. A
5. A
6. A
7. D
8. C
9. C
10. A
11. C
12. B
13. D
14. B
15. C
16. A
17. B
18. A
19. D
20. B
21. A
22. A
23. B
24. D
25. D

PART 10

ELECTRONICS INFORMATION

1. A
2. D
3. C
4. C
5. D
6. A
7. C
8. A
9. D
10. A
11. D
12. A
13. B
14. A
15. A
16. C
17. D
18. C
19. C
20. A

NOTES